THE SHADOW OF HIS SMILE
Brothers Together in Life and Song

John Benedetto & Patricia Benedetto

DEDICATION

The extended Benedetto / Bennett Family.
My wife Patricia, my brother Tony always supportive, sister Mary
always caring for us. Our Mother & Father. My son John, and
daughters; Ann, Lynn, Ciel. I love you, this is for you.
Jerry Perles, my first encouraging fan and publisher.
John

My Husband, Children and Our Extended Family
Those who have left our lives,
Those who celebrate life with us,
Those who will remain when we are gone, and
Those who will come after us.
Patricia

CONTENTS

ACKNOWLEDGMENTS

Abacoa Writers Group, whose support and direction is invaluable. A special note of thanks to Judy Lucas who founded this group, helping writers.

Judy Ratto, friend, editor, and was always there for me.

Rajeeyah Madinah, aka Gigi, Social Media Bootcamp, Marketing Guru.

Judy Martin, my daughter offering her endless confidence.

Kathy & Martin Peterson, my sister and her family providing patience and encouragement.

Ann & Lynn Benedetto, John's daughters, who gave their blessing and encouragement to write.

Tina Gerace, John's cousin, who took me into the fold years ago, the family historian.

Ralph Herman, John's friend and professional music director for many including Tony Bennett.

New York Public Library and Librarian Research Assistants; Eleanor Yadin & Jessica Pigza

Metropolitan Opera House and Historians Archives, Mr. John Pennino.

The Catholic Church Archives, Mr. Joseph Coen, C. A. Archivist, Office of the Archivist

Charles Rangel, Congressman, entered John's achievements in the Congressional Record.

Vance & Marcia Anderson & Seth Ferris, all close as Family, offering years of encouragement and moral support.

Nick & Fran Riggio's friendship and marketing support.

Dick Cami, dear friend and author, "Peppermint Twist".

Harold Holtzer, dear friend, author and Lincoln historian.

DOCUMENTATION

May 2nd, 1979

Dear Johnny:

Recently Rocky Graziano and I did a batch of commercials for different products, etc. In the course of talking about a commercial with Riccardo of Riccardo's Restaurant, your name came up. I said that I knew you and Riccardo (a wonderful guy) said that they all thought that you would be the star in your family. That you sang great!

How's Pat and the kids? Rocky and I may be coming down to Florida one of these days----so we'll all get together----and we'll see if you still pack a punch?

Things are going great for all of us up in NY except that we are getting older. How's Vince Auletta and Rita and their family? Say hello for Rocky and myself.

Take care Johnny---and if you have a record of your singing, please send it to me. I'd like to hear what you sound like. You know that you two guys always imitated me! ("I weft my heart in San Fwancisco".)

Getting ready to do Rocky's movie but we had some heart-aches with false starts recently. I don't want to work too hard any-more----everyone is dropping dead around us.

Take care of yourself Tiger and let me know how you feel personally and otherwise.

Your pal,

Eddie White

Hello Johnny
Where you been, will see you soon
your pal - 'champ' Rocky Graziano

CHARLES B. RANGEL
15TH CONGRESSIONAL DISTRICT
NEW YORK

COMMITTEE:
WAYS AND MEANS
RANKING MEMBER

JT COMMITTEE ON TAXATION

☐ 2354 RAYBURN HOUSE OFFICE
WASHINGTON, DC 20515-3215
TELEPHONE: (202) 225-4

DISTRICT OFFICE:
MS. VIVIAN E. JONES
DISTRICT ADMINISTRATO

☐ 163 WEST 125TH STREET
NEW YORK, NY 10027
TELEPHONE: (212) 663-35

PLEASE RESPOND TO
OFFICE CHECKED

Congress of the United States
House of Representatives
Washington, DC 20515-3215

November 22, 2005

Mrs. Patricia Benedetto
5930 Center Street
Jupiter, Florida 33458

Dear Mrs. Benedetto :

The enclosed plaque is a memento of the statement I entered in the Congressional Record in John's memory.

I believe that the principles under which he lived his life are so important that they should be memorialized in the official record of the Congress of the United States of America.

You and your family, again, have my love and condolences. I know that the holidays will be difficult for you. But I hope you will be soothed by memories of all the wonderful years you shared with John.

God bless you and the family.

Sincerely,

CHARLES B. RANGEL
Member of Congress

CBR/em

X

Congressional Record

United States of America   PROCEEDINGS AND DEBATES OF THE *109th* CONGRESS, FIRST SESSION

House of Representatives

IN MEMORY OF JOHN DOMINICK BENEDETTO
HE SHARED HIS FAITH IN ETHICS AND FAIRNESS TOWARD HIS FELLOW MAN

HONORABLE CHARLES B. RANGEL
OF NEW YORK

November 16, 2005

Mr. RANGEL. Mr. Speaker, I rise today to pay special tribute to my friend, John Dominick Benedetto, who died August 29, 2005, in Jupiter, Florida. His memory lives on in the loving embrace of his family and many friends.

John brought a breath of love and beauty to everything he touched, whether in music, the arts, in the preparation of foods, or in his creativity as an entrepreneur. In World War II, he served his country in the U.S. Air Force. But his appreciation for this land was manifest most deeply in his heartfelt concern for all of its people. He truly believed that every man, woman and child was due--without distinction--the fairness and justice that are America's promise.

In his unassuming way, John personified for me the great Godly virtue taught to us in the Gospel of Matthew: As you have done it unto one of the least of these, you have done it unto me. My love and condolences go out to Patricia, his faithful and loving wife of 28 years, their five daughters and two sons, their seven grandchildren, and of course, his brother, Tony.

For the information of my colleagues I submit the following obituary which was published in the *South Florida Sun-Sentinel* on August 30, 2005.

Benedetto, John Dominick, was born on March 18, 1923 in New York City, died August 29, 2005 in Jupiter, FL. He is survived by his loving wife of 28 years Patricia, his brother Tony, five daughters, two sons and seven grandchildren. As a young boy, John sang with the Metropolitan Opera Company, where his beautiful tenor voice resonated through the hills of Italy. His talent and creativity was a mainstay throughout his life, and manifested through his passion for music, life, art, and family. After returning from his tour with the U.S. Air Force during WWII, John became an entrepreneur whose passion for invention was nurtured through the development of many ideas and opportunities. As an innovative thinker, John thought about ways to make the world a better place to live and to foster positive social change. John loved to bring people together, whether it was for a small family gathering where he would create amazing meals with love, or simply sitting on his dock and fishing with a friend or relative. His travels and life's path brought him many experiences that were colorfully shared In anecdotes over a card game or an expertly mixed drink. John's charm and charisma attracted many friends, and allowed him to touch many people. John will be greatly missed. A private service will be arranged by the family for a future date. In lieu of flowers, the family thanks all who can please donate to the TRIPPS organization: 263 Shamey Lane, Kennesaw, GA 30144 - http://www.tripps.org/.

Rose Miniaci

August 31, 2005

Dear Pat,

My heart goes out to you at this very sad time.

Al and I loved John. I cherish the memories of his kind words, especially the beautiful birthday wishes he expressed to me.

John has left a wonderful legacy. He gave so much happiness through his magnificent voice and his personal touch. We will all have wonderful memories of this wonderful man.

If I may be of assistance to you in any way, please do not hesitate to call me. May God Bless you and your lovely family always.

Love,

Rose Miniaci

CHAPTER ONE

I am listening to the priest giving his eulogy for Mom. I have just flown in from San Francisco and driven from Kennedy airport to the funeral home. Anna had fifteen years of miserable sickness, and it's a blessing God took her. In fact, privately I would pray for her death so she would be spared the crippling pain. Her illness was an injustice that I never could forgive God for. I didn't fully appreciate her while I was young, but now I realize she should have been ordained a saint.

Father John is speaking, his tone matter of fact and unemotional. *How could they know, how could anyone know?* Then one thing Father John is saying hurls me back in time, "Thank you, God. Thank you for giving us Anna for seventy-eight years, for she touched everyone in this room. She set an example for all of us on this earth to follow."

At various intervals, I'm back in the funeral hall and the reality that my mom is in the casket. A custom I believe to be barbaric. I stare into my mom's still face as if some miracle will present itself — that she'll get up.

My head spins as my thoughts carry me back to my first meaningful inclination of family. The Lord has blessed me with vivid memories from childhood.

*****

I was one of three children; my sister, Maria, was the oldest. A younger brother was christened Antonio, but we called him Ninni.

I was the middle child, the eldest son, named Giovanni after my father. My mom was a young widow and had to raise her children without help. She never remarried or looked at another man the rest of her life. I scanned the room of relatives, I raced back into time. Before the funeral was over, I was to relive every heartbreaking and joyful experience of my early life.

The year was 1931, and the Depression had set in. The misery could not possibly be described, especially for those who had deep dignity and wouldn't accept charity. I was eight years old and already contributing to the family through my opera singing.

It was a typically cold January day on Long Island where we had moved from Mulberry Street in New York City. My parents felt their children would have a chance at life away from the hardships in the city. It was late afternoon. The clouds overhead turned dark moving as conveyers of evil. The howling wind would frighten me, seemingly communicating for the malevolent carriers above.

It was a tense time. My grandmother was gravely ill. It was a tense time for me as I was about to be introduced to death and suffer the loss of a loved one at the very young age of seven. In those days, especially in an Italian family, it was culturally unacceptable *not* to die at home. Emotions were high and children were subjected to death and unnerving ceremonies.

We lived in the proverbial cold-water flat. The rooms were railroad style, and in winter the children always ended up farthest from the only heat, which was from the black cast-iron stove. We had to beg, borrow, or steal whatever fuel we could find.

As I played in the street with my friends, from time to time I would look up at the second floor of our building, wondering what was going on. I had been chased out of the house as the guests arrived.

"What's happening at your house, Giovanni?" my dear friend, Herman, asked.

"My Nonna's very sick."

"Don't worry, Giovanni, she'll be OK," said Herman, compassionate even as a child.

"This will be the first year she hasn't gathered us around the stove to tell us the witch stories." Nonna used to turn out the lights and scare the hell out of us with legendary witch tales from the old country. The deep red glow of the stove would highlight the wrinkles on her face and the long wart on her nose. The shadows dancing on the kitchen walls cooperated with the dark mood she was weaving. I remember getting so frightened by tales of misbehaving children that I would run to confession and tell all to the priest. The amount of penance matched the magnitude of her frightening skills.

It was just about dusk when I noticed all of the windows were open. The wind eerily flapped the long crocheted curtains, which seemed to beckon me.

My Pop called out through the window, "Giovanni, come upstairs at once."

"Can Herman come up with me?"

"No, Giovanni. Come at once."

It wasn't like my pop to refuse a friend. I walked up the stairs slowly. The lights were out. The dark banisters and musty smell contributed to my dislike for the place, it was my first inclination that we were poor. I was progressing in slow motion proceeding up the stairway entering our dismal apartment we called home. As I entered from the kitchen through the railroad rooms, I felt the cold wind from the open windows. When I approached my Nonna's room, her gasping intensified. All the figures of authority in my life stood beside the bed; Mom, Pop, our family priest, doctor, and Father John who was giving Nonna her last rites as everyone bowed their heads in prayer.

A candle flickered at the end of the bed.

Her mouth wide open, my Nonna gasped for precious oxygen.

Most people were too poor to go to the hospital, so opening the windows in a home was a way to replace oxygen tents in the attempt to cure pneumonia.

Nonna was my father's mother, so he brought me to her side. My father spoke in a low, saddened voice, still kind and gentle as always. "Giovanni, come and say goodbye to your Nonna." Frightened, I moved to her side. Pop put his gentle hand on my shoulder. "Kiss her goodbye, Giovanni."

I bent over ever so slowly, though I remember wanting to get it over with quickly. I was about to kiss her when the first odor of death entered my life.

Her breath could only be described as macabre. I can close my eyes now sixty years later and still remember the odor as though it were yesterday. I remember feeling sick. Her skin was as cold as the ice box in the kitchen. At the peak of my fright, she stopped breathing as if someone switched off machinery. I learned then people die, and those with the power to protect can't forestall the one thing that must happen to us all.

*****

It was quite common in those days for the body to rest in the house until burial. I recall the arrangements being made. Uncle Frank had taken me with him when he bargained with the funeral.

"Now come on, Joe, I have seen the cops have not bothered you," he said to Mr. Morisco. While they bargained I wandered to the next room. Here sat caskets filled with illegal alcohol. Men were loading them into hearses.

When Mr. Morisco left the room I asked, "Uncle Frank, why were those hearses filled with alcohol bottles?" It was then I learned the main stem of the funeral-home business was smuggling illegal alcohol in caskets, using simulated funerals as decoys. It was Prohibition, and bootlegging was a big business.

"All right, Frank, this one is on the house," Mr. Morisco said. "In fact, anyone who passes on in your family is on the house. I respect what you have done for me and hope that it will continue. I just will never understand the fact that you refuse payment for your favor. You see, the boss accepts this as a constant cost, and he could well afford it. Besides, Frank, he loves you as though you were his own son."

It was all gibberish to me.

My Nonna was placed in the farthest room from the kitchen, and I vividly remember her look of death. I didn't like the cosmetics. Nonna never wore makeup, not even lipstick. Someone had applied colorful makeup, looking completely unnatural. I did know one thing: I knew she was dead.

I was frightened even more as the women started to moan and tell stories about Nonna's life in sad musical tones. This was a ritual hangover from the old country. The best was yet to come, for only three women were present. It would get competitive when the room filled with all my female relatives, to the point my ears rang and my brain felt as though it were leaving me. I felt a deep sadness, coupled with anger, anger with the knowledge my Grandmother would not want this display, and anger that I was subjected to this ritual.

That night, I was permitted to stay up much later than usual. Children didn't have to go to school. We had to be present for the relatives as a sign of respect and grief. Mom turned out the light when I finally went to bed. I was still awake when Nonna appeared in full life. I was frightened out of my wits. She didn't speak, just stared at me with a cold smile. I jumped up and ran into the mob of visitors, screaming; "I'm dying I need a priest." Mom grabbed me and escorted me back to bed, but I didn't sleep.

We lived near an elevated subway, and I counted the passing trains to stay awake. The night passed. I was still alive but none the best for it.

Early in the morning, people started arriving from all over the country. My Uncle came from upstate New York, cousins came from Pennsylvania, relatives on my mother's side came from New Jersey, many relatives I did not know.

I couldn't understand, with all of our poverty, why visitors came in limousines, Auburns, Cadillacs and Rolls-Royces. Mom's brother, Uncle Frank was the host and, I was to learn later, the ultimate leader of the family in every meaningful function. I liked him. We would develop a mutual respect for each other, even though we were so far apart in age. He was to be another significant influence in my life.

He placed the black wreath on the door while my other two uncles assisted.

"Frank, this is the middle, I'll put a mark here for you."

"That's not the middle, this is the middle over here, give me that hammer."

This was my first indication they were devoted followers, anxious to please him.

Frank was a very tall, dark, manly kind of handsome with a charm no language could describe. He was a pro. As head of the Democratic party, he was well respected. and the most important facet of his personality was his ability to persuade.

People came and went all day, relatives I hadn't met. Mom said, "This is your cousin, Rose, from Watertown, New York." And as grown-ups will do, she kissed me with her thick lipstick. I didn't like the feeling. My capacity for affection was narrow in those days, and these relatives were too much to handle. I peered out the window, longing to go out and see my friends.

I noticed a man emerging from a Cadillac limo. He stood beside the car door and slowly turned his head in all directions before entering the house. I wondered at his actions. He removed a black felt homburg as he walked in. I was impressed with his meticulous attire and his commanding authority. Uncle Frank embraced him, kissed both cheeks and then his ring.

Uncle Jim said, "That's the boss, Frank Costello, Uncle Frank's rabbi." Uncle Frank introduced him around. He played his part well with a solemn face that never changed.

"This is my nephew I was telling you about, the singer billed the Little Caruso," Uncle Frank said.

Frank Costello bent to see me. "This is the one you want me to confirm, Frank?" he said in broken English with a heavy Italian accent. Continuing, as he pats me on the head, "Frank, you are right as usual, he has the look of the hawk and the olive branch at the same time. He is a winner. I pick my horses this way, and I never miss."

They laughed and walked arm in arm as Costello spoke in his authoritative tones. "Frank, how about me introducing him to Petri, a friend of mine who heads the Metropolitan Opera chorus? They even have some solo parts for children in the *Bartered Bride* and *Gianni Schicchi*. If he is as good as you say, it would be a great background for his portfolio, and it'll expose him to travel."

Costello called to me, "Giovanni, I'm having a party at my house next Sunday. You can come and sing for us. I'll pay you. Don't be like your uncle and do everything for nothing." I smiled faintly but didn't answer.

"He'll be glad to come," Frank answered for me.

"I like you," he said, looking at me. "You have learned respect at an early age; you understand your uncle talks for you. . . Very good, Frank, when is the confirmation?" They embraced once more with the same kissing ritual.

My two friends Herman and Manny sneaked up the stairs during the funeral, and we exchanged news. I didn't get any sleep those three days, what with the trauma of Nonna's death and people coming and going all hours of the night.

Manny, always interested in the money, jumps in, "Have you heard about the huge new cruise ship 'The Manhattan' they are building in our harbor? It cost twenty-one million dollars!"

Herman, more interested in the spiritual, volunteers "Have you heard that the president, Herbert Hoover, will dedicate the new Empire State building on May first. He is going to turn on the light while he is in Washington! A miracle, right?"

"I don't think it's a miracle. I have kind of been hoping for a miracle this week. I need to get back to the funeral before my family misses me. See you at school in a couple of days."

The moaning and chanting were enough to set me off. This was my first funeral, and what was happening would have given Freud enough work for a century to come.

I was awakened at six o'clock in the morning, and Pop led me by the hand to the casket in the living room. I can still smell the flowers, that day I was robbed of the joy of their scent. The sadness has stayed with me until this day. Pop knelt on the prayer rail beside the coffin and gently pulled me down with him. We bowed our heads in prayer and then Pop said, "Giovanni, kiss your Nonna good-bye." A cringing shiver came over my body. I didn't want to do it, but I had to obey Pop. I wanted to scream but couldn't. I kissed her cheek — cold as an iceberg.

Visitors entered the room. My cousin Kitty was from the wealthy side of the family. She was my mother's sister's daughter. Her mom's name was Aunt Millie. She and her mother walked to the coffin and Kitty boldly rearranged Nonna's scarf and prayer beads, then bent over to kiss her. She was so brave.

My sister, Maria, and little brother, Ninni, now approached to kiss Nonna goodbye. The room followed suit. Then it happened. The funeral director walked to the coffin with a formal air. Without speaking, he looked slowly around the room as if signaling this was the moment to pay a last tribute, for he was about to close the lid.

All hell broke loose. Screams of agony rose from the women. When it seemed to peak, a star emerged just as in grand opera. Everyone quieted down, and Chica lapsed into a eulogy type of chant for an hour as everyone nodded approval as she recounted Nonna's life. The pallbearers lifted the coffin onto their shoulders, solemnly walked down the stairs, slid the coffin into the hearse, and closed the doors. Five limousines were assigned to immediate family, and the cars following us were countless. Although we had a large family, many were here to pay respects to Uncle Frank.

Uncle Frank guided me into his limo, and another tall dark man entered with us. This man kissed Frank's cheeks and said. "Frank,

Costello couldn't come. He had business, you know, so he sent me in his place."

Frank introduced the family and saved me for last, as usual. He beamed and patted my knee. "Pete, this is my nephew, Giovanni."

"Oh, this is the great singer of promise. Costello told me you would be at the party this weekend to entertain us. Great. You know it won't interfere with mourning because it is business. You'll be paid."

I nodded, feeling sick all over, as this is not the day to discuss money. This is my Grandmother's day, her last day. The next thing I recall is High Mass in church. The music was beautiful and helped to banish my developing migraine. I suffered violently from migraines, and music was the only cure. It was misty and cold when we proceeded to the cemetery, so cold that I could no longer feel my feet or fingertips. Father John expounded glowing words over Nonna's grave, and the casket was lowered into the place of rest.

At the quietest moment, Chica let out a shrilling scream. "I love her, take me with her! I don't want to live anymore without her here on Earth!" She attempted to jump into the pit, but my uncles, Jim and Dick, grabbed her. By now, my headache had returned. I was so frightened that my body pounded with pain from my kidneys to the top of my head.

When we returned home the mood changed, which confused me. The women cooked sauce for spaghetti and meatballs. Everyone was joyous, telling jokes and laughing. Pop joined in, so I gathered it was all right.

The men moved to the living room where the coffin had been. It still smelled of flowers, now mixed with cigar smoke. A great uncle produced the kind of cigar they called "guinea stinkers," so naturally the men in the family smoked them with pride. I decided to lie down in my room just off the living room. I could hear the men talking.

My uncle was questioning Pop. "Where is a copy of Nonna's

will?"

"It's in the strong box, Frank. Bring it out and we'll look at it."

A man with a boisterous voice entered. "I'm sorry I missed the funeral, but I had very serious business. I got away as quickly as I could."

Pop beckoned me. "Giovanni, come out and meet your Uncle Dominick." I obeyed and met my father's brother. I looked up at Dominick's bald head and porky, squinty eyed face with a tobacco stain running down the left side of his lower lip. On the rare occasions he didn't have a cigar in his mouth, you could see a distorted impression from where the cigar usually was.

"So this is your oldest boy," he said. He turned to me. "I have no children, Giovanni. Why don't you come up and live with me to help take care of my business? Then someday it'll be all yours." Instinctively I did not like him. I clung to Pop and thought, I never want to leave my Mom and Pop.

"Dom, how are things going in your general store?" Pop asked, holding me tightly.

"Just great, John. I've taken over thirty acres behind the river where the Indian caves are. The farmer couldn't make his payment to me, so I took his land."

"Did you have to do that, Dom? Couldn't you be a little easier on these people?"

"You leave the business end to me, John. You always were soft in the heart. Besides, I'm using the caves to hide good Canadian whiskey for shipment to Costello down here, and I'm getting top dollar. Don't look so worried. If anything goes wrong, I have Frank down here to squash it. I'm very careful. I work in the store as if this was my main interest, and no one suspects me."

"I just don't want to see you get in trouble, Dom. After all, I feel responsible for you. I brought you to this country, remember?"

Dominick scowled. "You're forgetting the respect. I'm your older brother."

Frank must have sensed trouble because he walked over.

"You're just in time for the reading of the will, Dom. Sit down, won't you?" Dom submitted and glared at Pop. I didn't like this man.

"Where is the booze, John?" Uncle Jim said. "Whoever heard of reading a will without a few belts beforehand?"

Pop slipped into the kitchen and brought out everyone's favorite: our homemade brew that all Italians made with anisette, Galliano, Strega, Sambuca, and brandied cherries. The men poured it, and Nonno, my mother's father, stood up with watery eyes, gray hair as silver as jewelry, a handle bar mustache, and cheeks as red as polished apples. He had the look of a handsome Santa Claus. "A toast to my daughter Anna and my son-in-law John who married in the true tradition of the dons of Calabria." Meaning, of course, they were first cousins.

Aunt Millie poked her head in. "Have you read the will yet?"

"Have you no respect, Millie?" her husband, Uncle Albert, said. "Her body isn't even cold yet."

"Well, she promised me the diamond ring, and its mine, no matter what."

I tried my best to put all of this into perspective, trying to organize people into the proper slots. How amazing, I found in later life, to be so close to the truth with little exception. For example, I figured out that Chica was a steady at funerals and paid with favor and recognition. It seemed to fulfill an outlet for her hostilities. Her husband Pasquale, known as Patsy, was mentally ill. He was committed to an asylum when he used part of the American flag to create his "united world" flag while preaching a united world to bring peace. He was an inventor who designed a periscope for submarines and tried to sell it to the U.S. government. They informed him he owed it to his country but would pay him ten thousand dollars. Patsy thought the price unfair, so he traveled to Italy to sell it to the Italian government. They stole his plans and deported him. This didn't help his frame of mind.

Patsy liked me. In fact, he more than liked me. He would say, "Giovanni, someday I'll build a new design in yachts, and you'll travel with me all over the world giving concerts. We'll live on the money you earn. Your talent and my boat will be everlasting partners." I believed him.

The day dragged on, and as life would have it, the men drank too much. Frank, who held his booze the best, never changed character. The husbands seemed to fight for their wives' claims on the few possessions Nonna left behind.

"I was in this very room when Buono Anima told me she never would forget my wife's services to her and promised her the china clock!" Patsy screamed, his insane eyes popping out.

"Listen, you degenerate runt, you don't even belong to this family, so keep your mouth shut," Dom said.

Patsy scowled. "I won't keep quiet. If your wife, Maggie, were here, I'd tell her how you take my wife every time you make a trip down here."

They were about to tangle when Frank stepped between them and told them they would have to leave if they showed any more disrespect. Pop stood by with a firm look of disgust. He was kind and gentle and surely didn't have the energy to say what he really felt. He loved his mamma, and she was dead. That was all he was really concerned about.

I went to bed listening to the backbiting. Patsy, seemingly the center of everyone's irritation, continued his accusations. Frank consistently played his role, knowing none of them had the guts or a real reason to fight.

I became more unsettled. I rested my head on the pillow, and my hallucinations took a far different form. It was a horrible dream, so vivid that as the years went by, I could feel the onslaught of the nightmare as I shut my eyes. I couldn't stop it. The figures were a bright whitish color, somewhat like Fourth of July sparklers. I couldn't distinguish them because of this.

It would happen, each and every time I had the dream, more

frequent in childhood than later in life. My body would tingle and increase in intensity, like an electric current running through me. Then I would hear the highest pitch of a scream. It was unbearable, as if it were the end for me; paralyzed and helpless. A pressure on my body, in my mind, felt as though I were being compressed. With every ounce of energy I could muster, I would shake myself out of the dream. My body would be covered with cold sweat, and the fear lingered until the first peek of daylight. When Mom woke me, all I could think of was seeing my friends, Herman and Manny.

I learned the last facet of an Italian wake. Visitors trickled in for the next few weeks. Women in the immediate family mourned for at least six months by wearing black and not attending joyful events. Meanwhile, the men wore black ties and the black bands on their jackets.

*****

I'm awakened by my favorite person, Cousin Irene, who is Frank's daughter. Of course, she can't know what was going on in my mind, reliving the past.

"You must be very tired, John. You fell asleep," she says.

I smile and squeeze her hand in warm affection of just knowing her. *How could I deserve her friendship through the years?* Irene has been forever supportive. God knows, I needed it, with what I put my family through at times.

Irene married the greatest guy, Peter Stora. A great husband and father, he became one of my best friends. He is a true war hero who threw himself on a hand grenade to save his men. He survived but lost a major part of his head. Peter had picked up my wife and I at the airport earlier today and took us to their home. Irene made dinner for us before setting out to the funeral parlor. Now she's waiting for me at the parlor entrance. I know she felt I was not up to this ordeal. She also knew I think putting loved ones on display was pagan-like. I smile and embrace her. "Thank you, Irene, but I'm ready for this."

13

My wife, Patricia, and I walk toward the coffin where my sister is standing. I embrace Maria for quite a while. She worked so hard taking care of Mom.

I look at my brother. If anyone knew the price of glory in show business, we would have no theaters. I could tell he's in shock, feeling isolated, not himself. *He has really become an island, no more jokes, no laughter. He is not Ninni anymore.*

My love for Mom is the only reason why I'm within these walls I resent so much. Aside from our public schooling, it was her insistence we go into private education in the arts. Thus my escape, falling into the past, reliving all the pain and joy of our lives with her.

CHAPTER TWO

Mom was always tired. She cooked us breakfast while getting ready for work. She had to work because Pop had a heart condition. It was so bad that the doctors ordered him not to climb stairs. Mom worked in a dress factory, aka sweatshop. She did piecework at a penny or two per garment. It was hell. Her average day started at seven in the morning and ended at six. Pop didn't have the energy to make supper, so she prepped everything and cooked it when she got home. Mornings were very sad for me because Mom and Pop would argue. I guess he felt guilty Mom had to work.

Pop had a way about him, though. He somehow would gather a smile before I left for school, say something meaningfully, and give me a big hug. I had to wear a starched white shirt, tie, and corduroy knickers with knee-high socks. Mom's insistence that I dress like this was responsible for me fighting each and every day of my school life. You see, the rest of the boys came from the same poor surroundings we did, and dressing shabbily was a status symbol of sheer toughness. My main adversary was a kid we called Babe. He was a ruthless, sadistic gang leader, and I was his special target.

I remember coming home in tears one afternoon because he and two of his gang members beat me to a pulp. I was sobbing, and Pop put his arms around me. "What's the matter, Giovanni?"

I told him what happened. Even though he wasn't allowed to

walk down the stairs, he put his coat on and took me by the hand to the dime store. I wondered what he was up to as I looked up at him with admiration. He walked me over to the section of baseball bats. In those days, they sold cheap bats fourteen inches long that could be concealed in a jacket sleeve.

Pop leaned over. "Giovanni, if there is ever more than one, use this bat. Don't be afraid." Even at my age, I understood his justification. This mild, gentle man gave me my first lesson in survival.

My life was so busy with differing activities, there was no personal time for myself. Like living with split personalities; I was attending public school, searching coal supplies, conservatory musical training, voice coach on Sundays, singing on radio stations, working in a drugstore weeknights and a butcher shop Saturdays. My spare time was laced with survival tactics in an area demanding animal instincts to remain in one piece. That, in a nutshell, was the reason for my headaches and hemorrhage nosebleeds.

The next day, Babe and three of his animals chased me for three blocks. I ran as fast as I could and slipped the bat into my hand, ready for battle. I stopped. As Babe rushed me, I closed my eyes and swung the bat shoulder level with every ounce of my strength. The bat struck its mark in Babe's windpipe. He fell, gasping for air. His three friends stopped short as I stood over Babe and threatened them with the bat. I felt victory for the first time as Babe struggled for air on the cold concrete. I knew Pop was right.

I went home, ran to Pop, and hugged him in some sort of recognition that he had helped me. He seemed to know; somehow he always did. I didn't have to work at the drugstore that day, so I ran out to play until Mom came home. It was near dark when I saw her slim, petite figure walking in the distance. She had to walk more than a mile from the subway every night after work. I zoomed up the stairs like a military messenger. "Pop, Mom is coming home!" I shouted.

"Go help her with her bundles." She would bring home extra work, as we owned a sewing machine.

"John, the Strega is coming tonight," Mom said to Pop as we walked into the house.

Pop's face tightened and turned pale. "Anna, what in the hell do you think you're doing?" Pop shouted for the first time. "It'll scare the boy half to death!"

"I can't help it, John. We've tried everything else, and she's been known to cure many children."

"You can't depend on old superstitions. She's no more than someone practicing witchcraft, even though they call it *malocchio* in Italy."

Pop was referring to the evil eye. If someone had put the evil eye on someone else, the Strega was believed to have the power to thwart it and cure the person I didn't realize they'd called her for me.

Mom put the dinner on the coal stove after I opened the little round covers and shoved in some coal to fire it up. Just as the water started to boil, a knock thundered on the door. I ran to open it and looked up at the new visitor. She was tall, dark skinned, with high cheek bones and slanted eyes, resembling an Oriental. She had a towel wrapped under one arm, and her look brought back to mind the funeral experience.

She stormed in and embraced Mom. "Hi Anna," she said. Mom took the tablecloth off the table and placed a small bottle of olive oil in the center.

"Is this the boy?" the woman asked.

"Yes," Mom said as Pop stormed out of the kitchen to his favorite sulking place in the living room. "Giovanni, this is Mrs. Bonura."

"Hello," I said.

"Whoever put the evil eye on this one was jealous of his beautiful eyes," Mrs. Bonura said.

"He's been having some trouble with them lately," Mom said.

"You see, what did I tell you?" she boomed. "Sit down, son."

I fell into the kitchen chair next to the table. She unwrapped the towel on the table to reveal a large crucifix, prayer beads, and cotton. She placed two candles beside a white ceramic bowl filled with water. "Shut the lights. I have to tell the spirits I am unafraid of them."

I was captivated, still unaware it was for my benefit. "Sit still and keep your eyes open," she roared.

The swarming lights of the candles seemed to change her face. I could swear it was Nonna. She dipped her thumb into the water and anointed my forehead with the sign of the cross. She closed her eyes and lapsed into a moaning wail of a prayer. She did this for what seemed like an eternity. Finally, she opened her eyes slowly and poured some of the olive oil into the saucer. I watched with eagerness, hoping she wouldn't hurt me. She snapped her fingers at the bowl of water, and two large globules emerged as peering eyes. She told me to close my eyes. She dipped her thumbs into the oil and rubbed them against my lids. She prayed again.

The Strega turned to Mom as I was developing one of my headaches. "Did you see the eyes? I knew it, he is cured."

I was beside myself. My head pounded to the point of distraction. I ran through the apartment into my room. I threw my pillow over my head and prayed to God for my survival. I didn't eat supper. Pop came into my room, kissed me, and threw the bedcovers over me. I fell asleep.

Two days later on Sunday morning, we got dressed, went to church, and came home. I had cancelled my vocal lesson because I was to perform at Costello's house that day. Frank was taking me to the event. I liked doing things with him and always was anxious to please.

He, like Pop, understood me. Mom dressed me in what was called a George Washington suit, made of shiny black velvet with a white satin shirt sporting long tassels down to my waist and the pants were above the knee. They kept my hair in a Buster Brown haircut because of my early career. Mom added Brilliantine to my hair to make it shine under the theatrical lights. Pop tucked my music in my portfolio and gave me a big hug and kiss, as usual, to wish me luck.

"Hurry up, Giovanni, we're running late!" Frank shouted from the downstairs hallway.

I ran downstairs to the most magnificent auto I'd ever seen. It was a deep, shiny maroon with a white canvas top. The tires had white walls with chrome spoke wheels. The hood seemed to extend forever with a chrome Greek mythical-like statue at the end, giving the feeling of flight even though the car wasn't moving. I fell in love with the smell of a new car. The leather seats had a most pleasant odor of richness.

I was spellbound as I turned slowly to behold the luxury of the interior. Frank started the engine, and the robust sound gave me the feeling of security. We seemed to ride endlessly as Frank was quiet. In my era, a boy my age didn't speak unless spoken to. I was hoping he would speak. I had so many questions. What was expected of me? Did they have a band or just a piano?

"These are very important people you are working for today, Giovanni," Frank finally said while puffing on a cigarette and putting his hand on my knee. "In fact, I have a surprise for you."

"What is it?"

"You'll see, Giovanni. If I told you, it wouldn't be a surprise, would it? I can tell you this: If I have anything to do with it, you're going to be a grand opera star. All you have to do is get the proper guidance and training. Listen to me, and you'll never need to worry."

I didn't quite understand his full meaning. However, I was satisfied something was being offered to me. I saw wonderful countryside as we entered a small town with a large canopy sign, Welcome to Glen Cove.

We turned left on a modest highway and drove through streets lined with magnificent trees. They shadowed the street from the sun's glare. The houses looked like castles. The road reached the water and turned north. It was truly a scenic view. We came to a dead end: iron gates between large marble pillars. Frank stopped the car and walked to a phone at the gate. He spoke into it, and the gates opened ever so slowly like magic being performed for my benefit.

Frank drove ahead as I swirled around to watch the gates close behind us. The drive was exalting. Long rows of glistening pines seemed to reach the clouds, but no house was in sight. Finally, we came to a long circular drive. A monstrous house of a deep brick color appeared in the center.

Cars were parked all over the lawn as we eased up to the front door. A huge black man opened the car door and greeted Frank. My uncle asked him how he was and how his family was doing in an overly warm manner.

"I'm doing fine, Mr. Frank. Don't you worry about me; Mr. Costello takes good care of me and Odessa."

As we walked to the house, Frank told me the doorman was the ex-heavyweight champion of the world, called Kid Candy. "Why isn't he still champion?" I asked.

"For one thing, he is old, for another, he got his bell rung against a fighter called Max Baer who could hit pretty hard." I wondered what happened to all the money he had made.

Two cathedral-like doors with hammered artwork led into the grandiose home. We entered, and I gulped. The foyer had to be eighty feet long and sixty feet wide with a Florentine-style fountain. Overwhelming marble statues stood against the circular contoured walls, and a huge glittery chandelier gave the room a full spectrum of color. Now I really knew how poor we were. I didn't think I'd ever see anything like this again.

Frank seemed to be aware of my shock, so he smiled and grabbed my hand. "Wait until you see the rest of it."

There was more? I noticed stairways followed the contoured

walls on each side of the room to an upstairs living area. I could hear murmurs, music, and laughter coming from another room.

Frank led me into the large area resembling a ballroom. It was awash in the glitter of lavish jewelry adorning both men and women, fine-fashioned clothing I hadn't seen in my short lifetime, men smoking cigars, and shockingly, women too. I hadn't seen a woman in my family smoke, nor at the concerts I had given.

Costello was perched on a large red-velvet captain-like chair handsomely trimmed with lattice. It was easy to see he was some sort of king in his own right. Most of the people who greeted him bowed and kissed his ring that sported a dazzling ten-carat blue-white diamond. Frank brought me to him when he was free. His cold black eyes seemed to bore through my skull. His expression changed when I bowed and greeted him with "*Buon giorno*, Don Costello." His hawk-like eyes softened and became watery, warm. I knew he was pleased and that this was important for Frank.

"I must talk to you about a most important matter, Costello," Frank said.

"Not now, Frank, this is a day for feasting. It isn't every day a man is celebrating his anniversary, and to Lauretta, such a great lady."

"This won't wait, Costello." Frank gave him a stern look.

Costello got up slowly and motioned Frank to follow him. "Bring the boy with you. It wouldn't be good for him to wander alone with all of these people about. He may give away the surprise about his performance. I am saving that for my wife until the last."

We walked into his den. It dripped Italian culture among the Tiffany lamps, a large picture of Enrico Caruso, a mandolin on the wall, and a record player with stacks of records strewn around, indicating constant use. I read some of the labels: Toscanini, Caruso, Volpi, the peasant singer Carlo Buti, and surprisingly, the great Irish tenor, John McCormack. I picked up the record curiously. Costello smiled knowingly.

"McCormack and Caruso were very close friends and admirers of each other's craft." He turned to Frank. "I keep it handy when I have any kind of meeting with the Micks."

"Exactly what I want to talk to you about, Costello. It looks as though we are going to lose Joe Coogan."

Costello lit one of his great uncle's black rope cigars. "What in the hell are you talking about, Frank? He is one of the most important and most powerful men in our machine. In fact, he is completely wired politically and in the church. Further, he is geared for governor of this state."

"Do you recall I was against putting him up as tax commissioner, and my reasoning was we wouldn't be able to save him if any investigation came upon the office." Frank extended his hand to Costello's arm as if to hold his attention. "When favors are done out of that office, the one liable for it could only be the commissioner because he is the one in authority."

Costello bit down hard on his cigar and snarled his mouth. "Who in the hell could figure *our* His Honor, Mayor Walker would turn out to be such a screwball? We had to save his neck through Joe's office, not for the money we would lose, but with his behavior, we couldn't tell if he would hold up under investigation."

Frank stared into Costello's angry eyes. "If we handle this clumsily, Coogan may tilt on us."

"What are you talking about, Frank? He is one of the best standup guys we ever had."

"I agree with certain exceptions. He is loyal if he perceives he is being treated fairly. If I recall, he, along with me, didn't want the job but was assured by your brother, Ed, he had nothing to worry about."

Costello slumped into his chair, grimaced, and clasped his hands. "I should have known. Every time my brother, Ed, brings me something, it becomes an impossible disaster," he said in a low monotone.

He pressed a button beneath his desk, and a gargantuan man

walked in with a low hairline, kinky hair, and enormous hands that hung much too low, like an ape.

"Bring Ed in here, and you stay, Frank. I want a witness."

Frank bowed his head. "Do you want the boy to leave the room?"

"No, it'll be good for him to listen. He may not understand now, but it'll be a good lesson for him to remember as he grows into manhood."

Ed burst into the room. "Everyone is looking for you, Costello. The cardinal is here, and you know how impatient he is."

"Listen, punk, and listen good. First of all, I made sure he was ordained cardinal, so he'll wait. I had no say in the fact that you would be my brother, so I have to tolerate you. Listen and listen close, Ed. Don't ever come to me with schemes, scams, ideas, or advice of any kind from this day forward. I am giving you fifty dollars a week to stay away from me. And don't ever use my name or reputation for anything you do in the future!"

Ed turned pleadingly to Frank. "What did I do, Frank? Me, his only brother! Why does he always treat me this way?"

Frank turned away as though Ed had committed a mortal sin.

Costello swung him around. "Why are you talking to Frank? I am the one you should be talking to, no one else. Ed, the only thing keeping you alive is that you are my brother, and Mamma is still alive. But don't push me, I warn you." He turned to the apelike man. "He deserves no explanation. Get him out of my sight, or before God I'll kill him."

My eyes widened, and Costello's expression changed. He looked down at me and forced a smile. "Don't worry, my godson, for you'll be a man. Real men are never talked to in this manner."

He made me feel secure somehow. He had a way about him that could scare you to death, or make you feel like nothing in the world could ever bother you. He pressed the buzzer once more. I noticed he never called the apelike man by name. He entered, and Frank spoke in a deliberate soft tone. "Bring Joe Coogan in here.

23

Tell him it is important."

Seconds later, a stately man walked in smiling. He was immaculately dressed with polished nails and an impressive diamond stickpin in his tie. His straight red hair was slicked back with a three-quarter part. "Did you want to see me, Costello?"

Costello brought his hand up in a cuplike fashion, rubbed his face, and looked at Coogan's pink face and sharp green eyes, seemingly deciding how to break the news. He walked to the window, opened the curtain with his right hand, and paused for a moment. "Frank, do me a favor and take Giovanni up to the artist dressing room so he can go over his music with the accompanist we chose for him." He turned to me and smiled. "This will be your big surprise for the day."

Frank once again took me by the left hand as I carried my music in the right. We walked up the stairs to a lush room harboring a beautiful Steinway piano. The room had everything. A makeup bar stood against the far left wall with lights trimming the edges of the mirror, along with a backless cushioned chair. Tasteful furniture accented the room. A tall, gaunt man with his back to us was playing a passage from Verdi's opera, *Aida*. Frank held me back with his hand on my shoulder and walked over to the man's side. "Mr. Petri?"

"Yes."

"This is the boy Costello was telling you about."

A very kind face turned to me. He held out his hand and stared into my eyes as if studying me, almost to distraction.

"What do you think you would like to do for us today?" he asked.

"*L'Elisir d'Amore*, the aria "Una furtiva lagrima.""

"Very good, I never expected that from a boy your age. Even though most of it is sung pianissimo, it takes a mature sound to get the meaning of the composer. A boy soprano could never make it sound right." He took my hand. "Give me your music, please."

I handed it to him. I could tell he was impressed as he said, "A special arrangement, eh? Written for you by Orlando Parado. I know he wouldn't waste his time for any kind of money. He only handles what he considers talent. You should be proud."

He started with an arpeggio, which usually signals the artist for his key. I didn't start. "Didn't you hear me give you your key, Giovanni?"

"Forgive me, Maestro, but if you notice the arrangement, I start four bars before the music."

"No signal?"

"I have perfect pitch."

He stared at me questioningly, beckoning me to start. I began, but he stopped before I finished the first line. "Right on pitch, Giovanni. Bravo, bravo."

It was old hack to me, so I was not impressed by his amazement; I would have been impressed had I known who Mr. Petri was. We were feeling each other out. Frank had left the room, and a red-faced priest entered. "I heard a beautiful voice as I was walking through the hallway, and my curiosity made me pop in. How are you, Mr. Petri, and what do we have here?"

"This is Giovanni, the protégé of Costello and Frank Suraci. Giovanni, this is Cardinal Patrick Joseph Hayes." I looked up at his round smiling red face and knew I liked him.

"Would you give me a private performance, Giovanni?" the cardinal asked.

"Surely."

"Do you have music to any of the "Ave Marias?" Petri asked.

"Yes, I do it in my church on all sorts of occasions for Monsignor Gibney."

"He is a grand friend of mine," the cardinal said. "On with it, on with it, Giovanni."

I sang with a height that couldn't be explained in language. The accompanist was superb, and the cardinal's presence seemed to lift the pressure of the past dark days. I couldn't help but give probably the grandest performance of my young life. As I noticed the cardinal's eyes fill with tears, I became emotional and sang as I'd never sung before. Both men embraced me and shouted bravos. Surely this was a grand day.

The cardinal wiped his eyes with a handkerchief and asked if I would perform this downstairs. "It isn't every day I have the services of such a super salesman to help me bring some of those heathens downstairs back to the church."

I was pleased. Mr. Petri went over a few things with me, then frowned when he saw an arrangement of Bruno Huhn's "Invictus." "Don't dare do this."

"Why?"

"It's an atheist poem. The cardinal would blow a fuse."

I was disturbed but honored his wish. It was my introduction to censorship. Although I didn't quite understand at the time, people in high positions did have the power to allow or disallow an artist's work. The apelike man entered and motioned to Mr. Petri that all was ready downstairs.

Mr. Petri gathered my music. "Well, Giovanni, before we go down, I want you to know I respect you as an artist. It is truly amazing, you have such a mature sound, with the range of a boy soprano, but the sound of a dramatic tenor. Your voice is not childlike, and if you use your instrument well, I predict you'll be one of the best of our time, Little Caruso.

"I'm going to give you your surprise now. I am head of the Metropolitan Opera Chorus, and I want you to start as soon as you can. Come to my studio at six o'clock Thursday for enrollment. Now I must warn you, you'll need to work as a team, and you won't have the freedom of movement you've been used to, but I'm sure the exposure will do you good, working with the top soprano singers in the world, and Toscanini is in the pit."

I was breathless and showed my eagerness, I'm sure. Mr. Petri put his large hand on my shoulder, and we walked downstairs together. When we got to the bottom, I noticed Mr. Coogan walking out of Costello's den with another man. I couldn't help but hear. "It doesn't make sense," he said, his head hanging. "All I did was what all my predecessors have done through the years, and the irony is the judge who will sentence me has been cutting money on these very favors for twenty years."

Their voices faded down the hallway. Mr. Petri and I walked into the grand room, where everyone was dancing the tarantella, a lively Italian folk dance. Mr. Petri led me to two chairs beside the bandstand to wait. Don Costello entered from his den looking concerned and troubled, but he quickly changed his expression and raised his right hand to stop the band. He walked over to the microphone and waited for everyone to notice him in the spotlight. He stood with all the stage presence of a pro until he had everyone's undivided attention.

He spoke quietly. "All of my friends, as you know my wife, Lauretta, and I have been married for twenty-five wonderful years, and I wish to thank you for your presence. Thank you for your wonderful gifts. I know it is your way of showing your love and respect for me." I looked at his wife, who didn't appear to mind the remark. On the contrary, she stared at him with deep admiration. "It is hard to believe we were poor immigrants a short time ago. With the help of God and my wife, Lauretta, things have turned out pretty good." The crowd quietly chuckled. After showering her with gifts, I sensed this was not enough. "Knowing how much she likes music, I've brought her a surprise gift. The next shining star in show business, Master Giovanni, who will entertain for you."

After the applause quieted, he added, "Remember, this is for my wife, Lauretta, I don't want to hear a sound."

Applause burst out once more. Mr. Petri strolled to the piano and brushed his tails back as he sat down. I took my place at the center of the stage. "I dedicate this song to Signora Costello," I said before proceeding to sing Gounod's rendition of "Ave Maria."

It was electrifying. The room's sound was better than Carnegie Hall's. My voice flourished throughout the ballroom, and Mr. Petri's chords so complemented my voice that I felt as though I had floated through an eternity of happiness. The crowd exploded with bravos and applause. Mr. Petri gestured for me to take bow after bow.

I couldn't help but notice how pleased Costello and his wife were. She hugged him. Remembering the ham Dick had been teaching me, I slowly turned while bowing until I faced the host and his wife. I threw them kisses, which drove the crowd to its feet.

Mr. Petri walked to the center. "I've never had the pleasure of listening to Gounod's rendition of this religious song." I noticed the cardinal nodding and staring at me with affection. "Now, I think I can persuade our Little Caruso to please us further. Maybe we'll get him to sing the "Vesti la Giubba" from *Pagliacci*." Everyone made all sorts of quiet sounds of approval.

When I finished and the crowd quieted down, I walked off the stage and sat in Frank's lap beside Costello.

Costello leaned over and whispered, "Bravo, my godson, you have done it well. I want to speak to you alone before you leave." I thanked him. Lauretta held my face in her milk-white hands ever so gently and kissed my forehead with her warm and tender lips. I liked her very much.

The crowd was thinning out, and Costello started to look tired. I thought he had forgotten, or he was just being nice about talking to me, but I learned my first hard lesson about him: When he said something, he meant it.

Costello leaned back to Frank and covered his mouth to say, "I'm going to talk to the boy in my den, Frank. If anything important comes up, I'll be in there." He led me by the hand to his office, where he sat in the dark and rubbed his chin as though needing a shave. This seemed to be a trait of his when he was about to tackle a problem.

"Sit down, Giovanni."

I was not quite on the chair yet when he said, "Do you know who or what I am, Giovanni?"

"You're Uncle Frank's friend."

He smiled. "A good observation, Giovanni. However, I'm a lot more. I have much power and influence, Giovanni. With this power and influence, I'm going to help you, and I'll tell you why. I'm going to talk to you as a man, because very soon you'll be the man in your family. You know your father is very ill, and they don't have a cure for him. I love your father, even though he is nothing like us, the leadership. He is a kind and gentle philosopher with enough love for all the United States and Italy.

"I'm a soldier carrying a banner for my people in a great country. As great as this country is, it has evil influences that exploit not only our people, but all the minority segments. Soldiers like me in every minority have grabbed the gauntlet to keep our identity. Remember, Giovanni, always be proud you are an Italian, for those Italians before you have given the world greatness. Michelangelo, da Vinci, Marconi, Verdi, Puccini, with many others, and we still have much to offer the world. It's important to preserve our great heritage. We're not all like those greats, so people like me who aren't giving a life to creation have the time to take leadership so we could protect them.

"Sometimes we have to do what is considered cruel, but unfortunately, someone has to sit in judgment of what has to be done for the good of all. A good soldier or general must have money. We couldn't accomplish our goal without money, for money is power when used wisely. To make myself clear, Giovanni, I'm going to use some of this found money to further your career, but you must promise to never lose sight of your heritage."

Not grasping most of his intent, I looked into his eyes out of affection. "Don Costello, I'll never forget my heritage, nor will I forget you. I know you are my friend, and I'll never do anything to change this."

He smiled faintly and whispered, "I know I have acquired a new friend." Then he rose in a sudden burst of energy. "It's getting late, and you have school tomorrow." He pulled a hundred out of his pocket. "Here is your pay for today, Giovanni."

I refused without hesitation, so he tucked it into my pocket. "I told you, you'd be paid for today. I know you think friends should do each other favors. Well, Giovanni, what you have done for my wife, Lauretta, today hardly makes this payment enough. Put it in the bank, or get some new arrangements . . . is that what you call the music?" I was embarrassed.

Frank and I walked to his car. "What's the matter, Giovanni? You seem so quiet," he asked as I stepped into the car.

"I'm tired, and I never knew how terribly poor we are."

I couldn't wait to tell Pop about all of the wonderful people I'd met and my job with the Metropolitan Opera, but I found Mom crying at home. Pop had been rushed to St. John's Hospital after another attack. Two of Mom's sisters were with her, and I was commanded to my bed. I burst into tears, afraid for Pop.

Little brother, Ninni, awakened and rubbed his eyes. "Don't cry, whatever is bothering you, it will go away." He came over and clasped my hand. Ninni was all of four years of age, I was seven, and our bond was in its embryonic state.

*****

Nearly forty-seven years later, little brother, Ninni, clasps my hand and quietly says, "Don't cry, we'll get through this."

Ninni is now fifty and I am fifty-three. Children no longer, we miss our mom terribly, feel lost, but still find solace in each other. I fall back into the past, searching for the safety of Pop's arms.

CHAPTER THREE

I was frightened beyond explanation, for I dearly loved Pop and had been exposed to death. I prayed to God as I lost focus. I couldn't conceive living life without Pop. Once again, I had a bad night with reoccurring dreams and fell asleep at the first peek of dawn.

After my usual quick awakening, I went to the kitchen table for my un-favorite porridge. My brother and I flipped the oatmeal at each other with our spoons. My sister warned us we'd get into trouble. We paid no heed, and our missed shots ended up on the wall. Mom entered the kitchen, and I scrambled to my room for sanctuary and to gather my books for school.

I walked to school with Herman and Manny and described the previous day. "Don Costello is my father's brother, you know," Manny said.

I didn't pay much attention because my mind was on Pop in the hospital, thinking I may never see him again, remembering what Don Costello had told me. I was very sad and didn't pay attention to my teachers. In fact, I had to stand in the corner several times, but I didn't care. *If God took Pop away, I never would love God again.* Babe or his gang didn't bother me; I think they had enough the other day. Herman and Manny walked me all the way home.

I was surprised to see Pop had returned. I was joyous and told him of yesterday's great events. I ran to my suit in the closet and retrieved the money to show Pop. He smiled weakly. "Fine, Giovanni, it looks as though you are on your way."

I told him all about my talk with Don Costello, except Costello mentioning Pop being so ill. Pop looked at me in his kind manner and filled my head with critical wisdom. "Giovanni, he's right, identity is most important in these times, but remember, you owe nothing to him or anyone like him. God gave you your talent for you to use wisely. Be polite to him, be grateful, pay him back with more than money, but don't ever let him or his kind steal your soul or dignity. If you don't understand all what I've said, remember well. It'll make sense to you as life unfolds."

I didn't know it then, but this was the first of a series of talks I wouldn't fully understand. Pop knew he was going to die and decided to teach me as much as he could before then. He somehow knew Mom wouldn't remarry and I'd be left without counsel in my formative years.

I went to my usual place at the front window in the living room where I did my homework after school. It faced two buildings on the side street. One was Ferrell's Funeral Parlor, and to the left was the huge Clover Laundry. Along the right corner of the building, a vertical pipe extended to the ground and elbowed out. It emitted a force of steam that could scald anyone within ten feet. We'd been told to steer clear of it.

The sun was setting, the time of day that made me feel the world was tired. Ferrell's place was another organized crime decoy for smuggling raw alcohol via dummy funerals. I noticed two men dragging another man who was struggling and digging in his heels. They forced his mouth onto the pipe, then tied his hands and ankles with what looked like baling wire. One of them grabbed him by the hair and wired his head to the pipe. The other man looked up as if to signal to someone in the upper window. Seconds later, a flow of steam rushed into the man's mouth. His body squirmed like a worm on a fishhook.

I was in a paralytic state. "Pop, Pop, come here quick!" I

finally screamed, forgetting excitement could endanger him.

Pop ran through the railroad rooms. "What's the matter, Giovanni?"

I stuttered in broken sentences.

"Calm down, I don't know what you're trying to say."

I pointed at the body wired to the pipe.

"Oh, my God in heaven!" He dragged me away from the window and held my head against his waist. "It's none of our business, Giovanni, forget what you saw."

How could I forget? I didn't understand Pop's reaction then, but I realize now that no explanation would have made any sense. He sat me down in the kitchen and sang a beautiful peasant song. He truly had a wonderful voice. Of course, I didn't calm down sufficiently, but it did distract me.

Mom came home at her regular time, tired and grouchy as usual. I ran to her. "Mom, Mom, you should have seen what happened across the street at Clover Laundry!"

"Will you give me a chance to sit down? I've been working hard all day."

I noticed a bandage on her index finger. "What happened to your hand, Mom?"

"I caught it under my needle, and it broke inside my finger."

The back of my knees tingled, and I felt responsible somehow. I wished Mom didn't have to work.

"Anna, teach me how to run the machine," Pop said. "I can take in homework so you won't have to work so hard."

"It's a cross I have to carry. You're not allowed to do anything, remember, John? I'll just have to do it myself somehow."

Pop slapped his hand on the kitchen table and shouted, "You'll teach me, or I'll go out and dig ditches if I have to!"

Mom shook her head and shrugged. "All right, John, I'll teach you."

My everyday chores now included picking up the extra

bundles for Pop's share of the work. He seemed much happier contributing to the house. He sang all sorts of Italian songs as he worked, often far into the night. I'm sure Mom never realized it, but he had his work cut out for him at the machine while tending to us. He positioned the machine by the kitchen window facing the backyard where he could watch us play most of the time. Needless to say, we gave his heart a few traumas.

My Thursday appointment at the Metropolitan Opera House came before I knew it. Mom took off early from work, and we took the IRT subway to 39th Street and entered the grand old building through a side entrance housing a circular marble staircase. Beside it was an old wrought-iron elevator. We rode to the first level. I could hear voices from each studio: sopranos, tenors, contraltos, bassos, robust baritones. Even with the discord of sounds, it sounded as if a composer were putting it together.

I felt a tinge of nervousness. Mom looked at Mr. Petri's studio number on his card. When we reached the end of the hall, she beckoned me and opened the door. In polite Italian manner, she said, "*Permesso?*"

Mr. Petri was sitting at the piano with a bevy of singers around him. "Entrare, Signora Benedetto," he boomed, pointing at a chair. She guided me over to it, but he stopped her. "No, the boy comes here by the piano."

He turned to me. "You are five minutes late. The first thing you learn is to be early, never late. I'll be with you in a moment. Just stand here by me and listen to a bunch of singers sound like a herd of pigs being slaughtered. Show these people a middle C." I did. "Give them a G." I did. "You see, this is a seven-year-old boy. Where in the hell did you get the idea you were musicians?"

He didn't seem to be the gentle, kind man I met at Don Costello's party. I wanted to crawl under the piano.

His voice quieted as he looked up at the high, regal ceiling. "What happened to the great stars of yesterday? The Buono Anima Caruso must be spinning in his grave thinking some lead tenor has to work with this bunch. We have two weeks to get ready to perform Bizet's *Carmen*. By God, you'll be ready, or I'll scratch out your vocal cords with my hands. Now, after listening to a small boy show you perfect pitch without the intro of piano, let us see if any of you can give me one sound on key with my help."

He struck another chord, cringed, and covered his face. "You sound like a high school band. One more time, please."

As he continued this line of disparagement, more boys my age entered, some appearing to belong, others with the same look I had.

"You adults can all go home tonight and pray to Jesus you're ready for me tomorrow night."

The young ones gathered around the piano as the others filed out. He passed out mimeographed sheets about the size of a checkbook and sat back down at the piano. "This opera is sung in French. For those of you who don't speak French, the words are written phonetically. That means it's written just the way it's supposed to be pronounced," he emphasized with impatience.

I was accustomed to different languages, for I had been singing in Italian, Spanish, German, but not French. The reality of where I was captured me, and I drifted to never-never land. I had the ability to absorb, perform, yet live in my own fantasy world. My teachers never knew of my escape mechanism. I never got caught off guard. At any moment, I could concentrate and hear the wildest chords of music and enjoy my own concert. I had favorite times and places for this, such as on the subway. Sometimes I would summon it if I was excited or if the situation was unbearable. Music was my medicine.

The lesson was over before I knew it, and Mr. Petri gave us a schedule for costume fitting. He led us onstage for movement and pantomime instructions, then ran down the list of cities where we'd perform that year. We'd receive eleven dollars per show in town, twenty-five out of town, plus expenses. "I'll see you all next Tuesday at 5:30."

Mom looked pleased as we walked through the darkened hallway. It was late and quiet now. The old-theater odor surrounded us, somehow far from offensive. In fact, it sparked images of the past greats who had blessed this hall, talents given us only once in a century, such as Caruso, Tagliavini, Stracciari, Titta Ruffo, Giovanni Martinelli. I was on a cloud. Mom was quiet. The next morning, I told Pop about my wonderful time at the opera.

After school, Herman, Manny, and I sneaked off to the East River. We were forbidden to go there, but it was our favorite meeting place. I gathered some branches and old newspapers to light a fire with those old-fashioned large Birdseye matches from Mom's kitchen, and I told them about my adventure the night before.

"You're going to be an opera singer?" Manny asked as he put three large Idaho potatoes he had stolen from Rocco's fruit stand on Astoria Boulevard in the fire. I smiled faintly and poked at the fire. I couldn't imagine being anything else. Then it dawned on me: I never bothered to ask what my two best friends wanted to be.

I handed Manny a hot mickey, what we called fire-baked potatoes in those days. "Manny, what are you going to be when you grow up?"

He became serious, so serious that he seemed adult. "I'm going to take Costello's place. He's my godfather, baptized me when I was a baby."

"We're going to be related, Manny. Your uncle is going to confirm me in church, and he'll be my godfather also." We smiled, feeling a deeper bond.

In chorus, Manny and I asked Herman what he wanted to be. We held pinkies and made a wish before Herman spoke. He was the most patient, careful thinker, as if liable for everything he said. "I want to help people. I thought of being a doctor or lawyer, but I think I'm going to be a priest."

"Great," Manny said. "With some of the things I'm going to do, I'll need a friend to confess to, sort of a partner."

We heated Manny's penknife, slashed our wrists, and swore loyalty and unity forever as blood brothers. It was getting dark, so we snuffed out the fire and headed home.

I opened the kitchen door with an obvious look of guilt. Mom was home early and grabbed me by the ear to smell my clothing. "You were by a fire, weren't you?"

The next morning, we had a surprise. I was not quite awake when I heard a husky female voice coming from the kitchen. I couldn't understand what she was saying in Italian. I ran into the kitchen and fell in love for the first time. Before me stood two of the most beautiful women I'd ever seen. They looked very much alike, probably seventeen years old, and were dressed the same. My mouth dropped open as I stared at the tall, slim girls in a black dress with chestnut hair, big blue eyes, and soft, wavy hair.

I suspected they were sisters. They had large leather travel bags with straps holding them together.

"Giovanni, these are your first cousins I've brought from Italy," Pop said. "They'll be staying with us for a while until they get settled. My sister's husband died recently, and I'm to be their guardian until they get married."

This was another introduction to Italian culture. You see, every Italian family had a woman who was the dealmaker, marriage broker, and she was rewarded for it. For example, the broker might arrange a union between a woman in Italy and a man in the United States. The broker would get paid for producing a husband and for the wife consequently becoming an American citizen. The broker usually was middle aged or older and shrewd, perhaps practicing a bit of witchcraft to cast a love spell. If the prospective couple was aware of the spell, they'd fall in love by suggestion.

I met my first marriage broker the next morning, the old mother of my deviate uncle. One look at her as she entered our kitchen, and I was afraid of her. She wore a stained apron over a black dress.

"This must be Giovanni, the singer, eh?" she said as her wrinkled skeleton fingers pulled a hard, stale pastry out of her apron pocket. "Here, Giovanni, I have blessed this. Eat it and evil will run from you."

I spun around to Pop. "Take it, Giovanni," he said, even though he looked disturbed. "It won't hurt you, I promise." I meekly obeyed and pretended to eat it. It made me sick.

Mom left for work, and the broker started her work. "Let me see the merchandise, John," she squealed.

"Anna, Maria, *venni qui al la cucina!*"

The girls appeared, and I was spellbound by Anna. I had most peculiar feelings about her for a seven-year-old.

The old witch looked pleased, but she downgraded them to receive a high broker's fee. "The older one is too skinny, and the younger one has hair on her mouth. It won't be easy getting them married, but if I really work at it, I think it'll be arranged. Write the remaining family and tell them it'll take cash for these two."

"I know for a fact you already have them promised, and the family is not as wealthy as you think," Pop said. "I'll do the best I can."

The old lady asked the girls if they were still innocent. The girls blushed at each other and bowed their heads almost shamefully. The old lady smiled knowingly and whispered to Pop, "They're innocent all right. What protection will they have until I can arrange a wedding date?"

"They have two brothers here. I've arranged jobs for the girls and will get them on the subway in the morning. One of the brothers will pick them up on the other end to take them to work. In the evening, we just reverse it. The rest of the time, they are in our personal care."

The old lady, looking smug and satisfied, shot up from her chair. "Well, I had better go to work on this right away. See you soon, John." Then to me, *"Forare malocchio, forare malocchio, piccolino."* (Pierce evil eye, young one.)

The family was later shocked to discover Cousin Maria somehow had become pregnant between subway stops. The brothers were furious. Virginity was a must. Without this, there was no marriage. So Maria was sent back to the old country, but her sister, Anna, later married.

*****

I worked very hard for Mr. Petri, and I was to appear February 7, 1931, for the first time in the children's chorus on the Metropolitan stage in the opera, *Carmen,* with Maria Jeritza and Armand Tokatyan.

I'll never forget such an enchanted evening. I slobbered in the smell of the theater. Hypnotized by the costume makers and dressing-room hustle, I got lost and ended up in the women's dressing room with breasts hanging out and nude women in front of mirrors. I threw my hands over my eyes, shocked.

"What are you doing here, little man, getting an education?" one of the women said, laughing.

I dropped my hands and noticed very little clothing on her. "I was looking for my dressing room, ma'am. Will you please direct me to it? You know, it's almost curtain time, and I'm not near ready."

She smiled, held a garment over her breasts, walked me to the door, and pointed. "There, right over there."

I sighed in relief and ran across the hall to the other boys dressing with Mr. Petri's help. "Where have you been, Giovanni? Do you think the audience is waiting for you? Here's your costume. Put it on, and be down at the side of the stage in five minutes."

A polished man with a concerned look approached us, and Mr. Petri introduced us. "This is Mr. Wilhelm von Wymetal Jr. the director and manager of the Metropolitan, boys."

Mr. von Wymetal eyeballed us as though we were merchandise, checking costumes, slanting some scarves, and unbuttoning some jackets. "Very good-looking bunch, Petri."

Then it happened: our cue. My heart pounded as we swarmed onto stage. My first view of the massive audience was breathtaking. The music was enchanting and brought forth much emotion.

I was ready for the opening act as urchins greeted Jose, "*Avec la garde montante.*" It was a night I shall remember and cherish forever.

*****

Life continued on with attending school and studying music. I worked in the drugstore and also the butcher shop for a man named Patsy. November was upon us with short and cold days. It was a busy month, rehearsing at the Met with Mr. Petri, voice classes with my coach, the part-time jobs, school, and two performances at the Met.

I was so excited preparing for one of my favorite operas, *Pagliacci,* and working with Editha Fleischer, a German soprano with the MET, and Giovanni Martinelli, the renowned Italian operatic tenor. At forty-seven, he had been performing at the Met for almost twenty years.

I appeared November 17th in the children's chorus on the Metropolitan stage in the opera, *La Gioconda,* with Rosa Ponselle and Beniamino Gigli as the tenor lead. Mr. Petri unnerved me by bowing down to whisper in my ear, "I have a surprise for you after the performance."

I was much too excited to pay attention to him. I rushed into my costume, a medieval motif with a red scarf wrapped around my head to resemble a pirate's child. I ran downstairs to the rest of the chorus standing in the wings with Mr. Petri, waiting for the stage cue. Mr. Petri was giving last-minute reminders. "Don't forget, boys, act natural. Do what all little boys usually do."

My friend, Roger, and I smiled at each other. We planned to play jumping jacks in front of the great ship as it landed.

The music surrounded my ears and gave me an indescribable high. I felt as though I was floating above the stage like Peter Pan.

The boy's chorus supplying the background of unrest, murmuring sounds, and the crowds moving about. The great tenor Beniamino Gigli appeared at the gangway of the ship. He raised his right hand, and the sweet, succulent sounds poured out of his mouth, seemingly with no effort. I was as spellbound as I'd ever been. In fact, I almost sat down to listen, until I remembered my instructions.

After the performance, reality once more invaded my private world. "Come to the piano, Giovanni," Mr. Petri said. "I have a solo part in the *Bartered Bride* for you."

I stood open mouthed. Mr. Petri seemed to smile, yet proceeded. When I finished, I hugged my maestro, picked up my music case, and ran down the dark corridor. I bumped into a large man in Viking garb with a soldier's horned helmet, flowing red curly wig, and beard.

"What's your rush, little man?" he asked in deep, pear-shaped tones.

"I'm going home." I rattled on as if I knew him, explaining I was in the chorus and wanted a career in opera.

"Sing a line or two for me, young man. I'd like to hear you."

Oddly relaxed, I sang a line from the aria *M'apparì* from the opera *Martha.*

"Bravo. It looks like my world will live on after I die. We have another Caruso in the bud. What's your name, young man?"

"Giovanni Benedetto."

"My name is Lawrence, Lawrence Tibbett. I'm a singer too."

I gasped and stepped back. "Lawrence Tibbett? Oh, my God!"

He gently laughed and bid his exit. "See you again, young man. I only hope I'm still around when you become a tenor lead so I can have the honor of being your baritone lead. They're not giving us many good tenors nowadays. The good ones are staying in Italy for some reason."

I was in a dream world. *The great Lawrence Tibbett actually talked to me.* The greatest acting baritone of his time. I couldn't wait to tell Pop.

It was late when I got on the subway alone, and it was just about empty. I liked to ride between the cars and hypnotize my mind into hearing innovative chords to the wonder of giant segments of voices. Always peaceful, happy, satisfying. It was a twenty-five-minute ride, but the longest I could stretch this phenomenon was about fifteen minutes. When the music faded, I played with the hitch wheel on the left side of every subway car, imagining I was driving the train.

I burst through the door at home about to explode with the night's events, only to find Frank in serious conversation with Mom and Pop at the kitchen table. This was a profound signal to me to keep my mouth shut.

"They have arrested our cousin, Mussolini, (not the dictator) in Calabria for murder of his wife and her lover," Frank said in a low monotone. "From the news I get from the family, he caught the young man he hired at the factory with his wife in a very compromising position. He strangled his wife after he tied the young man up, then dragged him to the salt pit, where he cut out his tongue, pushed him down the ravine, and shot him in the face with the sawed-off shotgun I sent him last Christmas.

"Of course, you must realize we have a big problem. The gold he had been stealing from the king's shipments, hidden in the mountains, can be lost. I know Musso has a map, but if it gets into the wrong hands, we'll kiss the money and Musso good-bye. Even if they find him guilty, it was a crime of passion; the sentence will be light. But if the king's men find out he's Robin Hood and has been taking the king's gold, they'll execute him.

"You are invited to our house for Thanksgiving dinner. Come as early as you please." Frank turned to Mom to discuss the Republican Party. All of my aunts were leaders of the party in our area under their big brother, Frank. He was a Republican, so they were Republicans. Years later, I found out he was as liberal as any Democrat; he'd just made his cradle with the Republicans.

I had already done one more opera that week, *Pagliacci*, at *The Gala Concert* at the Metropolitan. The silk costume felt so festive. The event was as much fun as it was exciting, singing in my big black polka dots. It was such a pleasure and honor to work with Beniamino Gigli again.

*****

Someone grabs my arm and shakes me out of my reverie.

"Your brother is back, John. Tony wants to see you."

It sounds like an echo chamber. I remember the last thing Mom said to me on the phone before she died: "All I want from you and your brother is to love each other and stay together until the day God takes you from the world. I didn't work and slave all these years for you to be strangers or enemies."

Oddly enough, she died in New Jersey while Tony, my wife, and I were together in San Francisco for Thanksgiving. This is rare because he's usually on the road as an entertainer. It is as though she still ruled our lives, even from her deathbed. I drift back to a Thanksgiving morning.

CHAPTER FOUR

Mom woke us early and bathed, rather scrubbed, us. I had to wear the Georg Washington suit. "When can I get this hair cut off, Mom?" I asked as she brushed my Buster Brown hair.

She just told me to sit still. All of us kids were excited about going to see Mom's parents for Thanksgiving. We loved Nonna and Nonno, and their dog, Prince. He was an Italian bull, a rare breed in this country. Nonna would slip a penny into an envelope on his collar, and Prince would trot down to the corner candy store where the proprietor would put a chocolate in it. Then Prince would trot back home for Nonna to give him the candy.

Today we were rich. We took a taxi because Pop couldn't stand and wait for a bus. At our grandparents' house stood two concrete lions Nonno had made, one on each side of the front door. They stood as guardians protecting the property. It was obvious Nonno was proud of his home, which he built brick by brick when he retired at age forty-eight, no easy chore during the dark Depression. He usually sat in a wooden chair in front of the house, never empty-handed, sometimes peeling fruit from one of his garden trees. This time it was a pear.

"Hello, everybody. Come children, give your Nonno a big hug," he boomed in his thick Italian accent as he stood up with his blood-red cheeks bunching up under a smile. His handlebar mustache tickled my neck, so I would tuck my shoulder to my cheek to protect my neck. I loved him very much.

Nonna emerged in her usual stately manner, her graying blond hair flowing as though in slow motion from the gentle breezes. She wore high button shoes and pilgrim-like dresses with high necks and lace cuffs. One by one, starting with the oldest, Maria, she handed us fruit out of the garden. We dashed to the back garden to torture the goat, half a dozen chickens, and three pigs.

My grandparents lived upstairs, and Uncle Frank, my mother's brother, lived downstairs with his wife, Emma and their four children; Tony, Bill, Irene and Jessica. I adored them from early childhood. Aunt Emma was Ukrainian, and a deep prejudice prevailed in those days. So when Aunt Emma and Frank courted, she carried a twenty-five caliber pistol in her boot every time she set foot in the Italian ghetto. It was a cardinal sin for two such ethnic groups to intermarry.

From what Pop told me, she was more than capable of using the weapon. The Russians executed her family, and she killed one of the soldiers near the border while barely escaping. Emma entered the United States under a refugee quota and eventually met Frank through his club when she needed a sponsor for citizenship papers.

She loved him, so she took all of the heat the Italian community could offer. She learned to speak Italian in addition to five languages. Emma learned to cook Calabrese-style Italian as good as my aunts. The daughters grew affectionate toward her, recognizing her quest of family acceptance. We all admired and loved her. Although a child, I recognized and respected her strength. If I wanted the truth, she was the one I could confide in. She was another positive influence in my young life.

The women were working in the kitchen, including Aunt Nettie, who lived with Nonno and Nonna in the upstairs of the huge house. She was an attractive, devilish flirt who would make Pop blush by teasing him that if she had a chance at him, she would grab it. Her husband, Uncle Tom, was tall, dark, and a dapper dresser with straight hair. Although gentle, kind, and sensitive, he seemed to idolize anyone who was opposite.

We were playing in the street and Ninni, although capable of walking, spent most of his time on all fours. Tom and Nonno were watching us from the front of the house when a big boy came along and pushed my baby brother to the ground. He was at least a head taller than me. It seems the Lord endowed me with timing in throwing a punch. As small as I was, I was told I hit like a hammer. I ran over and creamed the bully with one shot to the mouth.

"I'm going to get my big brother, you'll see!" he shouted as he ran away crying.

Tom jumped off the chair spurting in his thick Italian accent. "What a punch, Giovanni! What a punch! You should be the next world champion." He proceeded to tell everyone in the family.

When Mom heard, I caught it. "My boys don't fight like trash in the street," she said. I noticed Uncles Tom and Frank crossing glances, amused. Why didn't they defend me?

Dinner was called, and Nonno bowed his head in prayer. We started with an antipasto of sardines, provolone, black and green olives, pickled olives, anchovies, artichoke hearts, tuna fish, and celery stalks. Lots of conversation and gossip ensued, including stories of the two sisters Anna and Maria, apparently some off-color stories, judging by the undertone of laughs. "I'm the only one who knows how she got a belly full between subway stops," Aunt Nettie said.

Then came the minestrone soup as Nonno picked up his usual gallon of wine, always by his side at the dinner table. "This is the best wine I ever made. I knew when I bought the grapes it was going to be good, but never figured this good."

Everyone, except the women, picked up their glasses to be filled. This was how the old-timers commanded a compliment. Each of them praised Nonno as they tasted it, as if they'd rehearsed a speech all week. In those times, the young gave the old many pleasant reasons for living and feeling wanted.

Next came the pasta and meatballs, broccoli, pork and lamb soaked in pasta sauce, and salad. The eating intensified. Then came the turkey, golden brown with a rich Italian meat-and-spinach stuffing. It must have been superb to taste so good after everything else we'd eaten.

After the turkey, the women split into two platoons, either taking the plates off the table or bringing out fruits and nuts, such as alligator pears, chestnuts, walnuts, dates, and pineapple. Nonna seemed to have the honor of serving espresso. Again, only the men enhanced their coffee with spirits, such as Sambuca, Galliano, and anisette. The children were served cream soda, which was popular among Italians. Everyone sprawled on couches, chairs, on the floor, snoozing, snoring. I thought the holiday was over until Uncles Dick, Jim, and Albert showed up with guitars, mandolins, and a banjo.

My Nonno filled his glass of wine. His eyes gleamed as the men played a *stornelli*, one melody with improvised storytelling, like a folk song — some comical, sad, or risqué. They broke up and played a game called Seven and a Half, an Italian version of blackjack, but the king of diamonds was the hero. They played until the women beckoned them to go home, one by one.

That was an Italian Thanksgiving.

As we were leaving, Frank asked me how I was doing at the Met and told me how proud my soon-to-be godfather was of my performance. "I want you to come by here at 5:30 tomorrow."

The next day was Friday, and I didn't have school. I exchanged Thanksgiving stories with Herman and Manny. In those days, we dressed in costumes on Thanksgiving. We walked door to door and, rather than trick or treat, we chanted, "Anything for Thanksgiving?" We'd receive money, candy, fruit, etc. This year, though, we were doing it the day after Thanksgiving.

I dressed up in a clown costume from my closing number in *Pagliacci*. It was silk with large black polka dots on a white background. Herman dressed as a monk, and Manny sported a black mask as Jesse James. Herman predicted he'd get more donations as a churchman, while Manny thought he'd scare people into giving him more. But we all did well working what we thought were wealthy neighborhoods. Suddenly, I remembered I had to see Frank but didn't have time to go home to change. His house was about two miles away, so I ran all the way.

A big black Cadillac was parked outside the house with a man smoking a cigar. I walked through Frank's den entrance, strictly reserved for private meetings. I saw a dazzling glare from a ring behind the Tiffany desk lamp. It was nearly as enormous as the man wearing it with gray hair, penetrating blue eyes, and large jowls. His tie tack displayed a diamond as big as his ring.

"Dutch, this is my nephew, Giovanni," Frank said, holding my hand. "Say hello to Mr. Murano. He's going to handle your cousin Anna's wedding. He owns a club on Van Alst Avenue here in Queens.

"So this is the *cantante* Costello was telling me about. I'm sorry I missed the party at the house. I heard you were a sensation. Would you like to work special weddings for me, Giovanni?"

As Frank nodded approvingly I replied, "I would be honored, Mr. Murano."

His brow tightened. "He has the old manners, the kind of manners not from this country. It must be in the blood like his father. Yes, I know your father from the old country. Did you know your father used to climb up in the mountains surrounding Calabria and sing like a mockingbird? You could hear him over the whole city. If you have half the voice your father has, you'll join the great ones. I'll pay you twenty dollars a wedding, and don't worry about the music, I hire only the best."

I didn't know whether I liked him or feared him.

"Sit down, Giovanni, I'll be through in a few minutes," Frank said. "Dutch, you better take it easy. Times are changing. We're losing too many of our aces."

Dutch stood up chewing his black cigar. "Just tell those bulls to get off my back. I've been paying them for years, and if they keep this up, I won't stand for it. Frank, it's a matter of face, you understand? You know I only deal in booze. I take no part in the garbage-like prostitution and drugs You tell them, Frank, if they want a war, they'll damn sure get one, and that comes from Dutch Murano's mouth direct."

"We have been *compares* for a long time, and you know I step back for no one. Trust me until this blows over, and we'll replace some of our key men. All I'm saying, Dutch, is don't blow your top over every little thing that jumps off."

"Your trust is never in question, Frank, but the judgment of some of those creeps is. You know damn well if we back down, even on the smallest thing, we're either out of business, or the cost of operation goes up. I'll make a deal. I'll back off if they stop picketing, fair enough?"

"I'll do the best I can, Dutch."

"That's why we all love you, Frank, you never con us. If you can do something, it is done. If not, you admit you'll give it all you got, and you give it plenty. We'll not expect more from anyone."

They embraced, and Dutch left as though he'd made his point.

Frank turned to me. "I wanted you to meet Dutch. He is a very powerful man, and as Dick says, work wherever and whenever you can. You never know who's sitting in the audience. You're very young and have nothing but time on your side. I wish I had your young start."

I kissed Uncle and embraced him. On my way home, I peered into store windows as usual. As I passed Merkel's butcher shop, a large chain in our area, I noticed a man with a pistol. I froze as the butcher, Mike, picked up a cleaver. I heard two shots, and blood flowed from Mike's chest. I couldn't move as a crowd gathered.

The police arrived. "Did anyone see the shooting?" one of them shouted. I was too frightened to speak.

"This little boy was standing in front of the window, officer. He must have seen the whole thing," an older man said.

The cop asked if I could describe the killer. I explained I didn't see him because his back was to me.

"What is your name?" the officer asked.

"Benedetto."

"They train you wops young, don't they? You must've seen him, you little guinea."

I felt as though it were the end of my life. "I'm telling you the truth, sir," I said instinctively. "Ask my uncle, I don't lie."

"And pray tell, who is your uncle that I should believe him?"

"Frank Suraci." I gulped.

Like some magic act, the cop smiled and shoved me away. "Go home, little boy. This is no place for a tyke your age."

I ran as fast as my short legs would take me. By the time I arrived, my throat pinched so badly that I couldn't speak. I started to cry, and Pop took my temperature in his gentle manner.

"It's 104," he told my mom. "We had better call Dr. Keisman."

They put me to bed, and my fever rocketed to 105 by the time the doctor came into my room. Dr. Keisman was a slight man with a square mustache and thick glasses, his hair combed straight to one side. "Let's open your mouth, sonny. Bad, Anna, very, very bad strep throat."

Pop clutched my hand. "Don't worry, Giovanni, the doctor will fix you."

All I could think was how he couldn't help my Nonna. Was he some sort of death messenger? I started to shake.

"Do you have some wood from an old egg crate, John?"

"Yes."

"Get me a stick of it about one-inch-wide and six-inches-long."

The doctor shredded the end and lit it with a match. When it was red hot, he blew out the flame and ordered Mom and Pop to hold me. They grabbed my arms and legs. He forced my mouth open and assured me it wouldn't hurt, then shoved the white-hot stick down my throat to burn my tonsils. The pain shattered my entire body. I couldn't even swallow. He said my throat should be swabbed three times a day with Argyrol antiseptic and to feed me nothing but ice cream before he asked Pop for two dollars.

I thought I was going to die, and I blamed Pop for the first time. Why didn't he stop the doctor from inflicting this unbearable pain?

Well, it was three days before Christmas until the pain left me and I could talk. I worried whether I could sing again, especially only four days until my next performance at the Met. But Pop assured me I would sing better than ever.

The preparation for Christmas was elaborate. It was our turn to host and the aunts came over to prepare for the biggest feast of the year. Mom made the fettuccine and spread it on newspapers all over the beds and furniture to dry before cooking. They crafted the elaborate pastries from the old country: cannoli, *piniolata*, cream puffs, soaked rum cake, *trufoli*, and a family secret called *frisquoliske* — pretzel shapes made from a light batter and covered with powdered sugar after browned. They melted in your mouth.

I was getting excited. We never trimmed the tree until Christmas Eve. The anticipation was healthy, and we seemed to have much more respect for the grand holiday. We still believed in Santa Claus, even though packages were sneaked into hiding places throughout the house. Before midnight, we had fish in the Catholic tradition, and at the stroke of midnight, scads of Italian sausages with thick, tasty Italian bread, a blessing to those heavy on spirits.

The children's anticipation mounted on Christmas Eve day. It was snowing wide, flat flakes in various patterns. I tried to glue my eyes to each one to single it out before it hit the ground. Then I noticed a trail of blood hitting the white-covered ground from the brow of Borghese, my uncle by marriage who lived in the apartment upstairs. Pop had sent him to buy us a tree because he couldn't handle it himself. A fine six-foot tree cost fifty cents if you waited until the last minute and were in the know. Apparently, Uncle got into an argument with the tree man, who split his forehead. But he did get a tree.

Pop shrieked as he entered the house. "Can't you control your temper, even on the eve of the birth of our Savior?"

"I need a drink stronger than wine, and don't lecture me, because I'm bleeding and you're not, John."

Pop burst into laughter and thanked him, then poured a glass of Galliano into a crystal pony. *Salute, fortuna per cento anni*! Luck for a hundred years. Pop downed the glass, which he rarely did because of his condition.

Cousin Anna came home from work with her brother as a chaperone. Needless to say, the security got heavier after her sister's incident. She washed her hands to pitch in.

"How are you feeling today, Giovanni?"

I blushed with adoration. "Fine."

"Are you going to sing carols with us tonight?"

"I haven't tried to sing yet. In fact, I've missed two performances and three lessons. I'm not sure if I can perform in *La Gioconda* in two days. But Mr. Petri told Pop on the phone that I don't have to worry, the position will still be open as soon as I get better."

Things seemed to quiet down about three o'clock. "Come here, Giovanni, on my lap," Pop said. "I want to talk to you."

Still a bit upset about the doctor, I walked to him with much less enthusiasm than usual. He was about to weave one of his stories that made little sense to me at the time.

"You know, you'll be the man of the house soon, and you'll be responsible for your mother, sister, and brother. Even though you are younger than your sister, you are the man, and you should be responsible. When years come upon you, you'll find yourself being very gentle with women. Remember Christ chose a woman to give him birth, and his mother was the Virgin Mary. You must always respect womanhood, no matter who or what they are. That is the first sign of real manhood. And by all means, never, ever strike a woman for any reason. For if you do, you'll lose some of your manhood."

"Tell me a story, Pop. Tell me one of your stories."

"When I came to this country, I came with some friends from my hometown. One of them said to me, 'Come on, John, we're going down to Chinatown.' What for, I asked. 'Oh, we found a place down there for five dollars where they give you a pipe to smoke and a bed to lie in, and you have the most fantastic dreams like Pinocchio.' It was just as they said. I had twenty-five dollars in my pocket, equal to three weeks' pay. So, I paid five dollars, and this Chinaman gave us a bunk. My friend, Jimmy, taught me how to smoke the pipe, telling me to breathe it deep and hold the smoke in my lungs as long as possible, then let it out as slowly as I could.

"Well, I did, and before I knew it, I was having the wildest dreams. When I woke up, I wasn't in the same place, and all of my money was gone. The same thing happened to my friends. 'Let's go to the police,' I said. Jimmy said we couldn't, because what we did was against the law, and we'd be deported. After that, no matter what Jimmy asked me, I said no, but we still remained friends."

I tilted my head like a puppy trying to understand, and Pop said I would understand someday.

The anticipation kept mounting as dusk came down upon us, another day waiting for our guests to arrive. The first uncle to arrive was Albert. He stood at the bottom of the stairs singing Christmas songs with his gut guitar. Pop grabbed my hand, one of the rare times he left the house. Cousin Sal came downstairs and joined us. The four of us were off to Dick's house to sing Christmas carols. Dick joined us, and we went to Frank's house. This went on until all of our guests were assembled. We walked home singing with at least twelve instruments playing merrily.

When we returned home covered in snow, the caravan members shed their overcoats to decorate the tree. The men drank heavily while Ninni and I boxed. "What a punch, Dick. Look at the punch this kid has," Uncle Tom said. "He's going to be a champion."

Mom roared into the room and hit my head. "Dead Champion."

"He's teasing me, Ma," I said, not realizing Uncle Tom was the catalyst.

The festivity grew and grew with the men drinking and playing cards, Pop singing tunes like "Come Back to Sorrento", "Way Marie," "O Sole Mio." I was enchanted by his voice as always. It was a pity he couldn't muster the energy for a career. What a loss.

Contare, sing, Giovanni," Pop finally said. I was surprised he asked because of my bad throat. I sang and, to my relief, it was just fine. In fact, it added a kind of gruffness, exciting for my sound, but I begged off doing too many songs. It appeared I might be able to perform tomorrow.

We were feasting on *pisha stoka,* which is dried codfish, and the homemade pastries. At the stroke of midnight, the sausage flew into the frying pan, and the homemade bread was sliced, while others prepared stuffed veal for the main meal the next day. The smell of sausage frying in olive oil was enough to make me regain my appetite.

The timing was perfect. Pop seemed to know just when to put us to bed before we passed out from exhaustion. He turned out the lights in the living room, except the glittering maze on the tree. I fell into bed. The last thing I remember was Pop saying, "Sleep well, little man, and before you know it, Santa Claus will be here on his sled from the North Pole. You'll hear his bells."

I don't know how they were able to judge our first cycle of deep slumber, but they knew. Then bells jingled as I rubbed my eyes, half awake. Lo and behold, I could see the wonderful rotund figure of Santa at our tree. I walked slowly to him as I noticed Ninni and Maria in the room. Santa looked like Nonno with his gleaming eyes and rosy cheeks.

"Ho, ho, ho, here comes little Giovanni. I have presents under the tree because you were such a good boy this year. Merry Christmas! I must go now. I have a lot of stops to make. So many children were good this year, my sled is heavier than ever, and my reindeer are getting tired."

I loved Santa in my dazed state. And that was an Italian Christmas Eve. Some relatives stayed overnight, especially if they did not have their own children at home.

We awakened early Christmas Day, and we feverishly opened our presents like an atomic bomb exploding, hardly looking at them before picking the next package. Paper littered the living room floor as our parents and relatives watched us in amusement. The women were in the kitchen preparing a big breakfast. When the excitement subsided, we settled down to our favorite toys. Mine was a hand glider, catapulted with a stick and rubber band. It was a beauty and flew endlessly.

I chose to fly my glider on the grass island in the wide street out front. Ninni followed me downstairs, and I gave him firm instructions to watch from the curb. But he crawled on all fours between two cars to visit me. I screamed as loud as I could as a car with airless tires hit his frail body between his collarbone and naval. Pop ran to the street. "He's dead! I know he's dead," he shouted, crying and picking up Ninni's limp torso.

He and Uncle Tom shoved Ninni into Tom's new Ford and rushed him to St. John's Hospital, notoriously called the butcher shop. I knew Mom would say, "I told you to watch your little brother. It's all your fault." And it was true.

Mom broke down, whimpering. "This is too much for me. What did I do to offend God? A sick husband, working, cooking, three young children, it's too much."

I saw the serious side of Aunt Nettie's personality for the first time as she spoke in almost godly tones. "Annie, if it is God's will, somewhere you'll have a reward."

Mom slumped in exhaustion. I ran to the sanctuary of my bedroom and fell on my bed, playing inventive chords in my head. My escape, thank God. I cried and prayed for Ninni.

I walked to the front window and waited for Tom's car to

return. When I spotted it a block away, my heart pounded so hard that it hurt. The car stopped in front of the house, but it seemed a thousand years before the door opened. Ninni ran out with a charlotte russe in one hand, a candied apple in the other, jumping and laughing. I wanted to strangle and hug him at the same time.

Pop brought him upstairs. "It's a miracle," Uncle Tom said, lifting Ninni's shirt. "Look at how deep the tire marks are across his chest, and he didn't get one broken bone. It's all of the fresh escarole he eats every week. The iron gives him sturdy bones."

Cousin Sal came downstairs, his usual nervous, comical self. He was the son of my uncle, the Borghese. Although hyper, he was funny and happy, always playing jokes on everyone. "Is the car all right?" he asked. He joined the Army in World War I but was discharged honorably because he was under age. He kept his Army rifle loaded with a sheet over it in a corner of his apartment.

At dinnertime, guests trickled in for a feast similar to the one we had for Thanksgiving. And the result was the same too: All of us fell wherever we could, too stuffed to do anything but snooze it off. We awakened occasionally when a visitor dropped by to wish us cheer. The men started playing cards as we played with our toys.

I went to bed with my glider in my arms, as though it were a teddy bear. In my child's mind I thought, *holidays erased some of the hurt of the Great Depression. Why didn't God make every day a holiday?*

CHAPTER FIVE

The day after Christmas I was to perform again in *La Gioconda* with Beniamino Gigli and Leonora Corona. My friend, Roger, and I smiled at each other as we repeated our jumping jacks in front of the great ship landing. As the music surrounded my ears once more, I found it a miracle I was able to sing again. Pop had assured me I would sing better than ever. Well, he was right.

Following the performance, Mr. Petri informed me we were to go to Boston to perform *Carmen*. It was my favorite because we had a lot of freedom on stage, and Bizet's music was enchanting. I had to request a dispensation from school to accommodate the performances.

A couple of days later, Pop, as excited as I, led me by the hand to the home of my principal, Dr. Watson. It was rare for a female to hold that position. Later in life, I could understand why she was chosen. She was unique and a dedicated exponent of creative talent, and she knew how to motivate children. I grew to love her.

I remembered writing a poem in second grade. She demanded all creative work cross her desk. I was called to her office and noticed my poem in front of her. "Did anyone help you with this poem, Giovanni?" she asked in her quiet but firm voice, peering through her bifocals.

"No ma'am."

I love the trees. I love them all,
How do they feel when their leaves fall?

I wish I could make them understand,
That it's God's will all over the land.

"What were you thinking of, Giovanni, when you wrote this poem?"

"I don't know. I just think it's funny to love some things so much and not be able to know how they feel. How could we help them if we don't know?"

She smiled and walked around from her desk. "Do you mind if I put this on the main bulletin board here at PS-7?"

When I gave my permission, she framed it in front of me, led me to the board, and told me how proud she was of me.

We entered her house, done in early American with fine original oil paintings of Western scenes, from Buffalo Bill to Indians. Next to a spinning wheel in one corner was a mini replica of Eli Whitney's cotton gin. On her main knickknack shelf were hordes of early American platters with hand-painted scenes.

"Come in and sit down, Mr. Benedetto. You have a fine son. He is a good student, but most of all, extremely creative. Did you know he wrote poetry?"

"We know he has a great voice, but I never dreamed he could write."

"For a boy of his age, he may make some contributions if he follows through."

Dr. Watson looked me in the eye with her warm, sincere manner. "Giovanni, you should thank God for giving you such a wonderful father. My work would be so much easier if they were all like him."

I beamed, and I never remember feeling more fulfilled than at that moment. Pop and I strolled away as though we had made a great conquest.

*****

At nine years old, I could never have dreamed my trip to Boston would be such an adventure. It started with Pop sitting me down in the morning for the next chapter story for my posterity. He had been reading me the book, *Of Human Bondage*, while describing every meaning. Although I didn't understand most of it, I enjoyed his delivery. He finished the story when it was time to leave, as though he had planned it. Mom was at work, so he got me the bagged lunch she had put together and gave me my subway fare to Penn Station, our meeting point.

Pop hugged and kissed me good-bye, then looked at me with his soft green eyes. "Giovanni, you are a man now, and with manhood comes serious responsibility. I want you to promise if anything happens to me, you'll always look after your brother. He is very young. Even though he loves you, he resents all the attention you are getting. In a way, it is unfair to him, for he is a very talented young man, so be kind to him, and remember tolerance is a virtue. Do you understand? At times you'll find it difficult to understand him. Be patient with him, protect him, and love him. Will you promise me?"

A large tear rolled down his cheek. I looked into Pop's eyes. I adored him. As a father, he was a man for all seasons.

I took a deep breath. "Don't worry, Pop, I'll do as you say. Not just because you asked me, but because I love my brother and my sister. I'm nine and he is only six, so I watch out for him."

I was always saddened when I left home. I worried Pop might die while I was gone, but this soon left me as I got into the trip. Mr. Petri was standing in his usual black attire at the station with a music case in one hand and a black umbrella over his left arm. Much to his surprise, we were all there.

He sat with me for a time on our way. "Giovanni, you are about to have one the most wonderful experiences of your young career. The audience is primed for our arrival. The press has informed them how we shocked the New York audience with our *Carmen*, so everyone is excited. I promise you'll see a magic in theater. You'll never forget it."

We were about to have an excitement few people ever get the

chance of experiencing. The train moved ever so slowly until it stopped. The conductor directed us onto barge-like rafts with heavy rope ties that were pulled from the opposite shore. I was too fascinated to be frightened. When we reached the other side, a train was waiting to pick us up. On the next train, I sketched what I'd seen.

I saw a cow on top of a barn roof, a truly distorting site. The barn was half submerged in water, and the cow seemed to be waiting patiently until the flood subsided. I munched on my favorite candy, a Mr. Goodbar, as I watched, as though it were put there for my entertainment. We arrived in Boston rather late, but Mr. Petri took us to a chain restaurant called Childs. We felt so grown up because we could order whatever we wanted. I picked Boston baked beans with franks and spaghetti with a glass of milk. I gulped it down too quickly, which gave me a stomachache the rest of the night.

The following day, the great Baccaloni played with us with Toscanini in the pit. As usual, the music swarmed my body and soothed me.

On the way home, they must have rerouted the train, for we didn't pass the flooded areas again. All I could think of was telling my parents and friends about my great adventure.

*****

New Year's Eve was upon us before we knew it. Mom came home early in a down mood. "What's the matter, Anna? You look tired and irritated," Pop said.

"That dumb Dubinsky!" she shouted. "He ordered us all to Madison Square Garden. When we got there, his henchmen put up a large sign in the center of the ring that said, 'We want strike.' Then they had the gall to hold it up and order us to read the sign out loud. So I ran down the aisle onto the ring and pulled the sign out of the goon's hand. I turned to Mr. David Dubinsky and told him a thing or two. I told him we didn't want a strike. We were on piecework, and we had family to worry about, and when the day would come we'd be considered so stupid as to follow anything they would say, there would be no Italians left in the garment industry."

"You did that, Anna?"

"I did, all that, and they took my picture as I was bopping the goon over the head with the sign."

"What paper is it to appear in?"

"I think the man said it was the *Daily Mirror* or something. Can you imagine him pulling such a stunt? It's hard enough trying to raise a family without all of this other garbage going on."

I could tell Pop was hurt by the remark. He walked to his room. Mom mumbled as she started to cook supper.

*****

It was two Saturdays after New Year's Eve and the night we were to celebrate Anna's wedding at Dutch's Tavern. I was delighted to be the pillow boy in a Catholic wedding. I was excited until I learned I had to wear my George Washington suit, which I was beginning to despise. In my mind, my Buster Brown haircut and this costume were synonymous.

After going through the ceremony and photography, we proceeded to the tavern for my first football wedding. They were usually in a hired hall with a polished wooden dance floor and a four- or five-piece band that sounded like sick cats. They played everything from mod tunes to ethnic. The food consisted of hard roll sandwiches wrapped in waxed paper: ham, cheese, prosciutto, salami, bologna, liverwurst, etc. and Italian pastries. My favorite was the mini custard cream puffs.

The bridesmaids would enter to music and form two aisles with the male ushers on each side of the dance floor. The immediate family, maid of honor, best man, and priest sat on the dais, to be joined later by the bride and groom. The bride and groom would enter last and dance to "Let Me Call You Sweetheart." The family would cut in to dance with the bride and groom. Everyone stood and applauded when the father would dance with his daughter. The bridesmaids and ushers joined in while pictures were taken before the whole hall came to the floor as the music changed to an Italian waltz.

The beverages were kegs of beer and wine, with hard liquor on the dais. Later in the festivity, everyone would line up to present money envelopes to the bride and groom as the parents collected and guarded them.

The sandwiches usually would be placed in an area resembling a hat-check room with a counter. Guests at the counter would yell for a sandwich, or some guests would yell from their table. The server behind the counter would throw the sandwiches, much like throwing a football. Italians were masters at associating mimic names of people or situations with a sense of humor.

At this wedding, I met relatives I'd never seen before. It felt like I was related to the whole world. A bunch of relatives were from Mulberry Street, an area that not only was the heart of the Italian ghetto, but was also the pulse of everything illegal among the American Italians.

I was amazed by the number of young people who came by our table next to the dais to thank Pop for bringing them to this country, and further surprised most of them had stayed at our home until they got situated. I must have been too young to remember them.

Pop called me over to introduce me to two women. "This is your cousin, Nettie, and this is her sister, Cathy. I took care of them when their father died. Their last name before they were married was Alioto."

They were very pretty, and I wondered why they never visited our home, as so many others did. As they walked away, I questioned Pop about this, and he took a deep breath. "You'll find most people who come to visit only do so when they need something. The trick is to understand this weakness in people. Remember what I have just told you as you grow up."

Before he had a chance to finish, Uncle Jim ran over to Pop.

"We're going to have trouble, John! The two families have had a lot to drink, and the groom's family is bringing up what happened to the other sister between subway stops. You know Anna's brothers, once they explode, there'll be blood in this place."

Forgetting his illness, Pop ran across the dance floor. He seemed to plead with both sides, but to no avail. It almost got out of control before Dutch Murano went to the bandstand to call for quiet. The respect of his leadership was obvious; everyone quieted down as he drew his cigar to his mouth, showing off his ten-carat diamond pinky ring.

"I am proud I was invited to this wedding, and further proud the family decided to have it in my place. . ." He paused for a moment as though taking the pulse of angry crowd.

"We have weddings here all the time, and we've never had a cop called, nor a stick of furniture broken. I know you people who are so close to me will have respect. Trouble will not occur with the ladies and gentlemen I know you are." A flourish of muttering rose from one side of the room to the other like an ocean wave. "My gift to the bride and groom, at my expense, is the presence of a wonderful talent. Although he is a relative of yours, you must recognize he's on his way to becoming a star. It's only a matter of time. Frank, Mr. Costello, myself, and others are getting behind his career. I would like to present proudly, Giovanni Benedetto, Little Caruso."

Not expecting this at this time, I didn't feel my confident self, however, I walked to the stage and bowed as people cheered. It was hard to control them. Uncle Dick ran up and whispered, "This is no different an audience than any that's restless. Dig into your bag of showbiz tricks, Giovanni, and get their attention first. The rest will be easy."

My mind was muddled, but somehow I instinctively walked over to the groom's mother with the microphone. I paused for the audience to realize I wanted quiet. I took her hand and said, "I would like to dedicate this song, not to the bride and groom, but to the one mother who is represented here. For her, I would like to sing 'Mama.'"

The room exploded. Everyone stood up, cheering, whistling, stomping feet. I really didn't have to sing with this intro, but I did. I tore the house apart and then did "Come Back To Sorrento". The crowd was wild. I remembered Dick's advice to leave them laughing, and it would have been sudden death to do anymore in this situation, so I walked off. When I got near the end of the dance floor, Mr. Murano clasped my hand bringing me back for another bow, waving his right arm high, as though he were responsible for my being there. I didn't know he had shoved a twenty-dollar bill in my hand when he grabbed it.

The next day was Sunday, my favorite day because, every once in a while, I had nothing to do.

Sometimes my teacher would cancel Sunday lessons, so Pop and I would sit and talk. He was quite a storyteller and would mesmerize me by the hour. Later, at home I felt clean and blessed when we returned from church. When I received communion, I didn't touch the host with my teeth, for this was considered a mortal sin in those days. I didn't even take a glass of water until after communion. Having gone to confession earlier, I felt pretty secure.

Pop called me over to sit on his lap. He was a pure genius at getting into a story differently each and every time. This would hold my interest because I didn't know what was coming. He told me about his first job and why he quit.

"The only job I could get was a motorman on the trolley from downtown New York clear up to the Bronx. Well, Giovanni, I could take orders from a boss out of respect, but I saw red when I felt he hated me for the part of the world I came from. You see, everyone on earth, because of the way we live, must draw a line of what to stand for. We grown-ups call this dignity. You must decide as you grow where this line is."

The moment Pop and I finished, I noticed Ninni peeking

around the corner, his expression not happy.

Now later in life I know he felt neglected. After all, the first thing visitors would ask was, "Where is the Little Caruso? . . . John, you should be very proud of him," or words to that effect.

A sibling rivalry was being developed as though it were being planned. Ninni was strong and knew how to fight back. Ninni craved the attention, developing a drive in him as strong as the Rock of Gibraltar. He couldn't know how much I loved him, so he was reacting to an injustice done to him. Our great bond would survive, but certain areas would remain sensitive to him.

"Ninni, come over here, I'll tell you a story," I called out. Ninni came forward, stopped, and sang "Mammy" with Al Jolson's takes. Pop and I broke up, but not giving him recognition for a wonderful voice. This was nearly criminal; we should have realized. Ninni always came on like a humorous mimic. We didn't know he was desperately crying out for recognition.

Dick came by, dapper as ever, in his usual good mood. "I have a message for Giovanni from the cardinal. Giovanni, he wants you at the cathedral next Saturday for a wedding. He wants you to sing the "Ave Maria" for a well-known businessman's wedding. He told me you'll be paid fifty dollars because the man is a wealthy member of the parish."

I was to find out the groom was Angelo Marinello, a man of great power, and although allegedly legitimate, would get adverse publicity linking him to Costello, the man who was to become my godfather.

"Go see Frank sometime this week," Dick said. "He wants to talk to you about this wedding. Evidently, they also want you to perform at the festivity after the church stint. It's a good deal, Giovanni. It'll be at the Waldorf Astoria. This is big time; the most important people in the country will be present. I even heard a rumor the Vanderbilts will be there. They are the richest family in New York City and have a lot of influence."

It was late on a Tuesday evening when I arrived at Nonno's

house. As usual, big cars were parked out front. I walked into Uncle Frank's den, where three men sat talking quietly. My future godfather seemed to be the center of interest. Frank ordered me to sit down. I'm sure they thought I was too young to figure out what they were talking about.

"I'm telling you, Frank, I don't trust the little bum. I just had a big argument with him. He's a cheap little hustler who would sell his own mother, not for money, but for something worse: Glory. Can you in your wildest imagination believe this kind of attitude with me? A man who has turned mayors into governors? I proved this to him, and he still acted like his own man." He leaned forward for emphasis, holding his cigar with the mouth end protruding. "Listen to me, Frank, you stay where you are with the Republicans." Frank started to butt in. "Hold on, Frank, listen to me. I engineered this whole thing, brought us this far, didn't I?" Frank slumped back. "I have to help the little punk, and the only way he'll win is to split the ticket. He'll win with the minority vote because the do-gooders forced the indictment on Walker. This will give him just enough votes to get in. I already have a name for the party. Here, it's written here."

Frank picked up the wrinkled paper and read it slowly. "Fusion, Fusion Party."

"I like the sound of that. You spearhead the whole deal and, as usual, as far as the whole country is concerned, Frank, you are just a Republican leader here in Queens. That's the way we play it, because I'm going to be sure you never get any dirt on you, Frank. You're the only one who has the brains and loyalty I need in my organization and doesn't have the kind of ego that eventually gets everyone in trouble. You know how I love and trust you, Frank. Have the same love and trust in my judgment."

"I always have."

My eyes were starting to get heavy from all this talk I didn't quite understand. Mr. Costello started to get up but paused.

"Another thing, Frank. I had a meeting with the young lawyer,

Tom. I checked him out through his college. They tell me he is some sort of a genius and wrote some of the best briefs they'd ever seen in the history of the college. I decided to plant some seeds. I advanced him enough money for his law books and am allowing him to use one of my downtown lofts as an office. He's the beginning of a real viper. He grabbed at it, thanking me, kissing my hand. Can you imagine, Frank? . . . Oh, yes it looks as though Coogan is down the shitter. What a shame, he could have been president, governor for sure. What class, he is holding up like a Trojan, not complaining, not uttering a word. If we had more guys like him, we'd take the country in less than four years, with or without a president.

"One last thing: New Orleans, a key town for the organization, as it is a port, so I have feathered it with musicians to give it the home of Dixieland image. We want to open a lot of clubs down there. Actually, the real purpose is for harboring some of our boys down there at no cost to us while we wait to move in on the dockworkers. We'll organize all of the docks within ten years. The Vanderbilts want it, so you can bet we'll get a lot of side assistance with press and so on. Remember, Frank, the people want change. Hoover is a lame duck; Walker is a washout. We do it just like we fix a fight. We sneak in LaGuardia, help the *storpio* in a wheelchair, and by the way, I met what everybody thinks is a kook in Louisiana. His name is Huey, governor. He's as crazy as I am. We had a meeting with him, and I'm satisfied. I'm going to give him the usual juice to win the Senate — money, bodies, the usual stuff, you know."

Mr. Costello finally rose to his feet to exchange good-byes. He kissed my forehead, motioned his two friends, and they left.

"Giovanni, let me talk to you about the wedding at the cathedral," Frank said. "It's very important for all of us, you and me included. I'll pay for your teacher to accompany you for this one. I want an actual concert. It'll not be too far into the festivity because everyone will be boozing, so I'll arrange for you to come on as soon as the preliminaries are over. Now, I'm going to describe where the Vanderbilts will be sitting with this diagram Costello left with me. At some point, you dedicate your main song to their table. The family is well aware of why this is being done. Do you understand, Giovanni?"

"Yes, Uncle Frank. Don't worry, I'll please them."

Frank patted me on the head. "I know you will, Giovanni, I know you will."

*****

A commotion and rumbling brings me back. It is a fiasco as Tony enters the room. I grit my teeth at the behavior of some of the visitors in the funeral parlor. It is as though they want to ask Tony for his autograph. I can tell this shatters him, but he keeps his cool.

Tony and I find a secluded family room downstairs and chat about anything to distract us. If we discuss what's happening, we might explode and blow the dignity of the funeral. I tell him I'm proud of his boys, and how well they handled details while we were away and kept the publicity of the death away from the newspapers, for the last thing we want is a ballyhoo of media at a time like this.

A ghost appears, I think it may be Cousin Sal. I can't believe it until he introduces himself as Sal's son. I tell him how much I loved his dad, and I was sorrowed when he passed away. I notice he combs his hair like my brother and emulates Tony's every take. He says he's singing in clubs on Long Island but is only getting requests for Tony's hits. I realize he has joined the ranks of the copyists, the followers living on false hopes. Anyone in show business will admit, out of all the entertainers in the world, there is only one Tony. He has endless energy, tremendous charisma, and many times over has been called the greatest showman of our time.

CHAPTER SIX

After I left Frank's, I ran all the way in the dark to the small factory to pick up Pop's work. The owner lived an apartment in the back. They were called subcontractors in those days. The lights were out, so I pounded on the door, knowing I'd get in trouble if I didn't return with the work. The apartment door opened inside, and the little Jewish man came to unlock the factory door. He was nice with warm eyes.

"Take it easy, take it easy, son, I'm coming right now. Giovanni, you're late. We're eating supper, come in and wait a minute while we finish."

We walked through the factory into a small apartment where his wife was sitting, and he introduced me to his daughter. She was in a wheelchair, and her head rolled as though it would fall off her shoulders.

"This is my daughter, Sarah." I moved to shake her hand, but he held me back. "Don't get too close. She doesn't know how to shake hands. Sometimes she even bites, not because she's vicious, but because it's her way of talking."

She started to moan and mumble, stretching her arms toward me. I felt sad as I watched her helpless hulk. "Would you like some chicken soup with matzo balls, Giovanni?"

"No, thank you." I just wanted to get out of the place.

He rose from his chair and grabbed a large bundle wrapped in brown paper and tied with white jute cord.

"Here's your father's bundle. His name and address is written on it, see?"

I nodded, clutched the bundle, and ran all the way home. By the time I reached the top of the stairs, I was wiped out and breathing hard. I heard Mom's thunder.

"Where have you been? Do you know how late it is?"

I explained everything, and then at the supper table, I told them about singing at the cathedral and at the Waldorf with the Vanderbilts. After the meal, I leaned against Pop's chair to get his attention. He rubbed my head and asked about school and my voice lessons, if he could do anything to help, then lapsed into one of his stories preparing me for a fatherless future.

"Let me tell you a true story. When we all came here from Italy, my friend, Jimmy Pulimani, and five other guys went to Central Park Zoo. We were feeding the elephants some peanuts. Now, Jimmy was a clown and was torturing the elephants with empty peanut shells, especially one of them. Well, we left not thinking much about it, and about six months later, we went back to the zoo. You wouldn't believe it, Giovanni, but the elephant Jimmy had been teasing before lifted his trunk and blew a wad of mucous all over him. It took five handkerchiefs to wipe him off, and it still wasn't enough. You see, Giovanni, an elephant never forgets."

Mom looked around from the kitchen sink. "Did you do your homework yet, Giovanni?"

"No, Mom, I didn't have a chance yet."

"You have time to listen to a story. Get to your work at once, do you hear?"

Pop pushed me gently away as we both smiled. I finished my homework in my room. Before bed, I thought about Babe and our supposed truce. Herman, Manny, and I were to meet him and his gang to make it official. I couldn't wait because I'd been panicking every day, not knowing what Babe's gang had in store. Herman, the peacemaker, assured me all would be well. The anxiety must have affected me, for I had another one of my reoccurring nightmares.

I missed Herman and Manny, but I ran into Babe on the way to school. He beckoned me, but I stepped back. I had learned to never trust him. "I just saw Herman and Manny, and we decided the meeting will be in the Tisdale Lumber and Coal yard by the river after school," Babe said.

"I'll be there, Babe."

After school, I walked to the lumberyard. It looked sinister with piles of cut wood in symmetrical rows for a mile or so on one end and mountains of coal on the other from where we'd steal for our stoves.

I crawled under the fence through the hole we'd cut and walked down the main aisle slowly.

I felt a twinge of danger, call it ESP or what have you. I called out for my friends, but no answer. Then I remembered they were to stay after school. Babe was out for foul play. I turned for the fence, only to find Babe and his gang blocking the way. I ran through the lumber, but they split up and cut me off about halfway to the river. I didn't have a chance. They beat me until every bone in my body screamed in pain. They used short pieces of two-by-fours on my rib cage and shins.

Babe grinned from ear to ear. "If you admit you're a lousy wop chicken-shit grease ball, we'll stop."

I knew somehow this was one of those lines of dignity Pop had been trying to tell me about. The more I refused, the more they beat me.

Finally, Babe paused to look at my bloody body. "He really is a stubborn wop. Let's tie him up and throw him behind one of the lumber piles."

They tied my wrists with baling wire behind my back so tight they bled. After they left, I felt more alone than ever. All sorts of frightening thoughts raced through my mind. I pictured my skeleton rotting with no one finding me in this desolate place.

Hours passed, and it seemed more hopeless with each passing minute. I started to sob. My ankles and wrists were bleeding from my struggle for freedom.

As in a dream, I heard a scratchy voice with a crackling laugh. "Well, well, well, it seems as though we have a problem here."

I struggled to turn over and looked into the face of a hobo with beady eyes, long, dirty hair, long nose hairs, and bright-red alcoholic skin. Yet, he was a welcome sight. He gently untied the wire and used a soiled red handkerchief from his back pocket to wipe away most of my blood. He asked who did this. He made me feel secure, so I explained everything and said I was afraid to go home because I wasn't allowed in the lumberyard. He looked at me with a compassionate expression and paused before he spoke.

"Well, I did have some very tight appointments to consider, but I'll put them aside and come home with you. Perhaps if I explained, you may not get into trouble."

Still sobbing, I wiped my eyes and thanked him. He gripped my hand, and somehow I knew I wouldn't get punished as we headed to my house.

When we arrived home, Pop ran into the lavatory for sterilized cotton and the house favorite, peroxide. He wiped and bandaged my wrists and ankles. Much to my surprise, Mom intently listened as the man described how he found me. She interrupted him to ask if he would like something to eat.

He looked at her with his watery, beady eyes. "Thank you, no, ma'am, but it does get cold where I sleep in the lumberyard, so if you have some soft spirits, like wine, I'd be forever grateful."

Pop rose from his chair and grabbed a bottle of Nonno's guinea red from the kitchen cupboard. "Did you have your small bat with you today, Giovanni?" he asked as he poured the wine.

"No, I didn't think I needed it anymore."

"I'm going over to Babe's house and have it out with his parents," Mom said.

"No you won't, Anna, this is something Giovanni has to work

out for himself. If we do it, he'll be in danger all through school. He must settle it himself. If he finds he can't, then we'll do as you say. Giovanni, you use your head and take care of this once and for all."

I reversed in my mind what Babe had done to me, only this time I would be in control and with my friends. The next day at lunch period, Herman, Manny, and I discussed my plan. Herman was to call another truce meeting and tell Babe I'd had enough and wanted to make peace. It would take place in an open lot near Hopkins Hill, one of our favorite play areas. We used to roll homemade wagons and abandoned car chassis with wheels down the hill. They would freewheel for about two miles. In the winter, we'd do the same with our sleds. The lot adjoining the hill was quite large, the tall weeds missing this time of year. I instructed Herman to tell them we'd bring bottles of pop as a peace offering and to request they bring glasses or paper cups. One more requisite was to match our number of guys.

Babe agreed, and everything was on target. My plan: Control the bottles until empty and then cream the gang with them until they hollered, *"Uncle."* I wasn't worried about Babe reneging because the field was so open. We'd be able to catch any foul play in time to flee.

After school, we bought the pop and headed to the battleground. We reviewed our plan over and over to ensure our survival. I wasn't worried, for my two friends had more guts than a hundred Babes or any of his men.

No one was there. "I wonder if this is a double cross," Manny said, looking around.

"I don't think so," Herman said. "Besides, we have our escape route figured out."

My heart pounded, not of fear, but for revenge. I imagined all sorts of destruction for the Babe gang. Finally, we saw three of them coming over the hill. I was amazingly calm with my bat up my sleeve and the large bottles of Hoffman pop: orange, lime, and cream soda. Three bottles for three heads and a baseball bat for a bonus. We had arranged some large rocks to sit on and made sure the gang would be directly opposite us where we could keep our eyes on them.

Babe looked even more confident when he noticed the bandages on my wrists still staining blood.

"I'm glad you guys have decided to call a truce. It's stupid to fight with each other, especially when we're the toughest guys in the school." He motioned his boys to sit down. "Why don't we join forces? Then we could do anything we wanted all over the neighborhood."

You see, we anticipated Babe would try some kind of coalition. He'd been after us a long time to join his little army, and that's why he attacked us. Being a lousy poker player, I showed anger. "Who would be the leader?"

Cool, calm Herman butted in and winked at me. "Who cares who the leader will be as long as we're together?"

"It's okay with me. I don't care," Manny said, smiling.

Babe looked as pleased as a cat drinking a bowl of milk. "Well, it's settled then. I'll be the leader."

We sat around planning mayhem at the school, including slashing Dr. Watson's tires. Babe gave us detailed orders as to who would do what. I was getting impatient, wanting the taste of his blood, the memory of my ordeal at the lumberyard still fresh.

We collected the bottles as we finished them. The signal was as Herman suggested a name for our gang, we would grab the bottles and go to work on Babe's bunch. It came. I whipped out my bat in one hand, a bottle in the other. Herman and Manny grabbed their bottles, and all hell broke loose. We really did cream them, blood all over. I broke my bottle over Babe's crown. We had agreed he was mine. His two friends scampered and screamed over the rise of the hill. I had Babe pinned on the ground, pounding his ribs with my bat. I couldn't let go, my hunger for revenge too strong. Herman and Manny pulled me off as Babe screamed for his mother. I let it be known I wanted more of him.

Herman grabbed me from behind. "Enough, Giovanni, enough! Do you want to kill him?"

"Yes, I want him dead. He'll never stop bothering me, I know he won't!"

Babe looked up at me with his bloody face and jabbered like a maniac, swearing he wouldn't bother me again and offering for me to be the leader. "Just leave me alone, please, no more, please."

My arms dropped as I glared at him on the ground. "Babe, I'm going to let you go, but if you ever bother me again, make sure you kill me, for if you don't, I'll find a way to kill you, I promise you. Do you understand?"

He whimpered and held his sore ribs. "I promise you, I want no part of you anymore. I've had enough."

Babe was my first ruffian bully. He only had strength in numbers. He was just a frightened coward.

Herman and Manny picked him up by his arms. "If you ever break your promise and hurt Giovanni, you'll have to get Herman and me too," Manny said.

"I swear on my mother I'll never touch any of you again."

"Or anyone else for that matter!" our calm Herman roared.

The defeated warrior walked away with his head down, turning around every few steps to check on us. That was the end of the Babe episode until much later in my life.

*****

The next day, I strolled into Uncle Frank's Republican Club after school. Among other things, he was the Republican leader in the county of Queens. He was to give me final instructions for the cathedral and Waldorf affairs. The club was under the train elevator at Ditmars station in Astoria, Queens. Men always were hanging around the front door. I imagined they were what Frank referred to as leg men who helped during election time or emergencies. Most of them were older, probably retired, just wanting something to do. Others worshipped Frank and would do anything for him.

One of the men inside motioned me to the door of a private office in the back of the hall. I knocked, then found Frank in one of his usual meetings, this time with Mr. Costello, his chauffer, and another man. Frank looked disturbed as I sat down. They sort of stared at each other for a few moments in silence.

Costello finally spoke. "About that crazy Jew, Dino is right, when he's mad, he makes an Italian temper look anemic. Luckily, I'm one of a few people who can talk to him. What I am worried about is he and Lucky have become good friends, and Lucky is bad company. They're too much alike. Anyway, it's my problem. I'll settle it the hard way if I have to, and they know it."

His expression changed as he turned to me. "Giovanni, *come' stai?*"

"*Buono*, Don Costello, *et voi?*"

"*Sto bene*, Giovanni" "Sit down next me, I want to talk to you." Don Costello had a habit of starting off in left field with me. It was his way of handling children. I can look back now and know he loved them very much.

"You know, Giovanni, we Italians must all play a role in this country. The trick is to get many of us into important roles. Now, you are to play the role of a great artist. You're important to what we call image. It sort of takes some of the heat off the bad ones. We do have some of those also. You're showing us great promise, and I hope you stay with the gift God gave you.

Now he was getting to the point. "Saturday is very important for all of us. We're in negotiation with a real wealthy, blueblood American family for the first time. Now they need us, we don't need them, but they have to play the part. It's funny, with all of the art and culture Italy has given the world, and the Vatican being in Rome, the stuffed shirts still see us as sinister men carrying knives, killing, eating nothing but spaghetti. So we have to prove ourselves over and over, because they must have a defense for their other blueblood friends. But whenever they want to accomplish something heavy, they come to us. No matter," he said as an afterthought.

"Your part is a cultural one, Giovanni. I couldn't think of a better candidate to represent us in the arts. You are young, and your talent as an unknown will be much more effective than bringing a name Italian act. You see how important this is? Do you remember that early in your performance, you'll dedicate one of your best songs to the Vanderbilts? You walk right to the table and do it. Don't worry, it won't distract from your performance."

"I'll do as you say, Don Costello."

"Did you tell your teacher we need him for the whole day? We'll pay him for whatever student income he loses for the day."

"I called him yesterday, and Mr. Parado said he would cancel his classes for the day."

Mr. Costello raised his finger. "One more thing or two, I'll have my chauffeur pick you up at 10 o'clock. Wear tails with a cravat. Do you have one?"

"Yes, sir."

"Giovanni, what happened to your wrists?"

I pulled up my pants' legs to show him my ankles and explained everything.

"Manny, he has my blood." He turned to Frank. "My brother's oldest boy, I baptized him at birth, Frank. You're pretty tough like your Uncle Frank, eh? This boy, Babe, where does he live? I'll send someone to persuade his father it's not right to bother you or your friends."

I gave him Babe's address and last name. He seemed to handle it as important business and folded it into his big black wallet. "We can't have this, Frank. I know boys will be boys, but this is too much. I don't want Giovanni seriously hurt. This Babe sounds like the beginning of a young Turk."

Frank smiled and nodded. "I know this kid's old man, I'll handle it."

"One more thing, Giovanni, when you see the cardinal, you

bow and kiss his ring. Do you understand?"

"Yes, sir."

Uncle Frank hugged me, and I ran all the way home. The reason why I ran most of the time, especially at dusk, was I felt the devil was chasing me since Nonna had died. It took a long time to get over it.

It was the typical scene at the house: Pop slaving away at the machine, trying to contribute some money to keep us alive; Maria with her head buried in studies; and Ninni getting into all sorts of mischief. He kept us on our toes just trying to keep him out of the hospital.

Things must have been very bad that week. For supper, we had a large pizza pan filled with wild vegetables, such as broccoli rabe, fried in olive oil. That was it. I went to bed hungry. That was preferable to a night in the deep Depression when Mom cooked my favorite pet, a wounded pigeon I was nursing back to health. As we sat down, I had asked Mom what it was.

"Chicken," she said.

"Wow, this is a mighty small chicken."

"Just eat, Giovanni."

Then I recognized my pet! I was too young to realize Mom was trying to keep us alive. So many men had lost dignity with no work and cheap government handouts. Some were ruined for life, becoming lazy, giving up, and never to return to how they were.

I thought back on today's happening with Uncle Frank, Costello, and Dino. For the first time, I was sure none of us was in control of our destiny, and this day I was in the company of two giants.

CHAPTER SEVEN

It was Saturday morning, and I had a tinge of nervousness for some reason, probably because I was singing for the cardinal. It was the most important thing I'd done. Right on time, the black limousine pulled up at 10 o'clock.

Pop gave me his usual big hug and kiss, wishing me luck. "I'm very proud of you, Giovanni. I know you'll be the man of the house in the kind of tradition I'll be most proud of. Now, say good-bye to your mother and go."

I hugged Mom's waist as she scrubbed clothes on a washboard. "See you later, Mom."

"Do a good job, Giovanni."

I gathered my music into my briefcase and scampered down the stairs, three at a time, with Mom screaming, "Watch yourself, son! You can't afford an accident now. Do you hear me?"

"Okay, Mom, I'll be careful."

I wanted to ride in front with the chauffeur, but he directed me to the back. He spoke through a small intercom phone halfway to the cathedral. "Mr. Costello ordered me to put you in the back so when we get to the cathedral, your entrance will be impressive and formal. You know we never disobey Mr. Costello's orders, nobody dares. Perhaps you can ride in front on the way back."

I liked this man because he seemed considerate of how I felt.

Scads of cameramen and reporters were waiting at the cathedral. The chauffeur walked around to my door and stood like a soldier as I got out. "Kind of young for a groom, don't you think?" one of the reporters said. Laughter rippled throughout the crowd.

"Who is he?" one of them asked the chauffeur.

"He is the new singing sensation, Giovanni Benedetto. He's to perform here and then at the Waldorf. He's been tagged the Little Caruso."

One or two of the reporters took notes and asked me where I lived and my age. I felt quite important.

Mr. Parado, a slight man, was waiting on the front steps and appeared impressed. He wore a bit of rouge on his cheeks, for he had a waxy complexion. His red wavy toupee would jump up in front at his hairline. It never seemed to stick, which caused him to continually press it down with both hands. He had a way of swirling his head around when he accompanied someone, and sometimes he'd play with one hand as he pressed on the hairpiece.

He led me to a small room on the rectory side to rehearse. In the middle of my "Ave Maria," the cardinal appeared in his gown of splendor. What a costume! I knew it was sacrilegious, but he could do one heck of a show in that with the brilliant weaved beads and threads of gold. The jewelry looked as though it grew out of his body. He waited for me to finish.

"Giovanni, how wonderfully you sing. Your voice is so rounded and mature for your age. You have magnificent control. I just can't get over such a gift as yours. Well, we're almost ready." He showed me a picture of the main Mass hall and pointed at the balcony with the organ. "This is where you'll be singing from, Giovanni. You'll enjoy your sound as you've never before, I assure you. I can whisper from the pulpit and be heard all over the church hall. Artists have a tendency of shouting because of the size of the hall. It's a mistake, for they lose the shading needed for a good performance. Sing as though you have a high-volume microphone, don't push."

I knelt and kissed his hand. "Thank you, Your Reverence."

As I entered the balcony and walked over to the banister, the grandiose sight took my breath away. The candles were glittering against the stained windows, imported from all over the world, with bits of sunlight splashing against the statues of the saints. Painted murals and novena stations along the walls appeared to be a great massive ballet as the figures danced in the light. I was so enthralled I almost missed my cue the cardinal had arranged for me. In fact, I would have remained hypnotized if my teacher had not started his intro.

The cardinal was right. My tones flourished throughout the cathedral and enveloped me. I was in a trance listening to myself. It was a new kind of high. I never wanted to leave this spot. I was sure Gounod's "Ave Maria" never sounded like this before. I didn't even know when it was all over. I just stood spellbound.

The next thing I knew Mr. Parado was shaking me gently. "Well done, Little Caruso, well done. I've never heard anyone do a better 'Ave Maria' in my whole life, and I've heard the best of them. You should be very proud."

We gathered our music and walked to the rectory room for one more rehearsal before heading for the Waldorf. I realized I didn't remember any detail of the High Mass because the stained-glass windows, pictures, dancing lights, and the music captivated me so much and dominated my presence. I would never forget it.

Mr. Parado and I were picked up and taken to the Waldorf. As we entered the old, elegant hotel, I was overwhelmed by the Renaissance décor, the ultra-high ceilings, the hustling uniformed bellboys carrying luggage in the lobby. Mr. Parado led me by the hand to the info desk to ask where our dressing room was and to tell them why we were there.

The desk person was impressed. He hit a bell to beckon one of the hops. "Take Mr. Benedetto and Mr. Parado to room 1203." The hop took our music bags, and we followed him to an elegant room with red satin walls, original paintings, and French provincial furniture. A Steinway grand piano was in the corner. I walked around and touched the various materials, while pondering our cold-water flat in Astoria, Long Island.

Halfway through our rehearsal, Mr. Petri knocked on the door. "Bravo, Giovanni, Bravo," he said, applauding. "I saw the performance at the cathedral and talked to the cardinal. He was so pleased, Giovanni." He handed me a white envelope. "The cardinal gave me this to give you, payment for your wonderful performance."

I was shocked to see a fifty-dollar bill with a note from the cardinal, which read, "Thank you, Giovanni, for a job well done. This is a mere token of our gratitude and hope it'll help further your education in your field of endeavor." I shared the note with Mr. Petri and my teacher.

"You should keep this for your scrapbook, Giovanni. You never know, he may be the first American chosen pope," Mr. Parado said.

I sighed, slipped the note into my music case, tucked the money into my pocket, and thought how much this money would help Mom and Pop. Mr. Costello poked his head in. "It's time, Giovanni, they're waiting for you. By the way, we have Guy Lombardo's band for the festivity, so you're in good company."

Quite frankly, I panicked as I entered the grand ballroom. I guess it was just too much in one day: the large crystal chandeliers, the huge bandstand with twenty musicians in formal dress with gray-striped pants, the glare of the brass section, the waiters hustling and bustling, the crowd dressed as a fashion show, the women adorned in expensive furs and jewelry. My eyes stopped at a table covered in hors d'oeuvres of various ethnicities: lox, mini bagels, cream cheese, black and pink caviar, Italian cold cuts, provolone . . . The centerpiece was a huge ice sculpture of the bride and groom. A chef in a high white hat was serving people at the table. I was impressed, and wondered, *would I be able to get some of it.*

A drum roll, and Guy Lombardo appeared at the microphone

with a piece of paper and read, "Ladies and gentlemen, we have a wonderful treat for you: a new and great little artist who will give a concert for your pleasure. So let us all sit down and enjoy Giovanni Benedetto, or as he is better known, Little Caruso."

I walked down the center of the ballroom and bowed at intervals as the audience applauded. I was lucky, most of the guests had heard my "Ave Maria" at the church. I climbed the steps to the stage and shook Mr. Lombardo's hand, bowing. The house applauded louder.

Mr. Parado took his seat at the piano, and like an old pro from the things Uncle Dick had taught me, I tilted me eyes toward the lights so they would glisten and scanned the room until the crowd quieted down. I sang a light Italian folk song, then "O paradiso" from *L'Africaine*, which brought down the house. I carried the microphone onto the ballroom floor, and over to the designated table as the spotlight followed me.

"I wish to thank you all for your wonderful reception, and I would like to give much credit to my accompanist and teacher, Mr. Parado." The light moved to him as he stood up to more applause. I walked toward the Vanderbilt table and waited for the light to return, looked at the people in front of me, and smiled. "I would like to dedicate this next song to the Vanderbilts, mostly because of the wonderful contributions they've made to the Carnegie Institute and the Metropolitan Opera Company, keeping great culture alive." Everyone at the table beamed. "I would like to do 'Una furtiva lagrima') from *L'elisir d'amore*." I started it in soft pianissimo and performed one slow crescendo to the loudest fortissimo.

The house went crazy and shouted, "Sing 'Celeste Aida' (from *Aida)*, 'Vesti la giubba' (from *Pagliacci), 'Cielo e mare'* (from *La Gioconda*)." I bowed to the table and walked back to the stage as the audience still applauded. I felt a charge like never before. "Encore, encore!" I signaled my teacher, which quieted the crowd. "I would like to dedicate this song to the lovely bride and groom.

I'll sing, once again, the 'Ave Maria.'" When I finished, the applause was so great it brought tears to Mr. Petri's eyes, a great compliment.

Mr. Lombardo spoke as I left the stage. "That young man is truly a remarkable talent, and I'm sure the world will see much of him."

I was guided to the Vanderbilt table. "Sit down, son, sit down with us for a while," an immaculate man said. He had silver gray hair with a thin, waxed mustache, and his skin was like a wax dummy, so clean it shined. His cheeks were slightly pink, his fingernails long and pointed with chalkiness at the tips, and his diamond pinky ring could blind anyone. His lady looked like a queen with a diamond-studded tiara and at least four impressive rings glittering on the tablecloth.

She had a kind look as she spoke. "We wanted to thank you, Giovanni, for your wonderful surprise and for your wonderful performance. You have a marvelous talent, young man."

"Thank you, you are very kind."

"We're having a party at our estate at Oyster Bay in September and were wondering if you would give us the honor of performing for our guests if it fits into your schedule. I know it's a long way off, but if you know you're going to be free, we'd like to know as soon as possible. In fact, it would be even better if you could tell us before we leave."

"I'll ask Uncle Frank. He's here and he'll know."

"Which Uncle Frank is yours?"

I pointed at the next table. "Is that your uncle?" Mr. Vanderbilt asked.

"Yes."

He leaned over to my uncle. "Frank, come here, I wish to speak to you. Is this wonderful little man your nephew?" Frank beamed and nodded. "He is truly marvelous. We were just asking him if he could perform at the estate on Long Island in September and he told me he would check with you. This is wonderful, Frank's nephew, it looks like talent runs in the family."

"Anything for you. Even if he were full at that date, we would change it for you."

A man approached the table. "Come with me, the bride and groom want to meet you."

"Excuse me, thank you for your kind remarks," I said.

I was taken to the dais and introduced to the bride and groom, who thanked me for the performance. A man next to the bride handed me an envelope, and I thanked them, staring at the beautiful bride. She smiled and nodded, and I smiled back.

Mr. Costello approached me and clasped my hand. "Let's go upstairs to your dressing room, Giovanni, where it's private. I want to talk to you."

When we entered the room, I folded into one of the big chairs in exhaustion.

"I want you to know, Giovanni, I couldn't ask for more from anyone in my organization. Your whole approach was of a seasoned pro. I'm very impressed." I felt my eyes drooping. "I know you are tired, Giovanni, and you certainly are entitled to be, I just want you to know a few things before you leave. First, the envelope you were given had nothing to do with my deal, so here's mine."

That woke me up! *All of this money?* What would I do with it all? Then, of course, the truth pushed its way into my fantasy. I knew I'd give it to Mom and Pop. They were scraping bottom for my music lessons, and I was grateful.

"Giovanni, I don't know if you'll fully understand me, but you have my personal endorsement and loyalty for all time, even if I pass on. You see, I head one of the largest organizations in the world, and I'll inform everyone that not only you, but anyone in your immediate family, shall be protected for all time."

I couldn't grasp the enormity of what he was saying, but I felt a strong compliment. This man was my friend, and considering what was in store for me, I was going to need every friend I could get.

"Thank you, Don Costello, I appreciate your friendship and will return it in every way I can."

Mr. Costello relaxed into a chair and spoke in his usual whisper. "You know, Giovanni, I'm going to let you in on a little secret. The title don was given only to royalty or landowners in Italy, but when our organization was born, its purpose was to fight the tyranny of the landowners and the king. We were nothing but a bunch of peasants fighting for equality. Now we've gained money and power, it's ironic we're being called dons. I don't know whether I can appreciate the title or not. I guess you may not get the full meaning now of how I feel, but as you grow, you'll find out every man is a potential don if the right circumstances come his way.

"Well, Giovanni, I'll summon my chauffeur and get you home. You're very tired, I can see. Just tell your mother and father they should be proud God has given them this gift in you. I think they would like to hear this. I know how hard it is for them. *Arrivederci*, Giovanni. I'll see you, eh?"

This time, I rode in front with the chauffeur, and we talked all the way home. It made the trip seem short. "Do you like your job with Mr. Costello?" I asked.

"Yes, but this is only part of my job. I'm his personal bodyguard also."

"What is that?"

"Oh, I just protect him if anyone tries to hurt him in any way."

I don't think this sunk in at all.

I was loaded with anxiety when I got home and ran up the stairs with the three envelopes. "Pop, Mom, look at all the money I made today! The cardinal asked me to come back, and the Vanderbilts asked me to do a concert at the estate in Oyster Bay."

Pop beamed while Mom opened the envelopes. She whimpered as she held the money and her eyes filled with tears. "Look, John, just look at all of the money. We'll really use it. I just can't get over it. Giovanni, change into your work clothes. I have some work for you to do."

Pop looked upset but said, "Do as your mother says, Giovanni."

I went to my room a bit down. I thought she'd be so pleased. Now I realize she was toughening me up because I was going to have to make it without a father.

She brought me a burlap sack. "We need coal, Giovanni."

I headed to Manny's house. He was the best coal stealer in the neighborhood. I never told Mom we were stealing it. I told her some nice person gave it to us, but she probably knew the truth.

I knocked on Manny's door, and his Nonna answered. "Manny! Manny, your friend, Giovanni, is here," she shouted.

Manny ran to the door. "Just a minute, I want to get my sack too. I'll be right back, Nonna."

Off we went to the Tisdale lumberyard. I told Manny about my wonderful day, and his eyeballs popped out in envy. He mostly asked questions about his uncle, Don Costello, his idol. I laced the stories and made them even more vivid. Manny ate it up.

At the yard, we took our usual place behind the coal mountains, as we called them.

"A watchman is coming our way," Manny said.

My instinct was to run, but Manny held my arm. "If you run, he'll see us, Giovanni. Just sit here. I'll bury the sacks in the coal in case he catches us. Then, all he'll do is chase us and not call the cops."

We sat for what seemed an eternity. The watchman came right up to our coal pile. Manny squeezed my arm and held me down. My heart was pounding, and my nose started to bleed. "Take it easy, he's turning back," Manny said. I turned onto my back and breathed deep, pinching my nose to stop the blood. My nosebleeds could fill Turkish towels. "Let's get you home," Manny said. "You look awful."

"No, let's get the coal first, or I'll really have something to worry about."

We dug the sacks out of the pile and quickly scraped coal into them. We were almost done when I got the feeling someone was staring at us. I turned slowly and saw a pair of legs behind me. My eyes traveled from his shoes up to his glaring face. I was paralyzed as Manny continued scrubbing for coal and the man bared his yellow teeth. His face was red from the cold, and deep wrinkles ran alongside his mouth. I tried to signal Manny, but the man boomed, "Stand fast, you little dirty wop thieves! Don't you move, or I'll let you have this club over your hard heads." He swung it threateningly.

I don't know what possessed me, but I slung coal at his eyes. As he flinched, Manny and I grabbed our sacks. We ran like hell to our escape hole in the fence and made it. We knew he wouldn't chase us beyond the grounds, but we continued running until our lungs felt like they would burst.

Manny finally grabbed my arm and stopped. "Let's rest, the watchman can't catch us now. I'll tell you one thing, we have to find another coal supplier. I know another one, but it is much farther away. It's in the railroad yard at Queen's Plaza."

"Gosh, that's miles away from our house, Manny."

"Well, that's the best I can do for now. The only other way is to hijack some coal from the delivery trucks, and I can tell you those drivers are tough. If they catch you, they don't call the cops, they just beat the hell out of you. I know because it happened to me."

After resting, we walked home. The one gift nature gave us as youngsters was the ability to erase a bad incident in a hurry, or I don't think we would've survived those awful times. My face was stained with blood, as well as half of my shirt, and my nose still was bleeding slightly. Pop jumped from the kitchen table, where he and Mom were figuring out how to use the money I had brought home.

"Anna, get a cold towel. Hurry, he has another nosebleed. Do you have a headache with it, Giovanni?"

I put the coal sack into the large pail by the stove. "No, Pop, not yet anyway." I feared Mom's headache treatments.

*****

I was awakened at five o'clock the next morning. Much to my surprise, Uncle Frank was in the kitchen with his family, along with Uncle Tom and Aunt Nettie. I walked into the kitchen and rubbed my eyes as Uncle Frank spoke to me.

"We have a surprise for you. Mr. Costello invited us all to his new chicken farm in Smithtown, Long Island. Wait until you see it, Giovanni, the chickens are all fed by machines. A bell rings, food pours down a chute into bins, and the lights go on as the chickens eat milk and corn. After they eat, the lights go out, and they go back to sleep. It's a new way of doing things. The chickens get extra fat, and the meat is as sweet as sugar. Wait until you taste them."

As I became more awake, I began to get more and more excited. We all jammed into two cars and rode through the most beautiful winter land. Nothing could substitute the grand artistic work of nature bestowed on this area of the world. Smithtown is a little town, even today in the late 70s, in the center of Long Island, away from its two breathtaking shores. Lake Ronkonkoma, a beautiful Indian name, has sections running through the town. Lots of Indians lived on the island, and a large reservation was within a stone's throw of the town.

We drove through the miles of archways formed from trees. It was even more beautiful without the summer leaves. The glistening icicles and spots of snow hanging from the barren branches set an enchanting scene. I guess we rode about one and half hours while Uncle Tom named the little towns we passed through. Finally a sign post saying, "You are now entering the city limits of Smithtown."

We finally reached a dirt road, and Uncle Frank signaled to turn right with him. It was a wonderful sight riding up to what was supposed to be the farmhouse. It was more like a colonial mansion with a thatched roof. Off to the left was a small house for hired hands, and a beautiful huge red barn trimmed in white was in the background. I couldn't wait to get inside the house. I spotted Mr. Costello's limousine.

The chauffer greeted us. "Mr. Costello couldn't make it. He had the meeting with the boys from Jersey to clinch the whole coast of New York and New Jersey."

Everyone hugged Italian style, and he turned to me. "Giovanni, *come' stai?*" I ran to embrace him, and he said he would give us a tour of the chicken farm.

The house was a dream. Somehow I felt I had been there before. I eyed the large Arizona rock-decorated fireplace with colonial figurines seemingly dancing in the light of the fire. Above were two Civil War rifles, still loaded, I was told. The furniture from the Civil War period was highly varnished. Scattered on the walls were Indian trinkets: a bow and arrow, a large spear, and a rotted part of a totem pole that held its color. In the den was a pool table and a bar with two Civil War pistols hanging on the back bar. A large bear rug was spread in front of a smaller fireplace. I bent over to touch the teeth, a bit apprehensive it might wake up and bite me.

Frank bustled through the door with the chauffer behind him. I never saw Uncle Frank so angry. The room was dark and quiet, so they didn't notice me on the floor.

"Pete, what the hell is this broad doing here?" Uncle Frank said. "You knew it was a family thing. Are you crazy?"

"The whole world knows this is my *comare*. What in the hell is the difference?"

"If Costello ever finds out, you'll know it was the wrong thing to do."

"You're not going to tell him, are you, Frank?"

"No, but if he asks me, I'm going to make you tell him, because I never lie to him. That is the kind of trust we have. We would never lie about anything. What about your wife? Does she know where you are today? Suppose she shows up? I'll tell you one thing right now, my family will spit on you. Our women wouldn't stand for this kind of insult."

"Gee, Frank, if I knew it was going to be this much of a hassle, I would have left her in New York, but she kept bugging me, telling me I never take her anywhere, and when I found out Costello wasn't coming, I brought her along for a little company, with the long drive and all."

"How in the hell do I introduce her? You tell me. They all know your wife. What in the goddamn hell do I tell them?" Frank pointed his finger. "This is your baby, you introduce her. I'm putting it right in your lap where it belongs in."

"Aw, c'mon, Frank, how can you do this to me? What can I tell them? You're much smarter than I am."

"You should have thought of that before you came out here." Frank shook his head and turned in my direction. "Giovanni, what are you doing in here all alone? Go into the living room with the rest of the guests right now, do you hear?"

I ran out of the room. What would Frank do to the chauffer? Everyone was sitting down, and the lady in question looked uncomfortable. All the women seemed to look at her.

"I don't think we've been introduced. My name is Nettie, I'm Frank's sister." Aunt Nettie proceeded to introduce everyone in the room, but had the look of a woman ready for the kill. I'm sure she surmised all was not kosher. Upon the final introduction, she once again asked the lady who she was as the chauffer entered the room with sweat on his forehead.

"I'm one of Mr. Costello's bookkeepers, here to take inventory of everything on the farm," she said. "You see, he just bought this recently, and we haven't had the chance until today."

Pete jumped. "Yah, yah, that's who she is, the bookkeeper."

Aunt Nettie with her cutting Italian eyes spouted, "How nice, how very nice. Costello knows how to pick 'em. She's attractive."

With this, Uncle Tom poked her in the ribs.

"You folks make yourself at home," Pete said, squirming. "The ladies can pick out any chickens they want for supper. Mr. Costello wants everyone to be at home and have a good time. I'm going to show Giovanni, and anyone else, around the farm."

He wiped his brow with one hand and grabbed me with the other to walk to the giant barn. "This is the latest way of raising chickens," Pete said as we approached the barn door. "Everything is automatic, and the chickens end up better than the old way. These birds are white Leghorns, the best of all fryers."

A bell sounded for feeding time, and the lights turned on. The feed rolled down the chutes as the chickens frantically pushed each other for space through the bars. I was impressed, but the smell was awful. Pete led me to a room where an old man appeared to be putting green sunglasses on the chickens.

"What's he doing?" I asked.

"Well, you see, Giovanni, if two chickens have a fight and draw blood, they turn cannibal and will kill themselves off by the thousands. We found we could put these glasses on, and it seems to stop them."

I looked at Pete skeptically, thinking *The next thing you know, they'll be wearing bathing suits.*

Peter walked me around the property, opening doors to sheds, showing me the equipment, but I couldn't get the sunglasses out of my mind. When we went back to the house, the women were feathering the chickens in a production line. Aunt Emma was cutting their throats, and three large pots were steaming on the stove. Once the chickens were bled, Mom and her sisters dipped them into the water to soften the feathers. Next, they tied them upside down by the legs to strip off the feathers. I wanted to ask if I could do one but decided I better not.

Pete was watching, but his girlfriend was in the other room having no part of this action. His smile changed as he looked out the window. "Son of a bitch, here comes my wife up the driveway. She was supposed to take the kids to the movies. . . . Frank!

Frank!"

Frank ran to the kitchen. "What do you want, Pete?"

"She's here, my wife, she'll kill me."

The women were smiling and elbowing each other, ready to enjoy the slaughter.

"Quick, get her out the back door to the barn," Frank said. "Keep her hidden if it has to be all day. This must not happen, for everyone's sake."

"I won't be shoved into any barn!" the woman screamed. "I have as much right being here as she does."

"Fine, I'm sure you can handle her, but will you be able to handle Costello when he hears about it?" Frank said, taking her by the arm. "And he will if you two meet here."

She hung her head and walked out the back door with Frank. "You stay right here, Pete. Don't you move from this house until I say so, and *you*, woman, don't you dare come out of that barn if you know what's healthy for you."

Pete's wife blew through the door and almost looked disappointed when she found only the family cleaning chickens. She looked around the room.

"Hi, darling, what are you doing here?" Pete said. "I thought you were with the kids at the movie."

"I left them with your mother, Pete. I wanted to see the farm."

"You know my mother is too sick to take care of them. Go back this minute, do you hear?"

"I'll go back after I've seen the farm and visited my friends."

Pete looked worried as Frank appeared and greeted Pete's wife with much bravado. "Hi, Polly, what are you doing here?"

She frowned. "I came to see the farm, and my husband for a change."

"Good, good, it's good to have you here, Polly. I haven't seen you for a long time. You're staying the whole day, I hope?"

Pete, not understanding Frank's psychology, turned white. "She left the kids with my mom. You know she's sick and can't handle the kids alone."

"Well, Polly, it's still early," Frank said. "Why don't you go home, get the kids, and come back? Then we'll really have a swell time."

She looked sheepish. "You know, I never thought of that, Frank. I'll stay for a short while and go back. I'm sorry, Pete, I should have known better. But I'd like to see the new equipment in the barn. I heard it's out of *Flash Gordon*."

The women eyeballed each other as if watching the greatest show on Earth, and I could tell Uncle Frank was spitting mad. Pete turned pale again.

"Too bad, Polly," Frank said. "A lot of the chickens are dying, so none of us can go. We separated them yesterday because of it. They've contracted some disease and are killing each other."

As if cued, the old man from the barn walked in with a chicken all gouged out. "Mr. Frank, the glasses are beginning to help, but some of them are still attacking."

I just saw a master at work.

Her coat still on, Polly stood up in defeat. "Pete, I think I'll go home to the children. Try not to be too late."

"I'll bring home some of the cooked chicken."

"Don't bother, I have some sauce made, all I have to do is boil some water."

She left without an embrace. I watched her car drive off, amazed Uncle Frank improvised a master plan so quickly. He was truly a manipulator.

Maria was helping our aunts prepare the rest of the food, and Ninni was off playing on the floor. So I wandered through the house and opened closets.

I found an old shotgun and decided to play Daniel Boone. I put it on my shoulder, marched out the door, and walked alongside the barn. I looked down the barrel of the huge rifle and pretended to shoot various things. Then I aimed at some pigeons on the top of the house, only this time I squeezed the trigger of the double barrel. Much to my surprise, it was loaded and knocked me off my feet. Everyone flew out of the house. I didn't know it, but I'd blown a hole at the peak of the farmhouse.

Pop, white as a sheet, ran to me. I looked up as he glared at me. My arm felt as though it had been torn out of its socket. "Gee, Pop, I was only playing. I didn't know the rifle was loaded, honest I didn't."

"Get off your fanny and get in the house, Giovanni. Do you realize you tore the roof off the house?"

I started to bawl and ran into the house, only to fall into the hands of Mom. I couldn't sit for the rest of the afternoon. I felt the end of the world had come, especially when Mr. Costello would find out. I didn't raise my head through the meal. As the women cleared the dishes, everyone poked fun at me, so I ran upstairs to a bedroom to hide in a corner. Before I knew it, it was time to go.

*****

It was a warm Saturday morning in March, and Pop was shaking his head as he read his favorite newspaper. "Giovanni, do you remember the man who flew the airplane solo across the Atlantic in 1927 named Charles Lindbergh? I say solo because surely you remember my telling he was not the first person to pilot across the Atlantic. That honor belongs to two British aviators, [1] John Alcock and his navigator, Arthur Brown, eight years earlier in June 1919."

"Yes, Pop, I remember Charles Lindbergh and John Alcock."

"Well, someone kidnapped Lindbergh's son four days ago. This means someone stole his child and wants ransom, money, for his safe return. My God, the asking ransom is fifty thousand dollars. It seems as though they have a suspect — that means someone they think did it. His name is Bruno Richard Hauptmann, a carpenter and painter. The ladder used to get to the child's

---

[1] *"Tomorrow has Wings, Story of Captain John Alcock, first to Fly the Atlantic Non-Stop in 1919"* by Joseph F Alcock

window was his, and they found some of the ransom money hidden in a closet. Well, I guess they got the right man all right. The FBI was in on it, and when they go to work, they get things done."

"Why would anyone do something like that, Pop?"

"Well, let me put it this way, Giovanni, some people would do almost anything for money. . . . .Here's another interesting story. This man in India, Mohandas 'Mahatma' Gandhi, I know they'll kill him, like all the great men who try to help their people."

"Why is he so great, Pop?"

"It seems as though in India they have many British soldiers, and they have a law that most of the masses can get the death penalty if they touch anyone, even by accident. It's a form of pressure slavery never known in the history of the world. So this gentle little man is trying to change this without violence. But as history will tell us, when the British see he's making headway, they'll have him assassinated — killed that means, Giovanni.

"Wow, Pop, he must be something to get thousands of people to follow him. I wonder how he does that."

"He does it, something like you do when you perform, except he has a stronger cause and works on a much larger audience. They call it a form of mass hypnotizing. You are very young, Giovanni, but someday you'll find any one person who can get the attention of large amounts of people really has a gifted talent from God. It's not something you basically learn, though once you have this talent, you can learn to improve."

Pop could make anyone feel special, no matter what they did in life. This day he made me feel very special, very, very special. He made me realize what I was doing was important even at my young age. He clearly made me understand I couldn't take my gift lightly.

Pop followed the Lindbergh kidnapping every day. Like most people, he enjoyed second-guessing guilt or innocence, with one exception: His analogies were right on target. He had a God's gift also: perception. Three attempts were made on Gandhi's life in summer 1934, and he was later assassinated.

*****

With the arrival of summer, Uncle Dick began preparing me for the Vanderbilt affair at the mansion on Long Island. We were having one of our usual talks as he drifted into payment values. Although I didn't quite understand, I nodded in a sense of loyalty and confidence. Looking back, it amazes me how much an adult thinks a child understands, especially when so many singular words have multiple meanings. It is hard enough for a child to grasp semantics, much less trying to interpret life from an adult's point of view.

"Now, with the Vanderbilt party! Giovanni, this should be a great one for you. The whole scope of politics is going to be present, meaning anyone who is anybody will be present. Except for a few, a different set of people will attend. Even though you met the Vanderbilts at the wedding, remember they were invited by a different segment altogether, so you'll be exposed to a whole set of new faces, most of them blueblood millionaires, by the way.

"What I want you to do is prepare a couple of contemporary tunes mixed in with the heavy stuff to give it a hell of a pace. I can't impress enough how important this gig is, Giovanni. You're going to be at your very best by the time it comes around. In fact, I'm going to tell your mom you should ease up on your extra work until it is over."

At my next voice lesson with Mr. Parado, I related what Uncle Dick had suggested. "He said there would be movie people and Broadway producers attending, apart from all of the strongest politicians from all over the country."

Mr. Parado, who never said much, took out a book of show tunes. "Here's one for you, Giovanni. It's a well-written tune, and it plays in your range very well, 'Prisoner of Love.' "

He walked me over to the piano and went into the song with an arpeggio. It was beautiful. All I had to do was listen to the melody once, and I could pick up the lyrics and sing them with nothing but chords behind me. I had a wonderful feeling for the song. "Gee, this is a pretty song, Mr. Parado. I like it."

"I like it for you, Giovanni. Now we'll set this aside and look for one more." He feverishly thumbed through the pages. "Here, Giovanni, here's what we're looking for. It has some tempo and is very popular with the blueblood set. It's a tough tune, but you can do it, 'More Than You Know.' How is that for a title, eh?"

I felt this one as much as the first. We practiced most of the afternoon until I had them down. Mr. Parado looked pleased. "That's all for now, Giovanni. Take these lead sheets home and study them until you can do them in your sleep. Next time I see you, we'll polish any rough spots."

CHAPTER EIGHT

The next day, I met with Manny and Herman. Herman was all excited about a movie starting Saturday at the Meridian Theater about the famous Italian bandit's life, Mussolini. I didn't hesitate telling my friends he was my cousin. Their eyes widened and mouths dropped.

"Boy, he is your cousin!" Manny said.

"Yeah, ask your uncle Costello. He'll tell you I am telling the truth."

"We gotta go see it."

"I don't know if I can make it. I usually have to work or take lessons Saturday."

"Go ask your mom for one Saturday off, Giovanni. When she hears it's free because it's run by some rich man, I'm sure she'll let you go, especially when you tell her it's about your cousin."

He didn't know my mom; she didn't know the word <u>yes</u>. I trotted home and found her cleaning the kitchen. "Can I go to the movies this Saturday, Mom?"

"Where do you expect to get the money?"

"It's free, Mom, it's free."

"I know all about it, Giovanni, the philanthropist who gives little poor children the chance to see a movie, and I also know it's a movie about our cousin."

I should have known; she knows everything going on. "But Mom, my friends are going, and I want to go."

"Where do you get the idea it's free? You'll lose the pay you usually get for working, a dollar and a half, which means the movie is far from free."

Pop butted in with a rare contradiction. "Let Giovanni go, he's far too busy for a little boy. He needs some time for himself, Anna."

"Very well, John, but remember, you let him go, I didn't. When he gets spoiled, don't come to me."

Pop looked victorious. I ran and hugged him. "Thank you, Pop, thank you."

I was all jitters until Saturday morning. Mom fixed me a sandwich, and off to the movies I went with Manny and Herman. It was my first time at the theater. It was as long as a railroad car, and the seats reclined in a deep angle, which made you feel as though you were falling off a cliff. The theater was dirty with a musty odor. As we filed in, a brute of a man was holding a stick sawed off of a mop, similar to what we used to play stickball in the streets. He used it to push the free patrons into the aisles and would jolt them in the ribs if they didn't move fast enough. We were lucky to find seats together.

The story unfolded, just as it was told by my family. Then came the big surprise. A musician behind the screen played guitar when the movie showed Mussolini playing the guitar. Then someone shot a blank gun during the shooting scene, which drove us under the seats.

It had the same effect as an Alfred Hitchcock thriller. In fact, it was so exciting we decided to sneak back through the line for the second showing. Herman gave his usual profound advice. "Don't let him see your face. He has a memory like an elephant, I tell you, and if he catches you, he hits pretty hard with the stick, and you can't ever come back again."

We were so excited about the sound effects that we forgot fear. We got through but had to sit in the last row.

After I finished my sandwich halfway through the movie, a

man walked in with a large plate wrapped in a napkin. "Here's Tony's pasta," I overheard him say as he placed the plate on the shelf behind me. Although I couldn't see in the darkened theater, I could hear and smell.. "Make sure he gets it, I'm in a hurry." Well, the smell was too much for me. I sneaked the plate onto my lap and devoured it with my hands. I had nothing to wipe off the sauce all over my shirt, hands, and mouth.

Before I knew it, the lights came on, and a voice roared, "Which one of you little runts ate my lunch? I'll find out, don't worry."

As he stalked toward me with the stick, I started to shake. "Look out, Giovanni, he's tougher than my uncle," Manny said. "If he finds you out, he'll kill you."

My heart pounded louder, so loud I thought he could hear it. He stopped and glared at me like a wild animal. I think I died that Saturday.

"You little monster! I'm going to get you for this, you little thief. When I get through with your hide, you won't have enough to take home."

My two friends ran in different directions to confuse him. I crawled under the seats as he scrambled to see where I would come up. The Lord had blessed me with another talent: I could run, especially when frightened. If I could avoid him through half the theater, I'd stand a chance of running out the back exit doors. I flew down the last aisles with a grand cheering squad and the maddened theater manager screaming behind. I ran as I've never run before into the blinding sun. I scaled fences and ran across the busiest traffic intersection in town, right into the arms of the popular traffic cop . . . Peanuts.

He picked me up. His big red cheeks and Irish smile could win over the world. "Where in the hell do you think you're going, Giovanni?"

"I...I...I'm late, and I have to get home, or Mom will kill me."

"Well, Giovanni, you almost didn't make it in one piece. A big

Mack truck almost got you, and you never saw it."

If the big goon still was looking for me, he'd surely see me in the middle of Astoria Boulevard with a cop, and he did. He stomped toward me, waving his stick. "Give me the little thief! He stole my lunch."

I jumped behind Peanuts and held on for dear life. "Thief, you say? I know this little boy and his family, he is no thief. He may be a few other things, but not a thief."

"Don't tell me. Look at the sauce all over his face and clothes."

Peanuts covered his mouth to hide his laugh. "Well, if he is a thief, then he's my problem, not yours. On your way, I'll take care of the little bandit."

It didn't take me long to worry whether I was safer at the hands of the angry man with a stick, or facing Mom. Peanuts informed me he had to take me home and explain what I had done at the theater. The walk home felt like what I'd imagined the walk to the electric chair would be like. I sweated all the way, and rightly so. For a long time afterward, my butt was so sore I couldn't sit down without groaning.

*****

Time had come upon me. The big event, the Vanderbilt party, was at hand. Uncle Tom took me to a special tailor for a garment befitting the occasion. I couldn't believe people wore such clothes. I was fitted with a day formal: tails, gray pants with black pencil stripes, gray paisley cravat, a phony diamond stick pin, and spats for my patent leather shoes with high Cuban heels.

Uncle Tom was in my corner every minute as he spoke to the tailor. "What kind of a fit is this? Look at how the back of the neck leaves a wrinkle when Giovanni sits down."

"He has awfully big shoulders for a little boy, Tom, and this makes him hard to fit."

"You're supposed to be a fine tailor. Don't kid me, just finish it right. We'll wait right here until you are through, then we'll see in the final fitting."

"While we are waiting, Giovanni, how is that punch of yours coming? Boy, you have the punch of a champion. . . . Well, from what I hear, you're really going to rub elbows with the hoi polloi. All of the richest capitalists in the country will be at this affair. Listen to me, Giovanni, just do whatever Uncle Frank and Uncle Dick tell you, and you'll be in gravy, believe me. Besides you have the voice and talent to back it up."

"Don't worry, Uncle Tom, I do whatever they tell me to do. I know they'll help me better than anybody."

"Just remember for all time, they couldn't help you if you didn't have the talent, so you see, the deal is even."

The little tailor, who appeared to be five hundred years old with glasses on the tip of his nose and hunched over from his many years at the sewing machine, carried my jacket out of his workroom. "Here, boy, try it on and see if it satisfies your uncle's taste."

Uncle Tom smoothed his fingers over the jacket through my shoulders and shook his head. "Well, this is a little better but very good for a Sicilian."

"What the hell else can a Podargonian say? Your village couldn't shine the shoes of the village I came from."

Uncle Tom smiled. "Okay, how much for this?"

"Thirty dollars, and I'll throw in the stick pin in payment of your entertainment."

On the way home, Uncle Tom told me he was one of the finest tailors in the country. "I tease him because he's so good, and he likes it because he knows how good I am."

I didn't know why the whole thing enchanted me. I guess it made me feel grown up. I spent most of my life among them, so I wanted the kind of acceptance that came with maturity.

The morning of the big affair arrived, and Pop helped me with what he called the monkey clothes. "You're going to look so handsome, Giovanni, with these formal clothes."

I felt all dressed up and couldn't wait to look in the full-length mirror in Mom's bedroom.

Pop slipped on my jacket, attached my spats, and straighten me up. "Go look in the mirror, Giovanni, go look."

I ran to the mirror and thought I saw a handsome picture, although I'm sure I more likely resembled a chimpanzee with a Buster Brown haircut. It's amazing how tastes change with maturity. My hair shined with the horrible smell of roses from the Brilliantine that Mom sprayed from her atomizer.

The limo appeared, and neighbors watched as the chauffeur opened the door for me. We were to pick up Mr. Parado in the city, then double back to Long Island, an adventure in itself. We chatted all the way to the mansion and approached a small guard house on a private road. The driver presented the guard with some kind of card, and waved us through. We must have driven three miles along the winding, picturesque road until we turned off in front of a huge wrought-iron gate at least thirty feet high with a fleur-de-lis design, the usual telephone-buzzer system beside it. The chauffeur hung up the phone, and the gates opened. Several fierce-looking dogs were walking in the acres of lawn along the lengthy driveway to the house.

Ivy was growing over the gray stone of the cathedral-type house, seemingly smothering it. The parking area could fit fifty or more cars.

As I entered the palace the wonderful paintings on the circular walls stopped me cold. All were by one artist.

The realistic paintings depicted the Wild West: Indians, horses, wagon trains, forts, and fireside scenes. The plainsmen brought the period to life. I was so captivated that I didn't notice the throngs of people. In the center of the foyer was a beautiful rock fountain, surrounded by a low wrought-iron fence that was an umbrella stand.

The gracious Mrs. Vanderbilt greeted me. "Giovanni, I'm so pleased to see you again. I know today's party will be a tremendous success. Tell me what has been happening in your life."

I told her about the butcher shop shooting, the murder across the street from our house, Pop's illness, and how wonderful he was and his singing talent.

"I am so sorry to hear of your father's illness, Giovanni. I did not know he was also a singer. Now tell me about your career. How is it going? What kind of studies are you doing?"

I told her Uncle Dick guided me and Uncle Frank helped with his contacts. Her smile seemed permanent but sincere. She said she would introduce me to most of the guests after the performance.

"Then I want you to meet a very special person," she said. "In fact, he is some kind of associate of your Uncle Frank's. His name is Fiorello La Guardia. He's going to be the next mayor of New York, and he's most interested in talented people. You know, New York City is a very important place, and it deserves the kind of attention this fine man can give it."

I was taken to my dressing room with Mr. Parado. We looked at each other in amazement of the room decorated in dancing water like green shades. The piano in the center was a green antique color with gold trim, and a gold candlestick sat on the cover like a king's crown. The trim around the huge fireplace matched the wood of the piano. Large sheer drapes were the faintest green, and the tall windows overlooked a swimming pool and about ten cabana-like buildings. Miles of riding grounds encompassed the area with stables off to the left.

Mr. Parado joined me at the window. "How can anyone have so much money, and some so little? It doesn't seem fair."

"Gosh, Mr. Parado, so they own all this land with the house?"

"Probably this and most of the United States in one way or another."

We rehearsed the show, and a light flashed beside the door. "That's the signal for us to go to the music room. Now, she gave me a directional map of the house. Let me see, yes, we go left to the stairs and turn right until we see a large statue of Beethoven, then turn into the corridor until it ends and through double doors."

It seemed like miles. When we finally reached the enormous room filled with guests, a pantomime clown named Toto was performing. He could roll his body into a little ball in seconds. Amazing. He amused the guests to no end, and I seemed to forget my role, as though he was there for my benefit.

Uncle Frank broke the spell by tapping me on the shoulder. "You're on next, Giovanni, so give 'em hell."

Mr. Parado picked out the instrumentation and duplicated the charts for the small band. Mrs. Vanderbilt announced me and said so many nice things. I was completely relaxed. The two contemporary tunes mixed in with my standard repertoire enthralled the audience. Upon my last song, "E lucevan le stelle," I did something spontaneous.

"Ladies and gentlemen, I wish to thank you for being so kind and attentive, and I'd like to dedicate my last number to the next mayor of New York City, Mayor Fiorello La Guardia."

I found out afterward this was to be announced later in the day as a prelude to a fund-raiser. That's what they deserved for giving a kid my age that kind of information.

Luckily, it worked out fine, for the audience stood up and faced a short, dark man, his hair plastered over to one side. He wore a bowstring tie with a black suit and kept his right hand in his pocket with a rigid thumb protruding forward. He seemed quite pleased as he stood up to acknowledge the crowd.

I did my last tune, and the usual "Encore, encore" came. I did my favorite, "Vesti la Giubba" from *Pagliacci,* and left them screaming, remembering what Uncle Dick had told me, "Leave the stage when the audience is most excited, or always leave them laughing."

I walked off stage soaked in perspiration, and Mrs. Vanderbilt threw her arms around me. "Marvelous, Giovanni, just marvelous! You're such a talented boy. In all my years, I don't think I've ever heard a sound such as yours."

"Thank you so much, Mrs. Vanderbilt. I'd like to freshen up, I'm wringing wet."

"You do that, and then I have a very special person I would like you to meet. In fact, he is most anxious to meet you."

Excited, I zoomed through the corridor to my dressing room and back, just as perspired as before. Mrs. Vanderbilt walked me over to Mr. La Guardia's table. Somehow he didn't look real, perhaps because his features were so distinctive that they made him look like a mannequin.

She didn't even get the chance to introduce us. "Sit down, Giovanni," he said. "I want to talk to you. You know, besides being a fine artist, you have a shrewd political approach. You couldn't have had better timing when you introduced me." His eyes wrinkled into a smile. "I was beginning to think you upstaged me so I wouldn't stand a chance with these people. So, you see, you bailed me out."

I knew by his expression it was some kind of joke, so I smiled. "Here, Giovanni, sit down next to me so we'll talk."

I studied his face. The kind lines were unmistakable.

"What do you do besides your singing career?" he asked.

I gave it all to him, about my jobs, helping out in the house, and trying to make enough money to not only subsidize my schooling, but also help out because Pop was so ill.

"Giovanni, I don't quite know how I can help you, but I promise I will some way. I have one or two ideas. I'll let you know through your Uncle Frank just what we'll do. It seems to me you don't have much time to play any kind of sports, or even read the funny papers for that matter. And this really is not right for a boy your age, even considering your mature talent. One thing has nothing to do with the other. Maybe we'll find you the best kind of school that doesn't cost any money. No offense to your fine teacher now, but I get the feeling there is less chance for exploitation when a miner attends a large, orderly schools like

Juilliard. Those kind of schools deal on an artistic level of teaching, not a personal one, and eliminates ego that may affect a student at times. These types of schools have subjects covering the field of show business, and the artist comes out well aware of what he or she has to face up to in the world."

He still kept his small hand in his suit pocket and only moved his little thumb to make a point. Uncle Frank approached the table and shook hands with "the Little Flower", as he was called. "Success, Fiorello, success. We have all the heavies in the room backing your campaign, and I mean backing you across the board, not only with money, but in radio editorials, newspapers, the clergy, the whole ball of wax."

"Remember, Frank, I promised no sanctuary for certain elements in this town. I never gave you any fairy tales, and eventually, I want Tom Dewey as my district attorney for New York City, and you know where his feelings are. He has eyes on the governorship and then the presidency. And you know after talking and observing this man, he may just make it. He has the brain matter, and most of all, the patience. He also has the pulse on what's important to people right now and ten years ahead."

"Fiorello, it is my posture you get in as mayor. The last one has made things so bad, we have to restore confidence in the voter, Republican or Democrat. You make your promises on what you believe in, but remember, as a third-party candidate, you or anyone else must make friends with the devil, if necessary, to win with minority vote. One little bit of advice: This is one election in which no candidate should promise anything, including certain sanctuaries, unless they mean it. None of you can afford to go back on your word. These people are far too powerful to sit for double cross."

"Frank, have you ever seen two people eat an apple the same way, or chew gum, or peel a banana? I can give you one promise: If I headhunt anyone, it'll be in an approach no one has ever seen. I'll chew my apple my own way."

Frank looked disturbed. He didn't have his "altogether sure" look about him, deep lines distorted his forehead. His eyes seemed to sink into his prominent face, and his mouth grimaced. "I really like you as a person. I think you know this, Fiorello, and I'm not intimidating you in any way. Just be careful in your judgment, very careful. There's a lot more here than meets even the trained political eye."

"Don't worry, Frank, I know you're my friend. You stuck by me in all of my failures, which were many. But if I have to be careful, keep in mind everyone on all sides of the fence has to do the same. They had better not give me the chance for attacking them."

Frank lit a cigar and smiled. "At least we both know where we stand, dear friend." Frank took a lead pencil out of his pocket. In those days, this kind of pencil was some sort of status symbol. I couldn't take my eyes off the rich design in silver with deep vertical lines. The top and bottom had matching onyx, and the light from the crystal chandelier threw out prisms from the ridges of the pencil. It almost hypnotized me as Frank drew a schematic of the political wards and showed how he would engineer the votes to get La Guardia in with the minority vote.

"Well, Frank, it looks good in theory, and if you handle it exclusively, I know without a doubt it'll work."

Now I wish I had taken tablecloth, for its historical effort.

Uncle Frank rode home with me in the limo. We discussed the victorious day and the grandiose mansion. Before I knew it, we were at Uncle Frank's house. Mr. Costello's car was parked in front, and he was talking to my grandfather by the front door.

"Come in the house, I have your pay for the day on my desk," Frank said. I waited while he spoke with Mr. Costello in the den. Quite some time later, Uncle Frank came to me. "Oh, here, Giovanni. I forgot all about you. I know how tired you must be." He turned to Mr. Costello. "He did a hell of a job. I'll fill you in as soon as he leaves."

I said good-bye without opening the envelope and ran all the way home, for the limo didn't wait for me.

Frank arrived the next morning to visit Pop. I sat at the kitchen table and felt grown-up, though I never said anything. They had been discussing politics, Roosevelt versus Hoover, until we heard a scream. Mom had a habit of leaving sewing needles stuck in the corner of the kitchen chair, and Ninni had gotten a needle through the temple as he was crawling. His blood squirted with each pulse. Pop gasped and pressed his index finger on the hole. Ninni screamed and squirmed, making it almost impossible to hold.

"Oh, my God, Frank, he'll bleed to death! This kid will be the death of all of us sooner or later."

"It's a good thing I'm here," said Uncle Frank. "The car is downstairs, John. Let's get him to St. John's."

"He's getting to be a regular at the hospital, we might as well get him a steady room. Giovanni, you stay here. When Mom comes home, don't scare her half to death. Just tell her Ninni got a small cut and we took him to the hospital to make sure."

When they left, I persuaded Maria to explain what happened instead of me. She had turned white as a sheet and would have consented to anything. I threw my shirt on and scrambled down the street in search of Herman and Manny. I found them sitting in a lot with a third kid in the manner of old Indian tribes, pow wow style. "Giovanni, this is a new friend. His name is Vinnie, Vinnie Auletta."

I eyeballed him. He looked angry and tough, like a predator. I wasn't sure I'd like him, yet he was with my two best friends, so I extended my hand of friendship.

He didn't take my hand and instead asked, "Can you do a handstand?"

"I think so."

"Like this?" He not only did a handstand but cartwheels and back flips too.

"I don't think I could do all those."

"What does this little runt with the girl's haircut do?"

"He sings opera," Herman said.

"Opera?"

"Yes, opera, and he's our best friend, understand?"

"Okay, Opera." Vinnie finally extended his hand. "If you're an opera singer, then I'll call you Opera, okay?"

"Okay, Vinnie."

"What else do you do?"

"I play hockey, goalie, and I box a little."

He turned to Manny. "This little runt boxes with gloves and all?"

"He does. Believe it or not, he's good. In fact, he has guts and hits awfully hard for a little guy."

"Well, Manny, if you say so, I believe it, but he's such a little guy."

I told them about Ninni, and Herman shook his head. "That little guy was born for trouble, run over twice by an automobile, now this. If he survives, he'll be a good gang member."

"What are you going to be when you grow up?" Vinnie asked Herman.

"A priest."

"And you, Manny?"

"I'm going to be a racket guy like my Uncle Costello."

"Your uncle is Costello? Wow, some of my uncles work for him as drivers. He's heavy. . . . I'm going to do anything that puts a buck in my pocket, and I mean anything."

I don't know why, but I liked Vinnie even though he wasn't friendly. And we ended up watching each other's backs, a must in our neck of the woods.

By the time I got home, Ninni was back. Mom, looking belligerent by the stove, stared at me as if I'd committed murder. "Didn't I tell you to watch Ninni? Must I tell you every time he has a disaster?"

"Anna, it wasn't his fault," Frank said. "I was here, and no one could have stopped what happened."

*****

A few weeks later near dusk, I heard car horns and shouting, similar to New Year's Eve. Pop beckoned us to the window. "Frank promised us he would drive by with his car rally for Hoover. They have almost a hundred cars, a sound truck with big pictures of the president on the side, and two loudspeaker horns on the roof. Frank is inside making roving speeches for the election."

The sound grew louder as the cars drew closer. People twirled red flares out of the windows, the blur hypnotic. I stared so hard my head hurt. It was hard to believe you could hear Uncle Jim shouting over all the noise, "Hooray for Hoover! Hooray for Hoover!"

It was the first time I saw Mom and Pop lose control. They laughed so hard they held their sides, and tears streamed down Pop's face. "Your brother, Jim, has to be the world's champion when it comes to being loud. Did you hear him over all the noise, Ann?"

"I always knew he was loud, but never this loud. Come on kids, get dressed. We're going to the school. Frank is speaking tonight, and he invited us over."

*****

We filed into the auditorium, and an usher seated us up front in a reserved area. I was so proud when borough president Harvey introduced Frank as the next speaker. He looked so impressive with a midnight-blue suit on his six-foot-four frame. He was handsome and masculine with piercing eyes, which darted from side to side as he spoke in Italian. He was after the Italian vote. He truly was a fiery speaker, and the crowd gave him a standing ovation and screamed for more.

I had the same feeling of accomplishment as when I was performing. The same thrill came watching someone catch fish, as if I'd caught it myself. I was sincerely happy, not envious.

A disturbance broke out behind us. Dick and Jim swarmed all

over two guys. In fact, they beat the hell out of them before the police arrived. They arrested the guys covered in blood and didn't even question my uncles. Uncle Frank descended the podium and shook hands with his two brothers to congratulate them. "They were Baroni's boys sent to heckle us. You did a good job. I like the way you kept your eyes open. If they persist, we'll pay them a visit in force."

Jim held his swollen right hand. He was small but not timid. "Did you see the shot I gave him, Frank? Did you see him go right on his ass?"

"Yes, I saw it Jim, and if Hoover gets in, you'll get the job I promised you. Just keep up the good work."

Pop just shook his head in dismay.

"I know, John, but realistically we have to accept this sort of thing," Frank said. "It's been going on since the beginning of politics. I didn't invent this attitude, but I have to live with it. I have to protect our party position wherever I feel necessary, John. I have no way of stopping this. It'll be happening long after I am gone."

*****

Hurling back to the present, I begin to feel the hypocritical tone enveloping the room. There's no question some of these people are only here to see the famous 'Tony Bennett', and this bothered me, for Mom was a champion. She deserved the attention for her years of struggle, raising and teaching us without the support of a husband. People crowd around Tony, some looking to do business, others just to say they were at "Tony Bennett's mother's funeral". If it weren't for my wife's strength, I don't think I'll make it.

I sit down in nervous exhaustion and fall back in time once more.

CHAPTER NINE

Time seemed to fly by to 1933. I'm mature for my age, becoming a serious and responsible thinker.

At ten years old, I began to realize the sibling rivalry. Ninni still was emulating me in a comical sense, but now to the point of annoyance, especially right after a song or my scales. I did recognize he had one hell of a voice, very smooth though not an opera range. That, coupled with an uncanny aptitude for the arts, in particular drawing and painting.

One afternoon when I was practicing "Vesti la giubba from *Pagliacci,* I heard Ninni singing along from another room. His short vibrato and sweet tones were similar to Pop's. I tiptoed over, but he shut down. "Why are you stopping, Ninni? You have a very beautiful voice. I mean it, Ninni. you should practice with it."

He hung his head. "I can't sing as well as you."

"Let me tell you something, I never had your polished sound until I began studying with professional teachers. That means you are a natural voice, and who knows how far you can take your gift with training."

He looked relieved and sighed. "I do like to sing, you know."

"I know, Ninni, and I think you should sing every chance you can. You know something? I like to draw, but I don't draw very well. Maybe you could practice with me when I sing, and I can draw with you."

Ninni smiled sheepishly. "Yeah, that sounds like a good idea."

I know now this exchange formed a bond between us. However, outside influences wouldn't make it easy for my brother. After all, they couldn't possibly understand what was between us. They didn't do anything out of malice, just plain ignorance.

*****

Nonna, Mom's mother, had been in a coma for months after being very ill. Around-the-clock nurses cared for her in the house. Her children's dedication was powerful, especially her sons, Uncles Frank, Jim, Tom, and Dick, who was taking it the hardest. He had become despondent, so much so the family had to care of him. He moped in bed all day, refusing to work or leave the house. Mom brought him breakfast in the mornings on the way to work.

One day in my adolescent way, I decided I may be able to pull him out of it. "Aunt Ann, will you please tell Uncle Dick I wish to see him?"

"I don't know, Giovanni, he's not talking to anyone, not even me. I'm really getting worried. You know how sensitive he is. He usually comes out of these depressions, but not this one. It seems it is because of his mom's long illness, the expectancy of her dying these past many months. If she had passed away quickly, I don't think he would be taking it like this."

"Please, Aunt Ann, just tell him I'm here." She obliged, and I could hear her begging Dick to see me. Surprisingly, Uncle Dick emerged in his bathrobe. Usually so dapper, now his beard was thick, his mustache untrimmed.

"So you came to see your old Uncle Dudley."

"Yes, Uncle Dick, we all miss you, me most of all. You know, our long talks about show business."

"Is something wrong, Giovanni? Are you into some kind of trouble?"

"No, Uncle Dick, it's just I was so used to seeing you, and our talks were always helpful. Aw, you know what I mean."

"Yeah, I know what you mean, Giovanni. You've always been very important in my life, like a son. It looks as though I'm letting you down, what with your father ill and all."

"I wish I could say you're wrong, Uncle Dick, but you are important to me, and I wish you would come out once in a while. Not all the time like you used to, just once in a while."

"How do you like this?" he said to Aunt Ann. "My little nephew is here to help me when it's my place to help him. Tell you what, Giovanni, you just wait here. We'll take a nice walk to the candy store and shoot the breeze. I may even stop over at Frank's house."

"Gee, Dick, that's a good idea," Aunt Ann said with a look of surprise.

As we walked, I had a most rewarding feeling with Dick's hand on my shoulder as he told me Jack Haley, Jack Oakie, Bert Lahr, Jack Benny, and others started out in burlesque as chorus boys. He raved about the great duo, Buck and Bubbles, who worked their way up to more than $7,500 a week and $750 a performance.

After he picked up a rate sheet at the candy store, his favorite publication, we strolled to Frank's house.

"It's good to see you, Dick. We were getting very concerned about you," Frank said.

"You can thank our nephew, Giovanni. He got me out of bed, and let me say, he made me feel a bit ashamed."

"I just talked to the doctor, and he tells me Mom can't possibly last much longer, perhaps before the week is up. I suggest we all group here tonight in case she gains consciousness and through some miracle, asks for us."

"Good idea, Frank. It'll also give us the chance to make plans, the will and all, you know. We'll sort of push things around while we wait. Giovanni, you can tell your Mom to come over after supper. We'll all be here."

"Mom's been here every night, Uncle Dick, and Pop most of the time."

"Sure, I should've known. Forgive me, I've been out of touch, that's all."

The scene was not unfamiliar that Thursday evening, the waiting in sad anxiety for someone to die almost routine by now. Everyone was quiet at first, except for occasional updates from a nurse. Nonna's ever-faithful Italian bull was leashed to one of those large old wooden drawers in the kitchen. Prince, with the personality of royalty, was bright, alert, and proud. Nonna was the only one who could control him.

Pop, not feeling well, stayed home with little Ninni. The women chattered about what jewelry Nonna had promised them.

The door burst open. "A miracle has taken place upstairs," a nurse said. "She woke up. Color has returned to her face, and she acted as though she went to bed last evening. She requested her robe and went to the bathroom on her own. I just can't believe it. In all my years of nursing, I've never seen anything like it."

Nonno smiled and walked upstairs. The doctor allowed no one else. We waited what seemed an eternity for Nonno to come down and give us some news, good news. The women prayed to God with their rosary beads. Then in the most mystic manner, Prince started to howl. He sounded an eternity away, and tears streamed down his face as he pulled on his chain.

"Shut up, Prince. Don't you know Nonna is ill and needs quiet?" Uncle Frank said in Italian, the only language Nonna spoke and the dog understood, Prince paid no heed and howled louder as Nonno and the doctor came down.

Nonno was crying as the doctor held his elbow. "*Mia moglie è morta, a soli cinque minuti fa.*" My wife is dead, just five minutes ago. Everyone started to wail and sob. Uncle Frank mentioned the dog knew she had died. No one seemed to hear what he said, but the tale was told throughout the years.

As we cried, I was the first to notice Nonno had collapsed in his chair, so I tugged on Uncle Frank's sleeve. He leaned over him and beckoned the doctor.

The doctor lifted his eyelids and checked him over. "Don

Suraci has suffered a severe stroke and must be rushed to the hospital."

Mom jumped to her feet. "*Madre di Dio, ciò che sta accadendo!*" (Mother of God, what is happening.) She went into a hysteria I'd never seen before.

I started to cry. "Mom, stop, please stop." The more I pleaded, the more hysterical she became, so Uncle Tom, kind Uncle Tom, escorted me into Uncle Frank's den.

"Giovanni, *a zitto, a zitto.*" (easy, easy) You have to understand your mother is going to be like this for some time. It's her mother and father at one time. You wouldn't understand this at your age, but this is good for her. She's needed to blow steam for a long time."

"I'm afraid, Uncle Tom. I can't take her being like this. She's always in such control. It's not like her, and I'm worried."

"Now, Giovanni, you have learned a truth. It's not every day we learn a truth. Your mom is not made of steel like everyone thinks. She feels pain, anxiety, happiness, sadness, fear just like everyone else, and once in a while she has to let loose, because she holds so much inside. If she doesn't, she'll become ill. Let me explain it to you this way. Why do you think Christ innovated confession?"

"To wash us of our sins."

"That, Giovanni, is just a small part of it. Christ gave us the great invention of our mind, and in the mind, we have a part called memory. If too many bad memories go into this part of the brain, people get sick. He wanted confession to enable us to get rid of our guilt, as well as our sins."

Out of tragedy was born the most revealing evening of my life. I saw Mom relative to humanity and saw confession as a ritual of relief, rather than something to be afraid to tell the priest. Uncle Tom's profound words dug deep. I felt better than I had in a long time, as though I'd made a discovery I'd been searching for: forgiveness, peace of mind without guilt, and hope. Hope for my family especially my mother.

He wiped my tears and blew my nose. "Giovanni, are you ready to go into the kitchen and help your mom through this dark period? With your Pop not well, your mom is going to need your support."

"I'm ready, Uncle Tom. I won't let her know I'm too upset, I promise."

I walked to Mom and clutched her hand. She looked at me with admiration and love. "Thank you, Giovanni, thank you."

The hysteria intensified when the ambulance arrived, especially the women and Uncle Jim. Uncle Dick sat in a wide-eyed daze not blinking, as though in a trance.

Frank approached him when the ambulance left. "Dick, c'mon, we have to go to the hospital with Pop. Morisco will come by and handle the basic arrangements for us with Mom. . . . Dick, snap out of it and be the man I know you are. We have to go."

Dick shook his head like a fighter who had his bell rung. "Yeah, yeah, Frank, we have to go to the hospital. Don't worry, I'll be all right. I won't let you down." He started to cry like a baby.

My uncles left us with the women and told us they would call if they had urgent news. I don't think anyone heard them over the crying women. I admired Aunt Emma for being the strong one. I knew she loved Nonna as much as Mom and my aunts did. Yet, she kept her composure, knowing someone had to.

Emma consoled her sisters-in-law and Uncle Jim with back rubs, coffee and aspirin. Pop came to the house with Ninni to wait with us. Finally, Uncles Frank and Dick returned. Everyone was sapped of energy. Frank took off his coat as all eyes watched with apprehension.

He sat at the kitchen table as though trying to choose his words carefully. "Look, everyone, Pop had a severe stroke. Now let's all keep calm, and I'll give you the bottom line. It was bad. His left side is paralyzed, and according to the doctors, he'll never regain use of that side if he lives. And you know Pop, he won't tolerate being a cripple. The doctor claims anyone else would have been dead, being hit in that area of the brain. So we'll have to leave it in the hands of God and the doctors. Of course, Pop will miss the funeral, and that's good in my book. I don't think he could have taken it. We all know how much he loved Mom. They were like one person dedicated to us."

I looked at Uncle Frank's bloodshot eyes. He suffered from a malady the doctors called ulcerated eyes, and apparently the pain was brutal. When he got an attack, he would walk around for days with wet compresses doused with boric acid. Now I realize his heavy smoking habit probably triggered these attacks.

He looked at Mom. "I know Pop. If he's going to be limited in his movements, he'll not want to live."

"What are you suggesting, Frank?" Mom asked.

"Not what you think, Annie. I'm saying we all need to chip in and make him feel positive."

Mom nodded, and Frank turned to us. "And all of you kids, you must help Nonno also. Play Briscola, keep him as busy as you can, and see him at least once a day."

We nodded. I noticed Ninni looked serious for the first time. He loved Nonno and would do anything for him. Maria, calm as usual, reassured Uncle Frank with a smile.

*****

The funeral was behind us, and Nonno was out of the hospital. He perched in front of the house in an antique wooden chair, a favorite of Nonna's. The doctors had said he never would walk again. He swore he would cure himself. Nonno never allowed anything or anybody to take control over him. He was tough old Italian stock from Calabria, an area known for strong-minded people nicknamed *capa tosta* (hard head).

His therapy included eating organic vegetables out of his garden, mainly escarole, broccoli, asparagus, and potatoes. He never ate meat after Nonna died.

Nonno spent hours in front of the stone house he built with his bare hands, where he had retired at forty-eight. His eyes twinkled around blondes, and he would flirt with neighbors fitting that description. His self-made therapy also included pounding his lifeless leg with all of his might, and I might add, he was strong as a bull. He believed this might bring back the feeling.

Nonno did this for two or three months until one-day Uncle Frank and I were watching him from the window as he stood up, braced himself against the back of the chair with his good arm, and walked around the chair. Frank and I looked at each other in wonderment.

"I called in every specialist through Dr. Feinberg, and every one of them said the brain damage was irreparable. This is a miracle," Uncle Frank said.

It used to take four men to carry Nonno down the stairs in the morning and to assist him in the bathroom. Within a short span, Nonno could hold onto the wrought-iron banister outside and walk backward down the three steps. Then he would stare up at his two lion sculptures on each side of the steps before walking a bit down the street. He increased the distance each day, and within a few more months, Nonno would disappear down the block and return in the afternoon.

Frank couldn't believe Nonno's tenacity and strong will. "Giovanni, we all learn by this."

He became independent and sought no help from anyone. He had to have a reason for being on Earth: being self-sufficient.

Costello's car pulled up as Nonno was sitting in his chair. Don Costello kissed Nonno's hand and turned to me. "Giovanni, come, come with me. I have some news for your uncle Frank."

We walked to the front room. "Frank, we desperately need a senator from your district, number three. You know, one we'll trust. The reason I'm here is because the guy Tammany has picked is thus far unbeatable. You have any suggestions?"

Frank rubbed his chin with the back of his fist. "If it were anyone but Hendel, I would have an answer for you. I don't. He has it all: Harvard law graduate, model citizen in our community, and his taste in clothes is almost as good as Marcantonio's. I do believe he is unbeatable."

I knew by Costello's expression as he puffed on a De Nobili cigar, that he was weaving a trap for Frank. "You know, Frank, I've been thinking about this the past few days, almost to distraction. You know you're the one who should carry this weight. Yet, this is so important, I don't mind chipping in. I think I do have a candidate who might be able to beat this guy."

"Who might that be? I've been digging deep into every contact I have, and I can't come up with one name that would get a thousand votes against Hendel."

Costello grinned. "You forgot yourself, Frank."

Uncle Frank's reaction was frantic. "You're kidding? That would be like a real-estate man buying his own real estate. I'm an engineer, not a candidate."

Costello bit into his De Nobili. "Now calm down, Frank. I knew you'd react this way, and I know what you mean. Your contribution in getting the Little Flower elected was a stroke of genius. I'm not suggesting your expertise be inhibited. I'm saying you're the only one capable of beating this guy, and you know what I'm talking about."

"Let's say I do this insane thing. With one stroke, I'll destroy all of the confidences I've built up over the years. Everyone has been under the impression I never would seek office. That's why I can speak frankly to both sides of the fence."

Costello hung his head. "I'm surprised at you, Frank. Don't you think I thought of that? Yet, if we give this seat to Tammany, we'll retire until we get another shot at it, years from now."

"Let me take a shot at Hendel. If I promise him assurance of office, he may come over to our side."

"I thought of that also, Frank. We would give him the kind of ammunition to expose us as a corrupt party, and we would never recoup. That's out, Frank."

Frank slumped in his chair and asked for some time to think.

"Sure, Frank, this is Monday. We have until Friday, so I'll see you for lunch at Le Champs. We must move on this quickly with just two years until the election. Our PR must start now."

When Don Costello left, Frank sunk his face into his hands. "I never thought it would come to this. What a mistake."

I said good-bye to Uncle Frank, wishing I could help him.

"You have an offer also," Frank said. "When the political conventions take place, Costello wants you to sing the national anthem. This is quite an honor, Giovanni. Some of the greatest tenors have done this."

*****

One day, Uncle Frank spotted me on the roof with the pigeons and beckoned me down. "Giovanni, do you know where Nonno goes every day?"

"No. A couple of times I asked if I could go with him, and he got angry."

"He must not wander too far with his condition. Will you come with me? I want to follow him and see where he goes."

"Sure, Uncle Frank."

We waited for Nonno to turn the corner before we got into the car. Uncle Frank never went as far as the corner without driving. It was tedious because Nonno was slow, and our journey ended two miles away at St. John's Cemetery.

"What in the hell is he doing here? She's not buried here," Uncle Frank said.

He stopped to talk to a bunch of gravediggers who seemed to know him. Nonno handed them each a dollar from his wallet. "What in the hell is Pop doing now?" Frank said, scowling.

The laborers laughed, and one of them handed Nonno a shovel. He started digging one of the graves.

"Stay here, Giovanni, while I get the old fool out of here."

Frank bolted out of the car and pushed aside the men. "Jesus Christ in heaven, Pop, what in the hell do you think you're doing?"

"Digging a grave. What the hell does it look like? . . . Go away."

"Like hell I'll go away! You're coming home with me right now. Do you hear me, right now!"

"Now my son treats me as though I'm the son, giving me orders. If you don't stop, Frank, I'll backhand you across the face." The laborers laughed.

"You think this is funny?" Uncle Frank said. I'll knock you all on your asses! This is my pop and he's ill. If something happens to him, you won't have to worry about a lawsuit, I'll blow all of your brains out."

When he pulled his thirty-eight out of its holster, the laughter stopped. In fact, there was an air of solemn silence.

"Drop the shovel, Pop, or I'll see to it you're put in a nursing home at once, and you can't stop me."

Nonno looked at him like a child. "I've raised a traitor, a traitor, do you hear me? After all the sacrifices I made for you, you threaten to put me in some place to die like the old elephants, eh?"

"Stop the bull, Pop. First of all, this is bad for you. Second of all, if it ever gets out my father is digging graves with a stroke, Jesus, how will that look, Pop? I'll buy you ten shovels and a lot for you to dig in all day. Just get out of that hole."

The men helped Nonno out of the pit. He was mumbling a mile a minute as he rejected Frank's help to get into the car.

Nonno ranted all the way home. "It's not the same buying a lot to dig holes in for no apparent reason. The work I was doing is meaningful, and it's bringing back my blood circulation."

"Christ, Pop, I've never heard of anyone paying to dig graves. You've made a fool out of yourself and of me. I'm warning you: If I ever catch you again, I'll sign you into the nursing home, and I'm not kidding."

"If your mother was alive, she'd smack you right in the face, Frank."

"If Mom were alive, Pop, she'd kiss me on both cheeks."

"Heh, big shot, president of the bookstores. Now that you're a president, you're getting a screw loose somewhere. You know where."

Nonno was referring to Uncle Frank's honorary position as president of the Queens Library. He, along with a minister, rabbi, Catholic priest, and literary master headed the censor department and screened out books they deemed subversive. In those days, no one questioned this kind of position. In fact, it was prestigious, and there was talk about the Roosevelt regime choosing Uncle Frank for a very high state position before the year was up.

"Pop, I've had enough," Uncle Frank said. "Stop."

I looked in the rearview mirror and detected a devilish gleam in Nonno's eyes. I couldn't believe it, but he was enjoying the whole thing.

*****

I found myself in the clubhouse with Uncle Frank and Mr. Costello on an exciting, festive day. Beer trucks were rolling down the streets for the first time in years, people were celebrating and dancing in the streets, singing "Happy Days are Here Again." Bars were opening overnight on the corners.

Costello, watching from the front door, turned to Frank. "Pretty smooth, eh, Frank? It's amazing how we had the trucks, beer, and bars ready for this great gift from the cripple in Washington. Can you imagine how stupid they are up there? They honestly thought they'd put guys like me out of business by repeal."

*****

My train of thought is broken by the kind of Italian I've loathed all my life. He's a young Turk from Union City who had the audacity to come to *my* mother's funeral. He's the perfect duplicate of what Costello had predicted would come of the underworld sooner or later if control was let loose in the streets. His name is Moscone, dealer in all things degenerate.

He's a friend of a family member who invited him. I'm well tutored in how to handle his type. He has two lowlife henchmen with him who remind me of the company Ed Costello played with and who his brother so despised.

My lifelong friend, Uncle Tom, must sense something, for he walks over, holds my elbow, and darts his eyes at my wonderful wife, Pat. I sense her anguish. She's worried. She's seen my temper over injustice, and her eyes are telling me I shouldn't do what I'm about to do. I love her for it. Yet, it's as though something is being taken away for me.

Uncle Tom feels me shaking and guides me to the other side of the room. I start to cry, cry because this man is tarnishing a sensitive moment in my life. He's the last person I wanted to see at this wake.

Uncle Tom ushers me into the sitting room, and I slip again into the past, remembering how he admired my "deadly punch," which he obviously fears seeing tonight. I also remember his gentle manner, how kind he was to all of us, and how he adored Pop. To him, my pop was the total man, and he let everyone know it. As I slip back in time, I see Tom's face so much younger, dapperly dressed as always.

*****

Beautiful Aunt Nettie was in our kitchen, the favorite meeting place for all the sisters, and Uncle Tom was talking to me there.

"How many guys have you punched out lately, Giovanni?" Then turned to my father. "What a punch he has, John. When he grows up, his punch will be stronger than Jack Dempsey."

"That's all well and good, but he's going to be a great singer, remember?"

"He is already, John, but you can't deny he has a gift in that right hand for a boy age eleven."

"In this neighborhood, it'll come in handy."

"Giovanni, is Toscanini as tough as they say he is?" Uncle Tom asked.

"He sure is. All he does is stare at someone if they make a mistake. They don't even give an explanation, they just put their instrument in its case and leave."

"*Madon e a mia*. He must be Calabrese, Giovanni. I recall when your father and I went to see the great Caruso. We were late and standing in the foyer, but we could hear him through the thick oak doors. He was the greatest tenor of all time, you know. Many tenors will have heart attacks trying to live up to his lifestyle.. . . . By the way, Giovanni, when is your next performance at the Metropolitan?"

"Next Friday. We're doing *La Gioconda* with Giovanni Martinelli."

"Nettie, how would you like to go see our little nephew?"

Aunt Nettie reacted with her usual signs of excitement: blushing all over and her eyes growing three times bigger.

*****

It was Friday morning, but I didn't have to go to school, for we had rehearsal in the morning. Then Uncle Dick came by midday.

"Hi, Giovanni, how's the star making out?"

"Fine."

"Oh, I'm forgetting why I came in the first place, Giovanni. Frank is having a huge national political event at the Elks tonight, and he wants me to pick you up after your opera performance. It's on Long Island, so it's on the way home. You won't be tired, will you?"

"No, Uncle Dick. I'll wait for you at the 39th Street entrance backstage." I was about to do some more growing up before the full day was over.

La Gioconda was a wonderful performance and exciting each and every time we did it.

After the opera, Uncle Dick and I were off to the Elks convention. Cigar smoke hung like ugly clouds over the throngs in the dim hall. I didn't like the place, although it didn't affect how I performed. I had thorough control despite my age, thanks to my long talks with Uncle Dick.

A huge curtain opened to reveal a boxing ring on stage. Great, I loved to watch a good boxing match! Little did I know I was about to witness the most obscene act ever perpetrated on man. They guided six big blindfolded black men into the ring. The white crowd screamed, cheered, jeered, stomped, and whistled until the MC announced the ground rules.

"Gentlemen, no rounds, the fight is over when only one man is standing." the MC said to the boxers "At the sound of the bell, come out fighting. The winner will receive five dollars."

The crowd returned to a frenzy as the poor blind devils hit each other without mercy. The ring was covered in blood in no time. Eventually, two men were left, tired, weary, punching at the air. They hardly could lift an arm, but one of them finally struck the final blow. The black giant fell to the canvas as though he were dead. When they unmasked the survivor, I could see he was crying. This big hulk of a man was crying like a baby, and I couldn't help but cry with him.

The MC returned to the stage twice more before my performance. The last two acts were so inhumane, I can't ever repeat them. I wish my memories weren't so exceptionally clear.

Just before I went on, Uncle Frank came over to apologize for the indecency. "Giovanni, this one is important for me. I'll make it up to you. We're about to spring one of the most important political campaigns of our time, and I need all of the support I can get. I know you'll end this evening with some class, Giovanni, so give them hell!"

Like a miracle, I overcame the rowdiness, and the crowd applauded after each tune. As I finished, Uncle Frank and Uncle Dick hugged and kissed me. "You're ready for anything now, Giovanni, you're ready for anything!" Uncle Dick said.

Dick had preached to me that I had to be ready for stardom. I'd have to be prepared to work hard to hold on to it. Yet, despite all of the compliments, I still felt depressed after watching the unkindness that humanity could impose on each other. I shall never forget the futility of those acts. I forced a meek smile as people came by to praise me. I was tired, upset, and just wanted to go home. But I knew I wouldn't tell Mom and Pop about my night. I was ashamed for even being involved.

I thought to myself, it seems so many people are without dignity.

CHAPTER TEN

I hear Jim's voice booming throughout the funeral parlor. This was his trademark; he never could whisper. "Well, Jesus knows my address. When he wants me, he knows where to find me." Then he repeats this in his usual manner at least ten times. This takes me back to a Saturday morning visit.

*****

I was sleeping in late Saturday, being so tired from the ordeal I had the night before, when I heard Uncle Jim's loud voice in the kitchen. "Annie, Annie, I made a hell of a connection for Giovanni last night. I had this broad in my cab, and I could tell she was somebody, what with all her jewelry. She was telling me how she's connected with Paramount Studios, so I belted in a plug for Little Caruso. Well, by the time I got through, she told me if I wanted to bring Giovanni down for an audition at three o'clock today, she would be glad to listen to him."

"Boy, Ann, Paramount Studios is the largest movie company in the whole world," Pop said.

Off we went in Jim's yellow cab with him jabbering all the way, which gave me a headache before we got there.

Turns out Clara Stella only rented a studio in the Paramount building. After our intro, she said, "I'll consider taking him on. It'll be three dollars a week. I'll coach him and teach him some tricks. Of course, you have to understand that in most cases there will be no compensation, because it's not easy to get this kind of exposure, and artists are breaking down the doors to get these spots. I'll get him exposure. In fact, I have a spot for him on station WBNX with the great Carlo Buti, who is on Saturday mornings at eleven o'clock."

Back in the cab, Jim was counting all the money we were going to make.

"I think we should see Uncle Dick when we get home," I said.

"Why?" Jim said. "This deal is between you and me, and I see no reason why we should talk to anyone. Take my word for it, Giovanni, let's surprise all of them."

"I promised Uncle Frank if anyone gave me a deal, I would hand it over to Uncle Dick, and I will."

When I got home, the first thing I did was go to Frank's house. Luckily, Dick and Frank were in a meeting, but Frank looked concerned and Dick quite angry.

"Sit down, Giovanni, we'll be through in a few minutes," Frank said.

Dick resumed their conversation. "Frank, you know I'm through in show business, and I know nothing else. All I'm asking for is the right to book, and I'm not asking for much. You have so many friends doing it and affording them protection."

"Their days are numbered, Dick! And when the ax comes down, no one, yes, no one, will be able to help them. I know some of them may, by sheer percentage, miss going to the can, but you're my brother, and the one thing this family is, is legitimate and always will be as long as I have a breath in me. Pop didn't slave all of these years to end up with a hood in the family."

"Listen, Frank, I came here out of respect. Now if you won't give me your blessing . . . I think I deserve it. After all, I've done to help build your organization, without question, I say, if you want to own me, back me. If you don't, I won't feel any animosity about it. I will, however, do it on my own, and you wouldn't be responsible for what happens to me."

Frank fell quiet as he walked to the large oil painting of Nonno

over the fireplace, then stared into Dick's eyes. "Dick, this is what
worries me about you. You're slippery and clever. You feel you
have trapped me." Frank raised his hand. "Don't interrupt me,
Dick, I'm not finished. You're much too aggressive for this
business, and I can foresee problems you can't. When it happens,
you'll try the same tactics on me. So, I'll make you a deal. I'll fix
the operation for you, but then I'm finished. You and you alone
have to keep your nose clean. If you get into trouble, I wouldn't lift
a finger to help. I swear on Mom and Pop."

Dick grinned from ear to ear. "Frank, this is all I've been
asking for. I promise once I get off the ground, you drop all
responsibility, it's completely mine."

"Even if you face a jail rap."

"Even if it means a jail rap, Frank."

"Okay, you'll buy the bicycle store on the corner of Twenty-
Third Avenue. There's a grandfather clock there with a false back
door where you'll drop your tickets, Dick, and nowhere else,
understand? If you're ever raided, no one will look in the clock. If
you get clumsy and leave any evidence around, you're on your
own."

With this, they shook hands.

"What brings you here, Giovanni?" Uncle Frank asked.

I explained about Jim and Clara, and they became agitated.

"I know this broad, and I know her scam," Dick said once they
calmed down. "However, we'll use her, because she did get some
radio exposure for you. But I can assure you, Frank, she's only
valuable for a short time. The few bucks a week is worth it, and I'll
cover it so John and Anna don't worry."

"Dick, his management is in your hands. You know more about
the business than any of us. All I can do is lend contacts; the rest is
up to you. This is one area I have complete confidence in your
judgment, so this is your baby."

Frank detected I was worried and looked at me with his
piercing eyes. "Giovanni, don't worry about Jim. Talking to him is

our responsibility." He rubbed his chin. "Just get it out of your head, Giovanni. All I want you to concentrate on is your music and nothing else. That's all any artist is supposed to do: concentrate on their craft. Do you understand?"

I sighed. "Yes, Uncle Frank, I understand, but I don't want Uncle Jim to get mad at me."

"That won't happen. How is your Pop?"

"He's not been feeling well at all. We're worried about him."

"Well, don't worry, I made an appointment for him with Dr. Feinberg. He's the biggest heart specialist in the world. I got his kid out of a jam last week, so I figured he owes me. If anything can be done for Pop, he'll do it."

I got excited. Uncle Frank could get anything done, so Pop should be all right. I ran all the way home to tell Pop the great news. *Pop will be well, Pop will be well.* As night fell, I ran faster and faster until I couldn't breathe. I kept trying to blurt the news in the kitchen as Pop attempted to calm me down.

"What in heaven are you trying to tell me, Giovanni?"

"Uncle Frank has gotten the biggest specialist in the world for you, Pop, and he's going to cure you. Honest, he just told me."

Pop sat me on his knee. His eyes watered, but they had a warm look. "That is good news, but I want you to understand something: Nothing in this world is sure. After all, this doctor is not God. He may be the best, but he's not God." A tear flowed down his cheek. "What I'm trying to say is there may be a chance, but don't make up your mind it's a sure thing." He turned away from me. "You know, if God wants me for whatever reason, then all the help in the world won't change that, and if God wants me, you mustn't be saddened by this. In fact, you should be happy and proud. You understand?"

I sobbed. "No, if God wants you, I want you more. Besides, he has so many people he can choose from, and I need you Pop, I need you."

Pop embraced me as we cried and pulled a handkerchief from

his back pocket. "Now, now, Giovanni, you're not behaving like a trooper." His voice dropped to a whisper as Mom entered the room. "You see, when God made all of us, he had something in mind for each and every one. So you see, he has the right to choose who is best suited for the job he wants done. After all, he didn't leave himself out when he chose to die for all of our sins. He could have given anyone else this painful ordeal."

This wonderful human being with all his terminal health problems was trying to make *me* feel good. I loved him, truly loved him. He was my whole life, and after all these years he still is, to me and to so many people he touched with his wisdom and love.

"Where have you been all day, Giovanni?" Mom asked.

I gave her a detailed report, and she seemed satisfied.

"Take a bath and go to bed now."

When Mom spoke, it wasn't a request, it was a command. So I went to bed with my thoughts spinning in my head, trying to put everything into place. I was awake for hours, still rather confused.

*****

It was the next Saturday, and Clara Stella had informed Mom I was to do a show on station WBNX in the Claridge Hotel. I was to be there no later than ten o'clock for rehearsal, and the great Carlo Buti would introduce me. Needless to say, bedlam struck our home, for he was a national hero among Italians. In fact, women of all ages religiously listened to him on the radio. In most houses, women would hold coffee klatches for the mere purpose of listening to Carlo.

I entered the studio not knowing what to expect. I was very tense because I recalled Dick explaining how cold the radio media was because you couldn't interact with an audience. The studio was small with a baby grand Baldwin in a corner and a glass wall with men wearing earphones, working dials, adjusting the sound levels. It was up to the engineers to get each person's different sound level into the airwaves at top quality. A microphone resembling a large box camera hung from the ceiling. Clara walked to the piano with my music. She was not a good musician, and I knew I wouldn't enjoy it very much.

A man walked out of the glass-enclosed room and took me by the shoulder. "Giovanni, this is a microphone. Don't be afraid of it, it won't bite you. Just remember it only sends what you put into it. So if you do it right, this machine will send it right. If you don't, well, the machine won't."

This didn't help me relax at all.

The man positioned me in front of the mic and turned to Clara. "All right, Clara, let's try one for level." He returned to his room, secured his headphones, and signaled us. No sooner had I hit the first bar did he yell through the intercom, "Cut! Cut!"

He hurried back into the studio. "Giovanni, you'll have to stand back at least another four feet. I didn't think you had that kind of power." He marked the floor where I was to stand.

We did it again, and he returned with final instructions. "Now, Giovanni, you only have to listen to me. When I signal you with my index finger, you step over to where the X is on the floor. Now remember, don't wait, for radio time is precious, and seconds are important. Clara will be at the piano. Keep in mind you only have one take. You can't start over."

That just about did it. *Suppose I forget my lyrics. Suppose I get a frog in my throat. Maybe Clara will miss her cue.*

Carlo Buti entered with a kind face and introduced himself. "You must be the Giovanni I heard so much about. I'm most anxious to hear you. Of course, I have the easy part, I sing very light narrative songs from Italy."

Moments later, the countdown came, and an announcer appeared. When the engineer dropped his finger, the announcer started. "Ladies and gentlemen, welcome to the LaRosa Spaghetti Hour. Your host, Carlo Buti, will sing songs from the old country for your entertainment and pleasure." He shifted into his commercial, then signaled Carlo, who took his place at the mic and sang three songs.

"Ladies, I have a wonderful treat for you this morning," Carlo announced. "I have the pleasure of presenting, for the first time on radio, a talent you'll remember for all time. He is but a mere boy of eleven, but his voice is of a mature man. His name is Giovanni Benedetto, better known as the Little Caruso."

My heart pounded so hard I thought it would blow to bits. Then my head pounded too, and the pain was too much. The pounding even moved to my kidneys. *I'll never make this one. This is the end of everything. I'll never be able to perform again.* I wanted to run out of the studio but then noticed the engineer signaling me to the mic. I don't know how, but something took over in me. I sang my heart out. The minute it was over, I felt sick. I just wanted to go home. I didn't like radio. I couldn't wait to tell Dick. He would have an answer. Maybe he'd tell me I don't need radio.

I got home around two o'clock and changed out of my performing clothes. I went to Mom's side as she was chopping vegetables. "I heard the radio show, Giovanni, it was terrific. You should get a lot more work on radio after this."

Pop looked thrilled. "You should have heard it, Giovanni, it was fantastic. I'm so pleased for you. Mom is right, I bet you'll get a lot of requests to go back on radio."

I was ashamed to tell them how I felt. "Can I go out and play, Mom, can I?"

She looked at me sternly. "I think you should go down to the butcher shop and see if Patsy needs you. Do you want to lose your job?"

Pop looked down at the floor. I knew I'd get no moral support from him.

"Do I have to go, Mom? Can't I go out and play?"

"First go to the shop and see if Patsy needs you. If he doesn't, then you can play, but come and let me know what happened first."

I dawdled to the butcher shop, thinking the more time elapsed, the better chance I'd have of getting out of work. But the shop was full of patrons, and Patsy grinned sadistically. "Well, here's the child star, the opera singer, Giovanni Benedetto. Do you think you can give this establishment the honor of having you get to the back to bone some meat and make some sausage, eh? Don't think because you are on the radio anything has changed. You are very late, and you're lucky you have a job. If it weren't for your Uncle Frank, I'd throw you out on your ass. Get to the back, do you hear?"

Patsy abused me to no end, taunting me, working me to exhaustion, beating me, feeding me dog scraps, threatening me, and withholding my pay. I couldn't help but cry on the way home. My body was bruised from the beating, my hand hurt from several cuts, my bones were cold to the core from the cooler box, my back ached from the weight of the beef I carried around, and my mind was tortured. But I had one consolation: money to bring to Mom and Pop. And one more consolation at home: falling into bed and passing out into dead sleep.

The next morning was church day, and as usual, Uncle Jim made our house one of his first stops. "Hi, Giovanni, after thinking it over and giving it much consideration, I've decided to turn over the Clara Stella thing to Dick for your sake. I realized I'm really much too busy to give you the time you deserve."

I realized Pop was studying me. "Come here, Giovanni, I want to talk to you. You don't like the job at the butcher shop. Is it because you think it's is too low-down for you now you're an artist?"

"Oh, no, Pop. I like to work, and I love bringing home money. It's Patsy. I think, no, I'm sure, he's a very bad man."

"Why do you say that, son? We know his parents from the old country. I remember him as a kid."

"Well, Pop, he's always saying dirty things to women, especially when he's making sausage, pushing the meat through the funnel, asking them what size they want, and grinning at them like a rabbit."

Pop covered his mouth to hide a smile. "You know he does

look like a bunny rabbit with his long pointed ears, little mustache, and those buck teeth." We laughed. "Giovanni, you are a little young to pass judgment. Are you sure you're right?"

"Yes. In fact, a man came into the store to punch Patsy in the nose after he did it last week. Somehow, Patsy talked him out of it, but it was close, Pop."

"Is that the only reason you don't like the job? Maybe the work is too hard for you."

"I don't mind it, Pop, but he makes fun of me in front of the customers, asking me if I, the maestro star, wouldn't mind cutting meat in the back. And he feeds me the fat off the meat he feeds his dog."

Pop started to look concerned and scratched his face. "You have more to tell me, don't you, Giovanni? What is it? Tell me."

"Well, Pop, it's when he pushes me into the cooler box and hits me all over with a leg of lamb. It hurts, it really hurts."

"Come with me, come with me. We're taking a walk over to Patsy's house right now."

I got excited and forgot Pop's condition. "Let's go now, Pop, and I'll prove it to you. You'll see."

"I believe you, Giovanni, you don't have to prove me a thing."

As we neared Patsy's house, I noticed Pop had turned pale. "Aw, let's go home, Pop. It isn't important. I don't want to lose my job."

"I want to talk to you, Patsy," Pop said.

"What about, John?"

Pop started to shake. "First of all, my son has quit your job. Secondly, if you ever touch one hair on his body or say anything about his singing, I'll choke you to death."

Patsy looked frightened and babbled about how he pays me even when I'm late, and how he feeds me even though he doesn't have to.

"Shut up, you filthy pig!" Pop shouted. "If you ever did anything for my son, it was done in fear of what you really are.

One more time, Patsy, one more move on my son, and I'll kill you with my bare hands."

Pop's gentleness had vanished, and he looked like a man who would keep his promise. He'd made me feel secure, yet frightened me by stepping so far out of his character. Patsy backed into his house and apologized as he stepped out of the light into the darkness of his living room.

I knew Pop realized how I felt. He clutched my hand and explained his actions away in that wonderful style of his. "Giovanni, someday you'll have children, and maybe it's something God installs in a father. What I mean is, no matter how we feel about violence, there are times when we have to put our nonviolent philosophy aside and fight. Let's take war, for instance. I can tell you war is the worst sin of mankind. It's a kind of sickness where men kill men, or as in the last World War, brother killed brother, father turned against son, and all because of one man's lust for power, or to satisfy a sadistic drive. Like the Kaiser, for instance. Many men went to fight, even men who didn't believe in killing, for they were sure as long as this man was in power, their peaceful feelings were in jeopardy. These men went to fight so their children could grow up in a world without killing or fear. The same kind of peaceful man, when he finds anyone trying to hurt the ones he loves dearly, must take a stand to stop the bully, much as the man who goes to war. The peaceful man gives fair warning first. If the bully doesn't respond, then the peaceful man must take action. Do you understand?"

"Yes, Pop, and thank you for helping me. I love you very much."

We walked home hand in hand, a father and son, me looking up at Pop proudly from time to time. I was so happy he was my pop. By the time we arrived home, he was breathing hard and looked almost green.

"Oh, Ann, I feel terrible, get the doctor." He clutched his chest and slumped into the chair.

"John, don't worry, you'll be all right. You hear me, you'll be all right."

Pop fainted. For the first time, Mom looked scared to death. "Stay here while I go down to the store and call the doctor, Giovanni. If he comes around, give him the smelling salts."

Smelling salts were the answer to heart attacks, fainting spells, epilepsy, and anything else you could think of. Pop started coming around, so I held the salts under his nose. He whipped his head away and brought up what looked like a gallon of water. He struggled to breathe as though he were drowning. I helped him to the window and opened it for fresh air.

"It's all right, Giovanni. I just need a minute, just a minute, and I'll be all right."

I blamed myself. I'd never felt so bad. *If we didn't go to Patsy's house, this never would have happened.*

"Giovanni, get the big fan and plug it in front of me."

I ran to retrieve it from storage. Pop sat back in his chair and breathed in the cold air from the window as the fan directed it to to him. He threw his head back and took deep breaths.

Mom returned. "How is he, Giovanni?"

"He's doing better, Mom. See, his color is coming back."

"Oh, thank God, thank God."

The doctor finally arrived. He liked to use a door to explain a patient's condition. He would point at the square panels in the door to illustrate the location of main organs. The two middle panels were the lungs. The lower left panel, the appendix. The panel above it, the gallbladder. The one below the lung was the heart. I almost grew up thinking a person's inner anatomy looked like our kitchen door.

Sure enough, he walked Mom over to the door after his brief examination. "You see, Ann, he's a unique case. He's not having heart attacks as we commonly know them." He pointed at the panel representing Pop's heart. "The heart swells and presses against the lung right here." He pointed at the panel above it. "This causes the lung to fill with water, and it's just as though he were drowning. Now this alone is not dangerous. However, enough of these and he'll eventually have a severe heart attack. When it'll happen is not predictable. It's according to how strong his heart is and what kind of punishment it'll take."

"Thank you, Dr. Keisman."

The doctor turned to me. "How are your lungs feeling, Giovanni?"

"Fine. In fact, I can hold a note longer than my voice teacher."

"Amazing, simply amazing. I can't recall one case in all my years where a little boy had double pneumonia at eight weeks old and ended up with the strong lungs you have. You know, I knew your doctor. She was one of the first women allowed to practice medicine in this country. Dr. Berxtrum, quite a lady and quite a doctor. She is seventy-five now and still practicing, truly an amazing human being. Just think of what the world would have missed if they didn't allow her to practice. I heard she dropped all of her patients and stayed with you day and night until you were well, Giovanni. Don't you ever forget this grand lady. You owe her your life."

"I write to her all the time. She writes to me, always asking how my singing is coming along. In fact, she came to my last concert at Little Carnegie, and when I did 'Cielo e mar,' all she had to say was, 'Those are my lungs, Giovanni, take care of them.'"

He put on his battered hat and picked up his black bag with a serious look. "How true that is, Giovanni, how true. Well, good-bye all. Take care of John, Ann." And down the stairs he fled as though he had to catch a train.

Maria, Mom, and I stayed up into the wee hours until we were sure Pop would be all right. Ninni was too young to comprehend the gravity. *If he didn't go to Patsy's house for me, this never would have happened.* My guilt grew stronger until the day he passed away.

*****

I ended up curing my radio phobia by singing many times with the talented Carlo Buti. In fact, we became quite good friends despite our age difference. Uncle Dick often sat me down to advise me on my career and told me stories about the successes and failures of many artists.

Next thing I knew it was June. Summer meant we didn't have to go to school, and this sufficed for our generation. Our good times were soulful. In our apartment building, we had the Irish named Murphy, a Jewish family named Levine, and Cousin Sal's mother and father. Mr. Caramico, an Italian street peddler, ran a vegetable truck, and the Czechs named Jurich owned the building.

Mr. Caramico came down to our apartment while Mom was out shopping. He was always kind and jolly. "*Permesso*," he said through the partially open door.

"*Entrata*," Pop said. Pop poured a glass of our best red wine and put some cheese and hard bread on the table. "Sit down, Joe, sit down and make yourself at home."

Joe's eyes sort of crinkled and danced. "John, I can take the platforms out of my truck so we can take all the families to Oyster Bay. We'll eat on the beach, and while the women are preparing the food and watching the children, we men can fish for some of those big fluke they're catching right now."

"Gee, that sounds like a grand idea, Joe. It would be great for the kids. They have so little to do in the summer. Tell you what, Joe, I'll organize it. Each family will bring some food, and I'll ask for a collection of money for gas, bait, and beverages."

"Good, John. As soon as you have it all lined up, let me know. Oh, don't forget to tell whoever is coming that we're leaving at four-thirty in the morning."

"Pop, will I be able to go fishing too? Huh, can I?"

"We'll see, Giovanni, we'll see."

"Well, that was good wine, John. I have to go. Let me know by late this afternoon at least, so the girls can prepare the food."

When Mom came home, she seemed pleased to hear about the plans. Pop and I went up and down the stairs to each apartment to dole out responsibilities for the food. Much to my surprise, he didn't breathe heavy. The expenses came to sixty cents per person.

That night, I kept dreaming about going fishing, my obsession. Uncle Frank, who was an avid fisherman, had told me so many stories, and Pop had lived in the greatest black bass area in the world. Before I knew it, I was being called out of my room even though it was still dark.

I watched Mom finishing up her part of the food in the kitchen: veal cutlets Milanese, Italian sausage with bell peppers, and Italian bread with stuffed broccoli. I was frothing at the mouth. Pop brought his mandolin, cousin Sal his banjo, and his father a guitar. We made our way down to the truck. The morning air was wet and chilly but gave me a good feeling. Ninni crawled backward down the stairs, and Maria just walked quietly as usual. You never could tell what she was thinking. I was just the opposite, especially if I was happy.

We all piled in, and the men took a headcount before leaving. Even at this ungodly hour, we started singing. As the sun peeked out, I discovered this was my time of day. I felt so alive, the smell of the grass, the trees, the fresh hay in farm country, and clams and mussels mixed with a strong odor of seaweed as we neared the beach. I knew life had its moments for rich and poor.

The small, crescent-shaped beach was beautiful, so beautiful it took my breath away. The sand was almost blue white, and the water was a deep blue. On either side were huge rocks that looked like man-made sculptures, each a different color and shape. It was so unlike the commercial beaches everyone went to. Pop used to say he was sure most people enjoy being stepped on at Coney Island or Jones Beach. But here, there were no hot-dog stands.

We unloaded the pots and pans full of food, a half keg of grandpa's favorite red wine, paper plates and such from the truck. Then came what I'd been waiting for: The men started to separate the fishing gear. I was so excited to be grown-up, fishing with them. No one had fancy gear. In fact, the men attached sinkers to hand lines and threw them out. The hooks were tied on without swivels. I anxiously waited for Pop to hand me my line, but that never happened.

"When will I get my hooks, Pop?"

He looked down at me and placed his hand on my shoulder. "You're a bit too young for this kind of fishing, Giovanni. Have you seen anyone get a hook through a finger or in the face? It happens all the time if you're not experienced."

I started to sob. It was the first time I was really angry at Pop. He shook me gently. "Don't cry, I'm telling you the truth. It's not a matter of being careful. It's a matter of experience."

"Well, how does anyone get experience if they're not allowed to try it?"

"Tell you what, I promise you before the end of the summer, I'll take you where there aren't all kinds of hooks flying around, and I'll teach you how to fish. I promise you, Giovanni."

Pop wiped my nose and eyes with his hanky, but my resentment grew throughout the day. I stood on a rock where I wouldn't get in the way, captured by the men working the gear and occasionally catching a fish. My eyes filled with tears again as I stared at Pop. He looked in my direction and shook his head.

The men caught about thirty nice-sized fish. I watched in wonder as they cleaned and filleted them like surgeons, throwing back the innards for the crabs. Crabbing was another pastime here. This water yielded some of the largest and sweetest blue claw crabs in the world, so some of the men decided to net some. The creatures' dexterity fascinated me as they lifted their claws in anger. The women were collecting other goodies this great body had to offer: black mussels, cherry stone clams, middle-neck clams, and piss clams.

When the men threw the crabs into boiling water and cooked them alive, I was horrified. I couldn't help but imagine their pain.

The women covered the shellfish in baskets with seaweed and steamed them as they melted butter and garlic spice for a dip. No wonder I had acquired a yen for this kind of food.

I was to find out all of this was merely appetizers. Just imagine Mom's eggplant Parmesan, veal cutlets alla Milanese, stuffed beef broccoli, my aunt's Italian garlic bread, the Murphys' Irish stew with hard rolls, the Jureks' holubky (cabbage stuffed with rice and meat in a mild red sauce), the Levines' Jewish kreplach (stuffed dumplings) with bagels and cream cheese. It was obvious the ethnicities were competing with each other.

We stuffed ourselves until we couldn't move. The cool sea air seemed to have boosted our appetites. We devoured everything. Turning lazy, everyone scattered around on the beach and faced the summer sun. Uncle "Borghese" started strumming his guitar. One by one, the men with instruments joined in. Everyone was contributing their ethnic songs when Pop asked me to sing "Come Back to Sorrento."

Despite the feast, I was still angry. "I don't feel like singing. I'm very tired, if you don't mind."

I still can recall how surprised and hurt Pop looked as he cut away his eyes. He didn't say a word to me, which was worse punishment than yelling. "Well, it's getting late, I think we should pack the truck and go home before we get caught after nightfall," he said to everyone.

We journeyed home in the beautiful sunset. Our neighbors sang as Pop just stared at me. I was deeply sorry.

*****

Pop kept his promise and took me to the beach on a bus. He patiently taught me how to tie hooks onto my line and how to bait up. Even though he cautioned me on the no-nos, I was in a trance and I don't think I heard a word he said. I simply was happy he'd taken me. We sat on bedrock; I was told this was the only area in the world where bedrock was on the surface. The fishing was slow, but I was patient not knowing the tides had a lot to do with it. Pop looked glib as if he knew what was to come. The water kept creeping closer.

"Pull in your line, Giovanni," Pop said. "We're going to check our bait and put on some fresh ones."

Pop cut the squid into strips with a V shape at the end. "In the tide, the bait will flutter, and the split tail will anger the fish into biting."

We threw our fresh bait into the water, and was euphoric when I felt a strong tug. "Oh, Pop, I got a bite! I got a bite."

"Easy, easy, the way fluke bite, they tug away from your line. If you pull, they may scare. The first thing to do when he bites is go with him, give him slack, count to three, then pull, not too hard because the fluke has a soft mouth, and even if you think he's let go, pull in steadily. Remember he'll try to spook you, he's smart."

I was so excited I could hardly think about what Pop was saying, but I somehow landed a huge doormat fluke — a flat fish resembling a tabletop. Pop even got so excited he almost lost the fish in the net. No sooner had we unhooked him, and Pop landed one about the same size. Unhooked his fish, he explained they usually run the same size in schools. Pop looked at the two monsters on the sand. "I'll clean these, we'll gather some mussels and clams, and start home, Giovanni. We have more than enough for the table."

Back on the hot bus, we weren't very popular with our stinky fish, but this appealed to Pop's sense of humor.

Mom prepared the fish with garlic, olive oil, oregano, pepper, and salt, then topped them with stewed tomatoes before baking. We also savored corn on the cob from Nonno's garden. That night, Pop worked late on his machine, perhaps to make up for our fishing time. In the middle of the night, I heard Mom begging him to come to bed.

CHAPTER ELEVEN

Uncle Frank invited us to Nonno's home to celebrate the Fourth of July. I was thrilled because I didn't have much singing to do, either with the opera house or for Uncle Frank, so I hadn't seen him as much as I'd like. He was my favorite person after Pop. Pop liked Uncle Frank too, even though he didn't agree with many of his friends or the reality of politics. Frank's honesty and sincerity were enough for him. That morning, Uncle Tom drove us to Nonno's house in his shiny car.

This part of the family always had a wonderful time, never any differences or arguments. This went for the two generations. Everyone was on a high of friendship, hugging, and kissing.

Bill, one of Frank's children, was a couple of years older than I was. He looked up at the roof where he was breeding more than four-hundred pigeons. I always flipped when he invited me up to search for flying strays. We would send up a male hoping the bird flying by was a female thoroughbred. The male was supposed to entice the female back to the roof. Then we'd use a bamboo pole to guide her through a trap. The smart breeders would take captives to sell for feed or to breed. Once releasing a captive, you risked the bird flying back to its original owner. Bill had an expert reputation. When fanciers lost birds, they would approach him to buy back the bird. If the bird was valuable, he would horse trade them into giving up as many as five birds in return.

When things were slow, he would sell a dozen of his best

homing pigeons to the feed store for corn feed. One by one, they always came back. Bill and I eventually became sort of partners. That day, we caught three thoroughbreds. "Look at this white bootie, Giovanni, it's a beauty. We're going to breed this one."

I felt so important being involved. After all, Bill was older and Uncle Frank's son. We walked through the pigeon coop, which was built as well as some houses, into the breeding area with walls of cubicles for the mates to nest in and lay eggs. When the eggs hatched, Bill looked for a common disease that resembled skin cancer. If they had it, Bill would wring their little neck, putting them out of their misery.

Around noon, Aunt Emma looked up at the roof. "Bill, Giovanni, come down for lunch!" Her rasp came out in double and triple voicing, in harmony, actually. A guy on the *Major Bowes Amateur Hour* radio had won with the same impediment claiming to sing in harmony. Down through the roof we descended, down the ladder to the hatch, then another flight of stairs, and down into the kitchen.

Aunt Emma's potato salad, made with her homemade mayonnaise, waited in the middle of the table. It was my favorite dish at her home, so Bill and I feasted on it, along with deviled eggs. "Enough boys, you've had much too much. Do you want to be ill?" Aunt Emma said before chasing us out of the house.

When we went out front to play stick roller hockey, two police cars pulled up to the curb. Uncle Frank walked over to them, and we thought something was wrong. After some laughter and conversation, though, they opened one of the trunks. It appeared they were delivering confiscated fireworks to Frank. I never saw so many boxes of them: cherry bombs, buzz bombs, pinwheels, rockets, Roman candles, sparklers, and many more.

"That's good, boys. Come in for a glass of wine, it'll help you do your job better."

"Thanks, Frank," one of the cops said. "We'll have much more for you by this afternoon. This was our first haul."

Bill and I looked at each other wide-eyed, remembering getting caught with fireworks and turning it over to the cops. We were confused. Uncle Frank started setting up the booty in the side yard. He was truly a miracle worker.

Mid-afternoon, Mr. Costello's limo pulled up. Uncle Frank walked to the car window to chat. Mr. Costello spotted me playing in the street and motioned me over.

"How are you, Mr. Costello?"

"Fine, Giovanni, and how are you? How is your father feeling?"

"Fine, he's in the backyard. Do you want me to get him?"

"It's not necessary, Giovanni, just tell him I asked."

He turned to Frank with a concerned expression. "You must work very hard in getting as many subordinate Republicans in as possible. My men all over the country are on notice not to spare anything. Dollars are no object. If we get enough congressmen, governors, senators, and most of all, judges, we'll have a balance of power."

"I do have a kicker, Bertolli, the head of the Democratic Party, and I've made a bargain," Frank said. "No matter who gets in, we'll cooperate. After all, they're in the same boat. For example, we have Marconi up in the Bronx totally committed already."

"I love the way you move, Frank, with your attitude and brains. We'll be in control for a very long time. *Capisco, faglio mio?*" (Understand, my son?)

"I understand fully, and things will be put together properly."

Costello grimaced. "By the way, I'm tired of handing out dollars to my idiot brother, Ed. Besides, he causes more trouble for me with his mouth. Every time he gets into trouble, he uses my name to threaten everyone. The last time it was a newspaper guy, Walter Winchell. Now, you know, Frank, this could be damaging with a guy like him. So I decided to give Ed the freedom of the territory, like, let's say, from Astoria on out to the end of the island. Even though he'll get into trouble from time to time, we'll squash it a lot easier than in the city, don't you think?"

Frank vigorously rubbed his chin. "I guess what you're telling me is I'm responsible for your brother. I'll be honest with you, Costello, I'll do it, but I don't particularly relish the idea."

Costello smiled. "It'll be good exercise for you, Frank. Just think, I've been living with it all these years. Now you'll get a taste of the kind of patience I've had."

Then he turned to me. "Giovanni, you're getting quite an education. Very few people know how this world of ours is run. They're taught to believe George Washington never told a lie. By the way, I'll have some good news concerning your career. I'll give it all to Frank when I'm ready, then he'll explain it to you." He grabbed each side of my head with his big hands and kissed me on the forehead. "You are as my own son, and I'm very proud of you, for you are the future of the Italian people in this great country of ours, so keep up the good work."

Frank and I watched the limo speed down the narrow street, Park Place.

Frank looked like a child on the Fourth of July as he gazed at the sky. "Well, Giovanni, it's starting to get dark. Pretty soon we'll shoot off the fireworks.

My excitement was building to such a pitch, I felt I was going to explode myself. "Can I light some of the fireworks, Uncle Frank, can I?"

"Sure, Giovanni, as long as I'm there. You have to be very careful. I've seen people get hurt."

"I'll be careful, Uncle Frank, and will do just what you tell me, honest."

Just before sundown, the picnic table was set up with cold cuts, wine, pop, and the like. We ate and ate. Ninni was covered with so much mustard, ketchup, and chocolate, he looked like an ultra-modern painting. Ninni was a born showman. Now at eight years old he needed little encouragement. When he realized Bill and I were laughing at him, he slathered himself with every color of the rainbow. The more I laughed, the more antics . . . until Mom appeared. She took one look at him and spanked him on the fanny, then dragged him by the hand to the sink to scrub him down. He started to bawl.

Little did I know Bill had lit a ten-inch salute under my bench. After the shock of the explosion, my ears were ringing for an hour. Uncle Frank belted Bill, which sent him head over heels. Bill would never cry when he was punished, and this would send Frank into a frenzy. However, Bill hung his head and walked away. At the first sign of dusk, Frank emerged from the cellar with a bushel of firecrackers, from half-inchers to loud cherry bombs. He motioned me over to hand me a lit punk. This was a corn dog-shaped blossom from the top of a weed that grew in the swamps nearby. The fuzzy blossom would hold a slow-burning spark, just right for lighting fireworks.

By this time, all my relatives had assembled. I felt important as Uncle Frank lit the firecrackers using my punk, but I soon wanted to hold a firecracker myself. Frank must have sensed this, because he handed me one. My hands trembled from excitement and fear. However, that wore off after three or four explosions.

In the darkness, the fireworks dazzled. First, the Roman candles. Oh, how I enjoyed holding them as the brilliant balls shot out. I tried to count them but lost track because I was so distracted. Each ball came out in a different color, speed, and direction.

Ninni was handed a sparkler, and he looked as though he was handed the whole world. He stared into the brilliance that resembled thousands of stars shooting out of a fountain. He started to wave it in circles, figure eights, and designs. As soon as one sparkler would burn out, he'd ask for another.

The spectacular came around eleven o'clock. Pop and my uncles sat us down as we watched rockets burst into images of the American flag, Washington, and Lincoln. Then they lit pinwheels against the garage wall that spun so fast they hypnotized us. In the meantime, the police had brought more fireworks. My uncles lined up about thirty milk bottles as launch pads and gave us kids little punks. We tried to set off as many as we could at the same time, so each of us quickly lit two or three rockets, then tried to claim the one we lit climbed the highest.

The women built a fire to barbecue hot dogs, hamburgers, and spareribs. The festivity seemed endless to a boy my age. Such a fond memory, everyone happy.

It was obvious Maria was afraid of the fireworks. She stuck with the sparklers all night, and I threw firecrackers at her feet until she ran to Mom. Ninni picked up lit firecrackers and even lit a whole package. I never saw so many people scramble so fast. Uncle Tom ran behind Nonno's favorite fig tree.

It was finally time for the finale. My uncles piled the last three bushels about three feet high and threw flares at them. This ignited a fantasy that gripped me until the last explosion. I stood openmouthed, hoping for one more crackle, one more burst of color.

Then silence. The Fourth of July was a fond memory of happiness, display, and best of all, people who I loved dearly

*****

It was mid-summer of 1934, and Pop and I were sitting in the kitchen. He was shaking his head at the *Daily News*, his habit when he didn't understand something.

"What's the matter, Pop?"

"Just look at this front page. Our soldiers are shooting our own citizens in the streets of San Francisco."

I looked at the picture and noticed a soldier pointing a machine gun at the crowd.

*****

Cousin Frankie's voice shatters my half-conscious state and brings my mind back to the present. He's the son of Uncle Dick, a man I loved all my life. Looking at Frankie is painful because he's suffering from a rare disease, [2]acute systemic scleroderma. There's no hope because doctors don't know much about the disease. I can't help but pity him. It's another unfair act from God. Tears fill my eyes.

I'm not able to tease or con him as I did when we were children. He's turning to stone, his skin, his organs. His features are distorted, teeth clenched, a heavy curly beard. He embraces me in tears. He also loved Mom. I express my sorrow for his father's death and apologize that I couldn't find the strength to go to his funeral.

Frankie steps back and looks into my eyes. "I know how much you and my father meant to each other. You don't ever have to apologize. I knew you wouldn't come."

Uncle Tom whispers to me, "Johnny, I just saw your brother. I think Tony needs you. It looks like he's going to blow his stack. People are surrounding him."

I lead Patricia by the hand over to Tony. I grab his hand, nod excuses to everyone, and walk him into the private family room. We don't speak, but I can sense he's thankful. I study him and don't like the path my brain is taking. I don't know whether it took my mother's passing, or whether I'd given all I could. But I do know I've never had these kind of thoughts before.

I'm thinking, *in the Italian culture, as the older brother, I'm responsible for him.. Does he know some of the trials I went through just to satisfy his life's dream? Does he think it's worth it, or is he just playing the part? How much of his acceptance of fame and the sacrifices have to do with his ego, or is he as dedicated to his craft as he says he is? If it's ego, was it worth me playing the martyr the past twenty-six years? Was my thrill of watching him rise sincere, or was I watching what I could have been? Was I a quitter, or did I make an honest decision? Have I had deep resentment? Have I ever felt cheated? Were my cultural influences*

---

[2] Acute Systemic Scleroderma, is a form of sclerosis, an autoimmune disease causing the skin to harden affecting even internal organs.

responsible for what's happened to me? Is it fair for my wife and children to suffer for decisions I made long before I met them? Shall I bust out, stop playing the martyr, and show the thrust of my talents and energized ambition?

I look deeply into Tony's eyes, and think, *he's sad, not just because of Mom's death. He's truly an unhappy person, too many upsets, pressures, bad friendships. His faith in purity has shattered him. I know he carries the gentle feelings of Pop, even though he says he doesn't even remember him. Yet, his personality is split, and he has to live with both of them . . . loving humans, yet not trusting their motives. Feeling social, yet having to hide, or they'll pick him clean like desert vultures would an animal's carcass.*

He forces a faint smile, and we know we share a brothers' love. Yet, so many misunderstandings between us, never enough time for explanations. We've traveled in different directions, yet it's me he calls when he needs true judgment, because of my honesty, loyalty, and faith in this great talent. I wonder if he knows how much further he'll rise? I know. I know, for I've been his hope, his faith, and yes, even his engineer, although he's never known it. I did it so discreetly he'll never know, like one drop of water at a time, studying him so I could drop thoughts on him when he'd least expect it. He'll be the top of the heap.

I know what he's going through. I've watched audiences enjoying blood, screaming for more when champions were being mauled by a young adversary. I've seen the crowd yell for more as two cockfighters gouged each other's flesh. In an artistic world, these are the small sacrifices they make just to be where they are. Dedication is a mild word, for the pains these artists take are far beyond the demands of dedication. They keep taking it, and the crowds become more demanding through the generations. In the furthest reaches of time, who would give in first: the audience or the artist?

I carefully eye him. *How much humanity is left in him that's truly real? How much of him has become synthetic? Would it show in his work? Would it make him an efficient robot eventually? How horrible a thought — an artist of this caliber turning into a bitter machine just to satisfy the masses who have one thought, one constant drive: "Fall turkey, you've been around too long."*

I start weeping. Tony grabs my arm in sympathy, not knowing I'm crying for him and not Mom. Now I know why my mind keeps racing back into the past. I'm looking for answers, clues, a reason for all that's happened. Our lives are much too complex for any of us to just vanish into space without leaving something, a mark I call it, something to be remembered for or by. I can feel it coming, my thoughts spinning back, back, back into those times that were so different. How the world has changed, how people have changed. Have I changed? Would I allow this? More importantly, are my motives the same? Back, back to simpler, quieter times. Simpler quieter times?

*****

I was walking from the train after Mr. Parado's class when I heard sirens and saw blinking lights as I turned the last corner. My heart started to pound because I feared it was an ambulance for Pop. But he was standing in the front door when I arrived.

"Hurry, Giovanni, get into the house! There's trouble, hurry."

"What's the matter, Pop, what's wrong?"

"A man's been shot, and the killer may be trapped in the warehouse. The cops aren't sure if he got out. If he did, he ran across the roof into the house where the rabbis live down the street."

I ran upstairs as he ordered and sat by the living room window with sort of a TV view. A policeman started speaking into a megaphone. "Come out with your hands up, and you won't be hurt. You have five minutes before we open full fire on you. Listen, you don't have a chance, so surrender."

Seconds later, flashes from the roof with loud gun reports came, and Clark Street in Astoria exploded. The policemen returned fire for ten or fifteen minutes. I thought I was watching a movie until I was shocked into reality. One of the gunman's bullets crashed through my window, and I ducked. Even though I was scared, I returned to the window. Mom and Pop were watching the mad show, Maria was hiding under a bed, and Ninni was playing on the floor. Then the gunman stood up on the roof and fired his pistol at the police as if he wanted to die. The cops found their mark, and he fell into a swan dive like Batman onto the street. Mom buried her head in Pop's chest.

"He killed the old Jew tailor for a few bucks," one of the cops said. "Can you imagine? Such a nice old guy getting killed over a few measly bucks? He never hurt anyone in all the years I knew him. In fact, the irony is, if he would have asked the old man, he probably would have given him the money. I've seen him stake many a tramp to some dough. He was a soft touch."

Pop came up with tears in his eyes. "Mr. Levy was my friend. We used to talk almost every day. Why does God do this? I'll never understand. We have to go over to the house and offer help to his wife, Sarah. What will she do? She's old and has no one in this country."

"We all have our crosses to bear, John," Mom said. "Don't let it bother you. Remember, the doctor said you should control your emotions, or you may get an attack."

"You'd have to be made of ice not to have feelings when something like this happens, and I can't help myself. I knew him and loved him as a friend. Let's get our kids away from here."

Although I'd been exposed to conditions from our dismal cold-water flat to mansions, and to people very rich and very poor, I was still confused. I did get the idea you had to make a lot of money to escape the filth some of us had to live in. Yet, I was to learn too soon, although some made the money, they still lived in filth, and money represented different things to different people.

Someone knocked, and Pop motioned me to see who it was. It was Frank. I was always happy to see him. He and Pop sat down at the kitchen table.

"I got the information you wanted, John. I can arrange free transportation for the three kids as far as you want to send them, as long as someone is waiting on the other end. This way, they'll have a vacation, and it won't cost you anything."

"Frank, these kids are getting older, Giovanni will soon be twelve, and I fear if they spend another whole summer in this neighborhood, they're bound to get into trouble or hurt. I talked to my brother, Dominic, and he said he gladly would take them for the summer in the country."

"Are you sure you want this? You know what your brother is like, John. Even though he's my friend, he doesn't like kids, which is why he never had any."

"I discussed it thoroughly with him, Frank, and he understands the responsibility, I can assure you. And as for Giovanni, he needs time off from his crowded schedule. It's just too much for a child."

"I agree with you wholeheartedly, John. My only concern was Dominic's attitude, you understand."

"What's the next step, Frank?"

"Well, it is only August, but I'll arrange for you to fill out a form now for next summer, and the rest is history. In fact, it's better you do it right away, so the quota won't all be taken."

"*Gracia*, Frank, *gracia tante*."

Not long after, Manny got caught breaking into a candy store that was closed and lifting cigarette cartons. He was taken before a juvenile board and released into Uncle Frank's custody, because it was his first offense, and the judge was a friend of Frank's. Herman and I couldn't wait to ask Manny about his adventure. He was a celebrity to us now, a step up in our social circle.

"What did they do to you, Manny?" I asked. "Did they beat you?"

"Yeah! They beat me every night, but I wouldn't talk, not me. I'm tough. In fact, one time I hit a bull back, and he went to work on me with a rubber hose. That's so they don't leave a mark."

I realize now he was exaggerating, but I believed him at the time.

"It's okay, Manny," Herman said. "When we grow up and I'm a priest, you'll never get caught again. Can you imagine stashing stuff in back of the church? Who would ever expect it?"

"That's what I like about you. You got imagination. You and I are partners from now on."

"Hey, can you imagine if I were a bull, what a team we would make?" Vinnie said. "We would have the whole scene covered."

His uncle Costello's look came over Manny's face. His eyes exuded strength, determination, and leadership. It sent a shiver down my spine. The three of them went through the wrist-cutting ritual to exchange each other's blood for eternal brotherhood. I watched with a rejected look.

"Hey, Opera, you are just as much a friend as the three of us, but this is for the future of our friendship, and it ain't your bag," Vinnie said.

"That's right, Giovanni, you're going to be strictly an artist, and when we're all successful, we'll buy tickets to come to see you," Herman said.

I smiled in dejection and said I understood. I hung my head on the way home.

Uncle Dick stopped his car by me as I was walking. "Giovanni, come over to the store tomorrow. I have a surprise for you."

As I fell asleep that night, I wondered what the surprise was. A new booking date? A present? I couldn't wait.

I woke up early and strolled over to Uncle Dick's alleged bike store. He was sitting in a big antique rocking chair with four men around a poker table. He was awfully good, and the men were mad at him. I recognized two of Costello's men with their big cars outside, large light-gray Stetson hats, gray spats, and fat Havana cigars. No one came in to rent or buy a bike. In those days, bike rentals were profitable; very few people could afford to buy one. But all sorts of men were walking through with envelopes to tuck them into the grandfather clock in the far corner. They'd come and go without a word.

Dick finally noticed me. "Deal me out of the next few hands, I have some business with my nephew. You know who he is, the Little Caruso."

The men tipped their hats out of respect for Mr. Costello, I'm sure.

"I hear you work in your spare time, Giovanni."

"Yes, Uncle Dick, I work in the drugstore and in the curtain store from time to time."

"It must be hard getting around for you."

"Oh, it's okay, Uncle Dick, I get it done. I don't mind."

"Well, you know, I've been thinking, what with all the extra work, training, and school, you should have it a little easier."

My heart started to pound at the thought of owning a bike. This was a status symbol in my world. In fact, the only person with a bike in my neighborhood was the son of our landlord, Charlie.

Dick draped his arm around my shoulder and steered me to a row of fine wheels. "Giovanni, pick out what you like, one, that is, and it's all yours."

"Holy cow, Uncle Dick! You mean you're giving me my own bike?"

"Don't thank me, you have earned it. You've been a fine hard-working, loyal boy. And by the way, you're not obligated in any way. Uncle Frank and Mr. Costello are chipping in to buy this for you. After all, you do a lot of favors, and they're grateful."

I forced myself to take my time and not pick out a lemon. I'll never forget the feeling. I wanted to make it last as long as I could as I walked up and down the rows. *I can have any one of these, holy cow!* I finally stopped at a royal-blue English racer with metallic gold trim. It was a twelve-speed with brakes, a light front and rear, and an electric horn on the crossbar.

"This is the one. This is the bike I want, Uncle Dick."

Dick scratched his head. "Well, you have excellent taste, Giovanni. Why don't you ride it around the block a few times and make sure it's the one you want?"

"Can I, Uncle Dick?"

"Go ahead, Giovanni, and just drive it home if you like it. I'll catch up with you later."

I felt more and more like a king as I rode away. I felt like the whole neighborhood was watching in envy.

Will my friends be surprised when they see this! Should I let them ride it? After all, it's a very special gift. Yet, I could lose their friendship. All sorts of anxieties ran through my head. Yet, my neck and head stretched taller and taller as I rode through the streets of Astoria. Gee, Pop should be the first to see this. So, I pedaled home as fast as I could. Pop was working his machine by the window with one eye on the outside world. He walked downstairs and hugged me.

"How do you like your new bike, Giovanni? I really didn't expect such an expensive one, did you?"

"No, Pop, you should see how it rides, as smooth as Mr. Costello's Cadillac."

Pop smiled, then looked at it intensely. "Let me ride it 'round the block."

"Sure, Pop." As he pulled away, I realized he wasn't supposed to do any kind of exercise, and I worried until he reappeared at the opposite end of the block.

"It's a fine bike. You know, the Lord does move in funny ways at times," he said, looking me in the eye.

"He sure does," I said, not really understanding.

"Go ride your bike a while, Giovanni, and have fun getting used to it."

I rode off with one thing in mind: showing off to my friends. I caught up with them at the library atop Hopkins Hill. I liked going inside because it was beautiful and elegant, probably donated from an old estate. My friends were playing handball against the building.

"Wow, what a cab!" Manny yelled. "Where did you borrow it,

Giovanni?"

I took a deep breath. "It's mine, your uncle helped buy it for me for the favors I've been doing for him."

"I think I'll learn to sing opera. Can you teach me, Giovanni? If you get this kind of reward for singing, then I'm a singer." He mimicked me singing . . . badly, I might add.

"I think you'll get a bike quicker your way rather than by singing, Manny."

"Let me ride it," Vinnie said.

I handed it over, and he sped down Hopkins Hill.

"Hey, Giovanni, can we have a ride next?"

"Sure, you're my friends, aren't you?"

"Boy, a bike of our own," Herman said. "I'll bet we're the only gang with a bike."

"We'll pull some neat jobs with a bike like this," Manny added. "It sure is fast looking. Does it ride as fast as it looks?"

"Yeah, Manny, wait till you get on it. You'll see what I mean."

After Manny and Herman took their turns, all concurred it was the fastest machine they'd ridden. The sky started to darken, and I waved to people I didn't even know as I rode off. I felt like the big shot. When I got home, I ran upstairs and grabbed at Mom to come look.

"Well, Giovanni, you should be able to make a lot of money with this bike. It looks good and strong, and will last a long time."

"Yes, Mom, I can get a lot of jobs with this bike."

This act of kindness seemed to make the misery of poverty much easier.

CHAPTER TWELVE

"John, John, are you all right?" Patricia, asks.

"Yes, Pat, I'm fine. Why?"

"Well, I've been trying to talk to you for the past ten minutes, and you seemed to be in another world. You really had me worried."

I notice a familiar face in front of me, but I can't quite place it.

"Giovanni, it's me, your cousin, Johnny Fuchsia. Don't you remember me?"

I recognize his eyes and high cheekbones, but he's one hundred fifty pounds heavier. He still has that ingratiating smile, though.

"Forgive me, Giovanni. I know how hard this must be for you. I forgot . . . it was just . . . I was so glad to see you. I just forgot."

"No apology necessary. I remember only fond things about you. You were my father's friend, besides being a relative."

"You mean he was my friend. He not only brought me to this country, but my sisters as well." He turned to Patricia. "His wonderful father not only brought us here, but then in the midst of the Depression, he let us stay at his home until we got situated. What a man he was."

"What are you doing with yourself?" I ask.

"I'm still sheriff of Carthage. The times I waited to see if you would visit, you know the country around there is the prettiest in the whole world."

"In the summertime only."

We chuckle because the winters are brutally cold, and the snow piles so high that they have to dig tunnels out of their houses.

"Well, you can't have everything, Giovanni. You got to take the good with bad. That's what your father taught me when I was an anxious young man. You know, I was about to go bad, and if it weren't for your pop's infinite wisdom in handling dodos like me, who knows, I may have spent most of my life in the tank. Instead, I became the peace officer of a town where no one causes trouble."

I smile. "I'd heard through the grapevine you had a lot to do with the conduct of the young Turks in your area."

"Yeah, I did impose a bit of psychology on them once in a while, Italian style, but the parents helped. They were behind me one hundred percent. I couldn't have done it without them."

"You still had to gain confidence, didn't you?"

"Well, I guess you have a point. . . . Hey, where did you get such a beautiful girl, Johnny?"

"She has poor eyesight, you know."

"You take after your pop. You have the same attitude, but I think you inherited a realistic side from your mama."

Oh, how good it feels to be loved and wanted after all the hell I've been going through. Something good is happening to me, even with the tragedy of Mom's death. I'm beginning to make a slow, but sure decision. I'm beginning to feel like my old self again, full of fight, ambition, confidence, and best of all, I'm falling even deeper in love with my wonderful wife. I'm beginning to clear my mental decks to make much more room for her. She's not only worth it, but she also deserves every bit of it. She seems to know what I'm thinking, because she holds my hand tighter and tighter. She's smiling in that knowing way of hers, which has kept me off guard since the day I met her. Yes, I truly love my wife in a very, very special way.

My mind plays a song. 'Just around the corner, there's a rainbow in the sky. Let's have another cup of coffee, let's have another piece of pie.'

*****

I was in Frank's den listening to Costello. It had been almost a year since Franklin Delano Roosevelt was elected president. Herbert Hoover had been battered at the hand of one of the greatest orators of all time.

"Now, let's get down to business. Have you heard what my fool brother tried? He tried to bring in slots from New Jersey. He thought he had carte blanche because we helped the LaGuardia campaign. Here, look at the front page of the *Daily Mirror*. It shows our Little Flower with a sledgehammer in his hand busting more than one million dollars worth of my game machines. Can you imagine the fool doing a thing like this without consulting me?"

"You know, a move is being made on your brother, Edward. Everyone knows he's weak, and with the population growth here on the island, it's getting palatable for some factions to want to move in. If this happens, I know the kind of bloodbath that will take place. I'm begging you not to let this happen, or all of our plans will go down the drain."

Costello looked at his shined shoes and slowly lifted his head with authority. "I know who the factions are. They come out of Brooklyn. You know, Frank, the old man is mine, but this time they aren't listening to him, so I have to take a different course. On one hand, if I pull Ed out of this territory, it'll be a sign of weakness, and the wrong people will gain strength. On the other hand, if I call for a beef, I lose because my brother is a goofball. What I'm saying is, direct confrontation is out, and retreat is out, so I have only one alternative: We must squeeze them politically, put so much pressure on them they'll come to me on bended knee. Once this happens, we've won. No blood in the streets, no retreats, and we'll be in a stronger position. Can we pull this off, Frank?"

"Yes, Dewey is writing briefs for LaGuardia. He has much influence over the officers on your payroll. All I have to do is sell him on the idea we are cooperating, and he'll sic all of the dogs on these guys in the street. What it'll cost them in bonding costs alone will bring them to you. However, they want something in return. Even though they'll buckle under pressure, what they expect from you sooner or later is the demise of your friend, Lucky Luciano. They fear him, yet they have no respect for him. They want rid of him, rid of him as soon as possible."

"One thing at a time, Frank. I agree with them. He's a menace to all of us, but we have to do this properly, as you say. We don't want a backlash to hurt our years of planning."

Frank tightened his fist. "Why don't you get rid of the apes your brother has hired and put some brains around him? Could retard some of his crazy antics."

"Good boy, Frank, why didn't I think of that? In fact, I know just the men to throw around him. He'll never know what hit him when he starts doing everything right. Not only that, but with the boys I have in mind, the guys from Brooklyn will think twice before they dare make a move. . . . Well, enough of this, Frank. I have an audition screen test for Giovanni at Warner Bros. at the Queens studio."

"Giovanni, I have some investment in this company, so I'm talking to one of those fancy producers. It seems they want to produce some kind of Christmas Carol thing. Remember, it's just one of those short subjects they throw out once in a while, but many stars started this way, and the experience won't harm you."

Wow, the chance of being in a movie! My imagination was like a racehorse in its first start. Boy, I couldn't wait to tell Pop. Pop was a movie fan. He'd tell me gossip about Valentino, Eva Le Gallienne, Lillian Gish, Douglas Fairbanks Sr., John Gilbert. Yes, John Gilbert. He was the one who played the lover in so many silent films. Mr. Costello caught me daydreaming.

"Giovanni, are you listening to me? Cancel your voice lessons this Saturday and go with my chauffeur to Warner Bros. Studios. They're expecting you at eleven o'clock sharp. This means you'll have to leave the house around nine forty-five, putting you in the office fifteen minutes early. You're to see Mr. Darrell. He'll handle your screen test, and don't forget to bring your voice teacher with you. They'll want to make a track of your voice in the test. Now, I'm sure you want to run home and tell your father, so go ahead, Giovanni."

I ran the ten blocks so fast I think I broke Olympic records. I burst through the door panting. "Pop, Pop, I'm going to make a screen test! Mr. Costello set it up for me this Saturday."

"Wonderful news, Giovanni! I think you're ready for it. What a grand country we live in; anyone who has talent and the guts can make it."

My coach arrived at my house early Saturday morning, and we went over various materials we might use. Of course, we had no idea what this Mr. Darrell would ask for. However, it never hurt to go over the basics. At least, we'd be partially prepared.

"Just in case, Giovanni, I brought all of the charts with me. You haven't done some of them in a long time. Do you think you'll remember the charts and the lyrics if they choose one of the old ones?"

"Yes. Once I learn something, I never forget it."

"Listen to him," Mom said. "He forgets chores, homework, but never forgets what he learns. I'll remember this, Giovanni, when you tell me you forgot to do something for me."

I smiled sheepishly, hoping she was teasing. It was always hard to tell if she was kidding.

A horn sounded, signaling us the car was downstairs. I got the butterflies I usually got when entering a new medium. I knew nothing about movie craft, so I didn't know what to expect. But I felt letdown when we arrived. The studios looked like warehouses, and not very clean, I might add, with high cyclone fences around them and a guard at the gate. We were directed to the prim, young receptionist in the front office.

"May I help you?" she asked Mr. Parado.

"Yes, we have an appointment with Mr. Darrell. He's expecting us."

"What name, may I ask?"

"Giovanni Benedetto."

"Oh, Mr. Costello's protégé. He's expecting you. Just go into the third door on the left. His name is on the door; you can't miss it."

Mr. Parado timidly knocked on the open door. The man behind the desk was slim, bald, and well dressed with a bright diamond stickpin in his tie and a waxed mustache.

"Come in, come in. So you are the little Caruso we've heard so much about," he barked.

I didn't like him. For one thing, he talked like a girl, which wasn't funny. In fact, it made me feel strange. I couldn't warm up to him.

"You don't talk much, do you, Giovanni? From what I heard about you, I expected a more outgoing personality. Well, maybe you feel a bit strange and will get over it." He stood up. "I'd like you to meet Lillian Quinlan. She's one of the better managers specializing in show business for juveniles. That's you, Giovanni, ha ha ha."

"How do you do, Mrs. Quinlan?" I bowed to her.

"How do you do, Giovanni? My, what a polite boy you are."

How pretty. She had chestnut hair, emerald eyes, and she smelled nice. Mr. Parado introduced himself, and Mr. Darrell eyed me like some specimen in a test tube.

"Well, shall we get on with it?" Mr. Darrell said. "I like your hairdo, Giovanni. You'll photograph well, that's a plus. Don't you think so, Lillian?"

I felt he was patronizing me. I was an artist and a good one. I didn't need that just because I was a child.

"Let's take you down to costume and then to makeup. I'll explain the test for you, Giovanni."

"Thank you, sir."

"Oh, Giovanni, call me Tad. All of my close associates do. We shall be friends, eh?"

I was defensive as I gave him a quiet yes. We all walked over to a musty room with all sorts of costumes. It reminded me of the Metropolitan Opera House backstage; probably because of the old period costumes and the smell of theater were synonymous with this kind of room.

"Ronnie, this is Giovanni. He is here for a test. I want a medieval Italian costume for him. I hope we have his size."

Ronnie acted like a girl too, the way he talked and used his hands. I felt uncomfortable, but my voice coach seemed overly at home as I watched every eye expression between the three of them.

Ronnie disappeared for at least twenty minutes and returned with my garb. "Go over to the little room behind the curtain, Giovanni. If you need help, don't hesitate to call out."

I put on an ancient troubadour's costume, the kind worn in a king's court. The material was velvet, and the shirt was candy-striped silk with bolero sleeves and a red silk sash. The patent-leather red shoes displayed Florentine buckles. I felt comfortable in it because we used a lot of this style at the Met. I gazed in the full-length mirror as I positioned a red felt hat with a gold pheasant feathered plume, reminiscent of Robin Hood. This make-believe world always relaxed me. Exotic costumes gave me a sense of protection, as though I were someone else and not liable for anything. I opened the curtain with slight apprehension.

"Exquisite, absolutely exquisite," Mr. Darrell said. "His Italian coloring is perfect for this costume, more than I expected. Come a little closer in this light, Giovanni. Yes, very good." He placed his hands backward on his hips, once again like a woman, then motioned us to follow him to the makeup room. Another feminine male was waiting for us there.

"Well, this is the little boy you were telling me about, yes? Even better than you described. He's pretty. Sit here, Giovanni, under the light so I can go to work on you."

THE SHADOW OF HIS SMILE

The application was a lot more time-consuming and tedious than at the Opera House. It seemed to take hours. "Tell the photographer to hit the eyes," the makeup man said. "I assure you they'll bounce right off the film. Remember the eyes, they are really gorgeous."

I was feeling a bit edgy, and I noticed he was wearing lipstick, eye shadow, eyebrow pencil, and strong perfume. He also sported a large earring that dangled every time he bent over. I wasn't so sure I'd like making movies because the people seemed a strange breed.

Mr. Darrell placed his perfumed hands on both sides of my face and studied me. "Marvelous, just marvelous, Bruce. Now, let's get to the script. It's a simple one. You don't have to say lines, Giovanni. All you have to do is walk on this bridge scene and look up at the stars. You'll fake playing a flute. Pick whatever material you wish. All we want is to get the quality of your voice and how you'll photograph."

The first thing I thought of was "Una furtiva lagrima." My voice coach agreed it would be perfect with a flute. Mrs. Quinlan followed us to the shooting studio.

Mr. Parado was seated beyond the set at a grand piano. Mr. Darrell gave me last-minute instructions from the director's chair. "Now, before we shoot, Giovanni, let me put you wise to a few things. I'm going to ask you to walk over to the middle of the bridge from your left. Now, walk on slowly. Keep in mind everything you do is magnified five thousand times. So, if you as much as flinch or make a wrong gesture, it'll look five thousand times as bad. Completely relax before you let us shoot. If you make a mistake, we'll cut. Don't stop."

I was getting nervous as Mr. Darrell yelled, "Are you ready, Giovanni? Are you ready, Mr. Parado? Lights, action, camera, take one."

I was not used to the heat or brightness of the lights. They weren't like the ones at the Met. It was almost impossible trying not to blink. How did movie people work under these? I walked to the center of the bridge in slow motion.

"Good, Giovanni, excellent. Now sort of sit on the rail sideways, look up at the stars, and then down at your flute. Then bring the flute up slowly and look at it as though you're in love with it. Mr. Parado, just keep moving chords on him until he is ready to sing, then come in."

I took my time and somehow forgot about the cameras. When I finished the aria, the camera crew applauded. I found out later this was rare.

Mr. Darrell seemed most please, and Ms. Quinlan walked over to me. "Let's you and I have a chat, Giovanni, over here in the corner." She tipped up my chin. "You have a great talent. I think you warrant a manager. If you want, I'll come to your home and talk to your parents about handling you. I have handled many child movie stars, Giovanni, and I think with the proper guidance, someone to look after your interests, you'll go a long, long way."

"Well, I think Uncle Frank would be the one to talk to. He tells me most of what to do, Mrs. Quinlan."

"Good, but I still would like your parents to be at the conference. You see, they are really responsible for you, and some decisions have to be up to them."

"I'll tell them."

We waited about an hour to get the test results. Mr. Darrell came running in. "It's a bull's-eye, a wonderful test, Giovanni. Everything came off without retakes. I'm going to call Mr. Costello with the good news. I'm sure you'll be chosen for the Christmas feature and a lot more before we're through."

*****

I'll never forget that cold, misty day as we prepared for Mrs. Quinlan. Mom set out her best lace doilies and chinaware with homemade Italian cookies. Pop dressed in a shirt and tie. He was so handsome and debonair. I waited by the window, which was sweating from the cold and humidity. Mrs. Quinlan pulled up in a big dark-blue Lincoln with a huge trunk and a black leather roof. In those days, it would have been real leather.

"She's here! She's out front, Pop."

"Now, Johnny, calm down. Don't let her see you so excited. You're professional, remember?"

"Uncle Dick is here too!"

It didn't take long for her to win over Mom and Dick.

"Now that you've signed, I'd like to tell you something. I was told not to say anything before, which might have influenced your judgment. I was not at the movie studio by accident. Mr. Costello invited me, and I'm a good friend of the Vanderbilts, although I'm best qualified for what I'm about to do for Giovanni. Mr. Costello thought it of such importance, you make up your mind on your own.

"The first order of business is getting some personality pictures taken. I intend to put the picture on what will look like a postage stamp. Every letter we send out will have this stamp on the envelope. I'd like Mr. Parado to put together a chorus of six or eight girls to back him in concert. I'll get in touch with him."

Mom's eyes lit up. My mind leaped at the possibility of beautiful chords backing my arias. Working solely with piano was difficult, no matter how great the accompanist. A chorus sort of gave the artist buoyancy and afforded a high that couldn't be explained

"I have a great idea," Mrs. Quinlan said. "Let's celebrate by my inviting you all out to lunch. Do you have a good restaurant near here?"

"We have a fine little restaurant owned by my friend, Freddie, called Venice Gardens," Dick said.

Everyone liked Freddie for his magnetic charm and dignity. When we arrived, he gave us his usual warm greeting. "Here's a table worthy of such celebrity people, the best table in the house. And here's a special bottle of wine I made myself. It was so good I saved a bottle out of the barrel for someone special."

After our dinner, Freddie filled a glass for himself. *"Permesso.* I would like to make a toast to the next Caruso, and may he have a long, wonderful, exciting career."

We clinked glasses and drank. *A manager of my own. After all, how many people have managers? I must be good. Very, very good.*

*****

A few days later, Mrs. Quinlan took me to a photographer in Manhattan. After the photo session, she drove me to Long Champs, where I ordered a tuna fish sandwich with bacon.

"Giovanni, tuna with bacon?"

"It's really good, try it."

"You know it sounds so ghastly, I think I will. . . . I have some excellent news for you, Giovanni. LaGuardia has opened a city radio station, WNYC. Now, as Mayor LaGuardia's protégé, you'll be the featured talent on the opening day. Although it's only twenty-five dollars a show, it's in the massive lobby of Grand Central Terminal on the balcony. And guess what? A sixty-piece symphony orchestra will back you, and thousands of commuter travelers will see you, as well as being heard on radio."

I couldn't even imagine an orchestra that large. I was silent, then repeated what she'd said to ensure I'd heard her right.

"That's right, Giovanni, and guess what? You're the star of the show. You're booked for sixteen weeks. It's funny I was in the mayor's office on another matter for you. I was trying to see if you qualify for his new special arts training and he was talking about this show. When I mentioned your name he jumped at it and told me to make sure I told your Uncle Frank about it."

I could barely eat lunch. "How soon, Mrs. Quinlan?"

"Very soon, Giovanni. In fact, the problem we have is getting your charts written on time for the first performance. I promised the Little Flower I'd have them ready, so I need to get together with Mr. Parado right away. You'll be dressed formal in tails for every performance, and you'll be getting quite a bit of publicity.

It'll be written up in Walter Winchell's column and other gossips. The city will place a full-page ad in *The New York Times* with your picture right in the middle. I don't have to tell you, Giovanni, this is a giant step in your career, so make sure you get lots of rest between performances."

It was difficult for me to absorb it all. I was at a loss for words when I should have been asking a million questions.

She must have understood. "Now, as you think of any questions, write them down so you won't forget them."

*****

After all the rehearsals and my confidence built to a new high, I developed laryngitis so bad I couldn't even speak. With the performance looming the next day, Mom made me drink tea and honey, Pop fed me blackstrap molasses with hot mustard, and Dick gave me brandy and lemon.

"Why don't we call Mr. Petri? He handles important opera singers. Surely, he must know a remedy," Pop said.

"That's it," Dick said. "Why didn't I think of that?"

I was ready for a straitjacket, imagining myself on network, thousands of people walking by in the terminal, and me without a voice. I panicked when I remembered the sadist doctor burning my tonsils with an orange stick.

Dick, who had run out to a public phone, hurried back with a small orange box. "I've got it. Mr. Petri told me what to buy. He told me you should suck on this, and you should be all right by tomorrow. He said all the leading opera stars carry this with them wherever they go."

It was medicine licorice made with root and herbs, no sugar, but it didn't help. I also was not resting because I was waking up every fifteen minutes all night to suck on a licorice stick. It was so bitter, it gave me throat spasms.

I still couldn't speak when I arrived at Grand Central Terminal. I forgot it for a while as I walked through the wonderful advertising displays that served as performance backdrops on the balcony. Each represented a place the railroad could take passengers. One depicted mannequins snow skiing and riding a toboggan.

Mrs. Quinlan was in shock when she discovered I couldn't speak and saw how tired I looked. "Well, we had better cancel it, Giovanni. The worst thing you can do is give a bad performance."

I begged her to wait in a scratchy voice, as though a miracle could happen.

She waited so long, it became too late to cancel. I took my place, and lo and behold, I could sing when I opened my mouth! In fact, my voice came back with more resonance, and I lasted through the performance with bravos from the massive audience. Oddly enough, my voice died precisely as I finished my last aria. Mrs. Quinlan was impressed to say the least.

I had been too tense to enjoy the beauty of working with a sixty-piece orchestra, but I had many more chances after my ailment went away the next week. The number of people who came to watch the performances surprised us, and I started signing autographs.

One Saturday, Manny, Herman, and Vinnie showed up. I experienced a new sensation when I saw them: self-consciousness.

"Hey, Opera, you look good in the monkey suit," Vinnie said with his constant humorous expression. "It appears like you're going to be a star. Tell me, will you still talk to us?"

"Of course, I will. You're my friends. Nothing will ever change that."

"He's kidding," Manny said. "You know Vinnie, if he isn't kidding someone, he isn't alive."

I introduced them to Mrs. Quinlan, and she graciously offered them seats. But she sat them right in front of me, and I had to ignore all of their antics.

One of the guests that day was Richard Crooks. I sang with him in *Carmen* at the Met. And a man came on to perform sound effects he usually did for radio: from creaking doors to lions and tigers. The boys really would have something to talk about at school.

Mrs. Quinlan took us to an ice-cream parlor. "How'd you get here, boys? Did your parents drive you?"

The three of them looked at each other like they'd just robbed a bank.

"Did I say something I wasn't supposed to?"

"Oh, no," Herman said. "Our parents can't afford an automobile."

"Did you ride the subway?"

Vinnie laid his spoon down with impatience. "Our parents can't afford that either, lady. We walked across the 59th Street Bridge."

"You walked all that way just to see your friend? How noble. You're a very lucky boy, Giovanni."

I nodded as I stuffed my mouth with a banana split.

"Well, how would you boys like a ride home?"

"Yeah!" they chorused.

She looked sincerely satisfied. I really liked her. The ride home was an adventure for my friends. They ran their fingers over the rich upholstery, gesturing each time they discovered something new. They pressed the lighters in the ashtrays, amazed how they lit up. The small opera lights on each side of the back paneled windows entranced Vinnie. He kept switching one of them off and on as fast as he could.

Mrs. Quinlan peered in her rearview mirror. "How would you boys like to come to a party we're having for Giovanni? We're celebrating his first movie part. He'll start shooting next week."

This was the first I'd heard of it.

The boys got boisterous, all cutting in. "Wow, a movie! You're going to be a movie star!"

"It's just a short subject. I'm going to do a Christmas thing," I said.

"What's the difference?" Herman said. "People all over the

world will see you."

"That's right," Mrs. Quinlan said. "I don't think Giovanni realizes the impact yet, but people in the street will start recognizing him."

Somehow, I couldn't get excited. I think it was nerves, actually.

"Would you like to be dropped off somewhere?" Mrs. Quinlan asked the boys when we arrived at my house.

"This is fine," they chorused.

The four of us talked for hours in the street, fantasizing about how we would live after I became a star. I must have looked silly out there in my formal tails. Finally, I ran upstairs to tell Mom and Pop the news.

*****

I was now formally under contract with Warner Bros. Two days before the shoot, Mrs. Quinlan kept her promise. She rented out Venice Gardens and invited everyone. My family and I sat on a dais, and Mrs. Quinlan, Uncle Frank, Mr. Costello, Uncle Dick, Mr. Darrell, and my friends sat at a table in front of us. Uncle Dick danced almost every song with Mrs. Quinlan, which pleased me. Pop and Mom looked ever so proud as people came up to congratulate me. Freddy, as usual, gave us a feast to be remembered.

For the shoot, I had a chorus of six girls. Everyone was excited I did most of it without retakes because it reduced the cost of shooting. Mrs. Quinlan said the thirty-minute movie would be a good forerunner for future concerts.

Uncle Frank called. He still was helping me with my career, even with all of his problems. "Giovanni, I was talking to the Little Flower, and he informed me the city wants you for another sixteen weeks of concerts on the balcony of the Grand Central Station. You'll have several guest conductors, all on the level of Toscanini.

"WOW!" I yelled as I just about jumped out of my shoes.

"So get all of your charts together so you can decide what you want to do. You're going to be paid handsomely for this. It'll be broadcast on our city station, WNYC, every Sunday. Your first rehearsal is this Sunday at two o'clock sharp. Be on time. You know how these maestros are."

"Gee, thanks, Uncle Frank, this is great news!"

I ran into the kitchen where Maria was reading to tell her the news, and I was stunned she acted excited.

*****

It wasn't easy being a neighborhood celebrity. My film was released two weeks before Christmas, and the response at school was at extreme ends of the pendulum. I either had to fight or sign autographs. I don't think I would have made it without my three friends. And much to my surprise, my staunchest protector was Vinnie Auletta. He was tough and did indeed watch my back.

At the ripe old age of twelve, I found myself coping with strong mixed emotions. My headaches became stronger and more frequent. I filled Turkish towels with nosebleeds. Mom would rush me to our family doctor, and he would seal the capillaries to stop the bleeding. Dr. Weiss informed Mom my condition stemmed from my schedule and I should be into group sports and even a bit of fishing. Mother explained to the good doctor that her husband was practically bedridden, and I was contributing money for the household.

Dr. Weiss grimaced. "Well, Annie, as his doctor I must inform you about his welfare. Let's pray these symptoms don't progress, for if they do, you'll have a much bigger problem than worrying about money. The stress is causing an increase in blood pressure."

Listening to this, my mind moved in a direction disappointing to my parents, especially Pop. He was so bent on me becoming an opera singer and following through on my education. Then I realized I couldn't dedicate my life to the craft.

When I was in concert, I became another person. I had wonderful poise, and I was in command of my audience. Looking back, it reminds me of the fight trainer who finds a potential champion. His prospect has a superior physique and tremendous staying power, only to find his chin is questionable when he enters the ring. That was me abstractly. I finally realized I hadn't been a child for a long time, and I resented it. Although in innocence, my parents denied me the childhood I deserved.

Yet, I believed Ninni had the ingredients for complete dedication with his beautiful voice.

Contrary to the way he sounds today, Tony had uncanny breath control and a silver tenor voice with a tight vibrato. This was miraculous without formal training.

CHAPTER THIRTEEN

Before I knew it, summer was here. I had forgotten Frank's offer of transportation up to Dominick's for vacation. Mom and Pop decided Ninni was too young for the adventure. They addressed Maria and me to lay out their expected behavior of us. They sold us on the idea we would be very happy. I was excited because I loved train trips. I had taken many trains with the Met and somehow acquired a liking for the steam-engine odor.

Mom and Pop put us on the train late one evening, probably because it was the more available time with a special rate, considering the city was paying for it. Mom gave us last-minute instructions as she held brown snack bags for Maria and I. Pop looked pleased, knowing I wouldn't be pressured or getting into trouble on the city streets.

I recall the clickety-clack of the train racing northward upstate and the lonesome wail of the train whistle. It sounded alive, as if the train was calling out for its destination. I got up at least twenty times. I thought the ice-cold water at the cooler and folding paper cups were really something.

I also felt grown-up staying awake into the wee hours. Maria, who never was much impressed by anything, slept through most of the trip, so I got to make my own decisions. I was wide-awake when the train stopped at Potsdam and added more cars. The banging and jolting frightened me, but a kind conductor came over to comfort me. He even took me outside to explain the procedure.

We gained a few hours in transit, and it was only four o'clock when we pulled into Canton, a small college town with about five thousand residents, plus the agricultural students. Dominick's place was in a smaller town of one hundred-fifty residents, named Pyrites after a mineral that turned out not strong enough in deposits for mining. The people were mainly lumberjacks and farmers, and the Whelan family owned a small hotel.

Dominick was waiting for us, even though we were early. He hadn't changed a bit with his squinty eyes, bald head, and bull neck. When a blunt cigar wasn't in his mouth, you could see a round perforation there. He had a high, yet rounded voice, nothing like Pop's soft tones. It sounded forced or affected.

"Hi, Giovanni. Hi, Maria. How was the trip?"

"Fine, Uncle Dominick," I said.

"Come with me, kids. Carry your luggage, you're strong enough." He walked us to a new shiny Buick. "How do you like my new car? You know, I don't understand your father. He could have anything he wants if he comes up here and helps me run the business."

Dominick couldn't read or write, and his grammar left a lot to be desired. I couldn't help but resent what he said. I recalled Pop saying he brought Dominick here from Italy and gave him the money to go into business. In my mind, the business belonged to Pop.

As we drove through the country, it took my breath away. This was truly God's country. The landscape was like an oil painting of tall oaks, elms, weeping willows, fishponds, fast brooks, and wildlife. At least four deer scampered into thickets as Dominick, known for his heavy foot, sped on the narrow blacktop connecting The Thousand Islands, which was a bit farther than his house. In those days, this was a main highway to one of the most popular resorts in Canada.

I knew we were close to Dominick's home as he started to slow down. "Well, this is Pyrites. How do you like it?"

Accustomed to large cities, I wasn't impressed by the poorly constructed, aging wooden buildings, some of them falling down. It looked run-down and poor. At the end of town, we reached a two-story frame house with a general store and gasoline pumps. Aunt Maggie was rocking in a chair under a sign across the front that read Benedetto's.

I got the instant feeling she was tolerating us. As we piled out of the car, all she did was nod as though she saw us every day. She didn't even smile. She looked clean in a satin dress much too warm for the season with stunning satin-covered buttons from the hemline up to the closed Mandarin-type collar. The long sleeves went way past a ruffled wrist line with a pink organdy hanky dangling from the bottom of her wrist. She was holding a flyswatter, which seemed to be a serious business.

"Maggie, show the kids where they're to sleep. I have some customers I have to attend to."

She motioned us to follow her alongside the house. An intolerable odor turned out to be stagnant water. With no sewage system, the collected water produced slimy algae, and frogs seemed to make a home in it. We reached a side entrance and ascended the stairs to a large living room area with a small dining room just to the left. Blankets and a pillow were on the floor.

"Giovanni, Maria, here is where you'll sleep. Now, we get up early, five o'clock sharp if you want breakfast, and start our chores right after breakfast. Everyone here chips in and does a share of the work, whether it's butchering, sacking potatoes, or taking the counter in the store. We eat supper at six-thirty sharp, and bedtime is at seven. You must not use the toilets in the house; you may use the ones outside." She pointed through the window at an old outhouse across a small field. "Now, we don't tolerate laziness, fights, or being answered back. If any money has to be collected, either your uncle or I will take it. Church on Sunday is at six o'clock, breakfast afterward. You get a half day off Sunday if you finish your chores. Oh, yes, Dominick is very fussy about his chickens. Don't bother them unless you're ordered to feed them."

I wanted to go home. This wasn't my idea of fun. Besides, I didn't like either of them.

I heard a voice calling me. "Giovanni, are you finished with your aunt? If you are, come down here!"

I ran down the stairs around the back of the house. Dominick was holding a beautiful calf by a chain looped around its neck. I ran over, threw my arms around its neck, and admired its perfect markings.

"You're just like your old man," Dominick snarled as I stroked its back. "He was a sucker for all kinds of animals. Here, hold this chain while I go to work."

I did as I was told and noticed a mallet-type hammer in Dominick's hand. As he herded the calf, it instinctively walked in a circle.

"Hold him, Giovanni, hold him tight."

He waited until the animal was in full stride and smashed the mallet between its warm brown eyes. The calf shrieked like a child in pain and fell. I was in shock. He drew a knife honed to a fine point like a round dagger and thrusted it through one of its eyes. The animal was dead.

"Don't stand like an idiot, help me lift him on these wall hooks. I'm going to butcher him now."

I started to sob.

"I knew it, just like your old man, chicken at the sight of blood. Why do you think God gave us these creatures? To admire them?"

Once I helped secure the calf, I started to walk away.

"Where the hell do you think you're going? You're going to learn to be a man in a hurry. I'll get your old man out of your system." He emitted a dirty laugh.

I'd never felt so sad. I wanted Pop; he would understand. I watched him slit the animal's belly and cut out the innards. He scraped the waste out of the stomach. The lining looked like thousands of honeycombs, and the smell was ever so bad.

"This is our supper tonight. Did you ever have *tripa* (tripe)?"

"Yes, but I never knew where it came from. We always got it in tomato sauce."

"Well, now you know where it comes from."

I never wanted to eat tripe again. At the dinner table, I claimed I wasn't hungry.

Dominick gave me one look and said, "You'll eat it. Believe me, you'll eat it."

I stuffed it in my mouth and felt like throwing up with every bite. "May I go to the toilet?" I asked when I finished.

"You know where it is," Aunt Maggie said.

I ran across the field and opened the weather-beaten door. The swarming wasps and surrounding nests frightened me, and the odor was worse than the calf's slaughter.

I cried all night, and when the sun peeked over the horizon, I knew what it was to hate. *Oh, how I hated my father's brother.*

At the crack of daylight, Maggie started cooking breakfast. This was a little more like it: fresh-laid eggs, thick, country, cured slab bacon, homemade biscuits, home-fried potatoes, and a tall glass of milk. I watched Dominick gorge his food like an animal without chewing.

"Did you have a good sleep?"

I couldn't believe it, an attempt at concern or kindness? But I was wrong.

"You better have because you're going to find out what work is today. I need a hundred sacks of potatoes before one o'clock so I can get some of them to market. The remainder will stay in the store."

I looked across the table at Maria, who was expressionless, as usual.

He walked us to the back of the store where mounds and mounds of potatoes were in the middle of the floor with burlap sacks. "Now, here's a scale on the floor, weigh fifty pounds to the sack. Not once do I want to see any sack an ounce over. Now, you can put three rotten potatoes in each sack. The customers don't squawk at that many. I don't want to catch you throwing any of them away, I don't care how bad they look. Here's how you tie the top of the sack."

I thought it would be easy, but lugging around fifty-pound sacks got to be a little much. My hands grew raw. Around twelve-thirty, Uncle showed up with warm farm milk and two sandwiches made with thick slices of bologna. I was famished and gulped down my sandwich, but Maria beat me.

"Shake it, Giovanni, you only have a little time left to sack all these." He kicked aside some of the potatoes. "Leave these for the store; the rest have to be sacked."

The food and a bit of rest did me good, and my tempo increased. We finished on time. Dominick came in to spot-check the bags. He opened one bag and removed a potato the size of an onion. "This one was just a touch over, don't let it happen again."

It would have felt better if he'd hit me. We had been so careful. *Gee, how I miss Pop. I wish he was here.*

Uncle brought us a large bowl of spaghetti. "Here, Giovanni, feed this to the chickens. Just throw it over the fence, they'll do the rest."

Sometimes God does move in funny ways, for I found pleasure in feeding the chickens in the midst of my depression. I laughed so hard my gut felt as though it would burst. Did you ever watch a bunch of chickens eat spaghetti? It's better than Broadway comedy. Two chickens invariably grab one string of spaghetti like a tug-of-war, the envy of any athlete. You could bet a third chicken would run in and grab the strand in the middle. That third chicken would end up the winner every time. And each time got funnier.

But then the ogre shape of Dominick reappeared. "Go out to the front, a farmer is delivering cucumbers. Now be careful with them, Giovanni, they bruise easily. Once they're in the store, you'll see some empty bushels in the back. Fill them up and put them along the floor in front of the vegetable counter nice and even."

Dominick was keeping his promise: I was learning what work was. And I learned something profound: When a person isn't happy, work becomes intolerable. It was torture. I missed my friends and their acceptance of me. I missed Mom, and most of all, Pop.

My first day at the store counter was a disaster. I was bored, so I started looking over the merchandise on the back shelf behind the counter. I noticed a small colorful package labeled Apple Jack and smelled it. It had an odd odor, between candy and something I couldn't recognize. I opened it, and it was dark brown with a glaze resembling honey. I couldn't resist honey, so I bit into it. Unfortunately, I swallowed it before I realized it wasn't edible. This was my first introduction to chewing tobacco. Needless to say, I turned green and was ill the rest of the day.

Of course, this didn't faze Dominick or Maggie. I still had to put in my day's work while running to the outhouse every five minutes. I didn't eat supper that evening.

The next day, a wasp stung Maria's tongue after it landed on the bread she was eating. The swelling was so bad she started to choke and turn color. I was so worried. Dominick rushed her to a doctor in Canton about fifteen miles away. I was relieved when they returned, but Maria remained silent for days.

I continued to rub Dominick the wrong way, and he kept comparing me to Pop. I became fascinated with snakes. We had all sorts of specimens, and I would drape them around my neck and send Aunt Maggie into a frenzy. Her severe punishment didn't stop me, however, even after a large one bit my wrist. In fact, I still have a scar where Dominick cut into the bite with a Boy Scout knife to suck out the venom. He kept threatening to send me back, and I hoped he would.

My depression became critical with migraines, nosebleeds, and the return of my recurring nightmare. I'd rest my head on the pillow, expecting to hear shrieking, feel tingling all over as though I were being electrocuted, see vivid explosions and brilliant white, transparent human forms. In my mind, it represented purgatory.

One day, I was playing by the chicken pen and picked up two pretty black chicks. I was horrified when I realized Dominick was behind me. I remembered Aunt Maggie instructing me not to touch the birds, so I shoved them into my back pockets. Dominick sat me down on an old wooden bench to talk.

He didn't notice the squealing in my pockets because it blended in with the chickens in front of us.

When he left, I pulled out the chicks, only to discover I had broken their necks. I cried all day. When they asked me what was wrong, I just kept sobbing and said I wanted to go home. My depression got so bad one morning that I refused to get up, despite their threats.

"Leave him alone," Aunt Maggie said to Dominick. "He's spoiled. Let's see how long he'll stay in bed."

With this challenge, I huddled under the covers until I had to use the bathroom. No one was home, so I spurted it all over the rug in the hope it would earn me a trip home. All I got, though, was the beating of my life by Uncle and Aunt. I wanted to die. I felt hopeless without Pop.

Each day became more punishing than the previous. My anxiety built to such a pitch I couldn't enjoy anything. A beautiful river flowed across the street from Dominick's house. It was about a quarter of a mile wide, and the water was as blue as a clear sky in June. A bridge crossed from the gas pumps to thick woods and a hunting path beaten down by Dominick's many guests.

One Sunday, we were awakened at four-thirty for a hearty breakfast of pork chops, eggs, and honey-raisin bread. Some couples had been invited to a picnic, so we packed up food, fishing gear, and shotguns. This was to be the only day of the entire summer I enjoyed.

I didn't know Tom and Nettie were coming too. In fact, the picnic was in their honor. I'd never been so glad to see anyone in my life. As soon as they got out of the car, I ran to Tom and grabbed his sleeve. "Uncle Tom, can I go back with you? I want to go home. I miss Pop."

"Giovanni, it's not for me to decide. Dominick is in charge of you, so you have to ask him."

This felt like the end of the world.

We started to hike single file across the bridge continuing on the hunting path through thick woods about an hour to the campsite. I noticed Uncle was carrying a wicker basket over his shoulder. Surprisingly, the wildlife wasn't unafraid of us. About a half hour in, we approached a clearing with a small muddy pond. Green algae almost blocked the path.

Dominic walked over to me. "We're going to pick up fishing bait here. You can help. The frogs with the black dots are what we want. Here's the way you catch them."

He knelt by the edge of the pond, plunged his left hand into the slimy water, and moved it toward his right hand that was waiting to pounce on his prey. Sure enough, a frog jumped in the direction of his right hand. He grabbed it and threw it into the wicker basket. I had a lot of fun catching at least a dozen. We continued on once Dominic was satisfied.

I could tell Tom was not an outdoorsman as he stumbled and tripped through the woods. He strolled with the confidence of one walking along a paved city street and paid for it. We finally reached what looked like the end of the woods. A fast-moving stream separated the thicket, which continued on the other side. An eight-foot tall waterfall was to the left. I knelt down to feel the bright, clear water and noticed a man under the falls showering in bathing trunks. I didn't know how he could stand how cold it was. Melting snow from the mountains fed this stream.

"Father Brody, good morning!" Dominic called out. "Would you like to join us in some fresh trout or bass?"

"Love to, Dominick, just let me finish here."

This place enchanted me. How I'd love for this to be my own private place. Clean-cut holes a foot in diameter and two to three feet deep created a pattern on the white lime rock edges of the stream.

"What are these holes in the rock?" I asked Uncle.

"Old Indian tribes dug those out. When the spring waters would swell, then recede, all sorts of shell and fish life would remain in those holes for the Indians to eat. Pretty smart, eh? They must have been Italian Indians."

I didn't get the humor but found some freshwater lobster and a small trout in the holes. I presented them to Aunt Maggie, who was building a fire by the stream. The men started to catch one fish after another. A man named Freddie Scarfone seemed to have the best knack. He was later to become an associate in Uncle's business.

The water was so clear, we could see hundreds of trout stemming the tide. The sight of a huge black bass would stir the blood in a fisherman's veins. When I realized I wasn't allowed to fish, I became angry, then bored, and I wandered away. I found a pile of rocks downstream leading to a path on the other side of the stream, so I walked over into the thicket. I ended up stumbling on three caves, where I found arrowheads, flint rock, and old pottery. I rushed back to show them to Tom.

"Hey, Giovanni, where did you find these? This is what these archaeologists look for. I bet they're worth a lot of money."

"You'd better put them back," Dominick said. "The Indians around here don't like anyone taking these things."

I thought he was just being mean, so I kept them. Actually, he didn't want anyone discovering his liquor-in-transit hideout. By this time, the women were cooking the fish in black iron frying pans with pure salted butter. We had a feast by the edge of God's country. It was the first appetite I'd had in weeks, and everything tasted so good.

Tom and Nettie headed home the next morning, and I was sad. As we walked to the car to bid them good-bye, I heard Dominic tell Tom, "Tell John all is under control. The kids may be a little homesick, but they're getting over it."

I ran to hug Tom. "Take me with you. I don't like it here. Please."

"I talked to Dominic. He's in charge. He said you must stay the rest of the summer."

*****

The day finally arrived to return home. I was so excited I couldn't breathe.

"Well, you'll be older and stronger next year. We have a lot of work for you. See you then," Uncle said.

My spine tingled. *Wait until Pop hears about my summer.*

The trip home was just as thrilling as the one upstate, plus a bonus: I was heading home. I thought about Mom, Pop, Frank, Dick, Mr. Costello, my music. I didn't sleep all night just like last time. Mom was waiting on the platform when we pulled into Grand Central Terminal the next day.

"Where's Pop?" I asked.

"He wasn't feeling well. Don't worry, he's all right."

On the subway home, I chattered about my sorrowful time with Dominick.

"I hope you showed your uncle respect," Mom said.

I kept quiet the rest of the way, just like Maria. We found Pop working his fool head off at the machine. He didn't hear us enter because of the noise. I wondered how the neighbors tolerated it, but somehow everyone in those days pulled together. They understood survival was a group effort.

Pop sensed us and bounced off his chair to hug Maria and me for a long time. When I saw his joy, I decided to keep my misery to myself.

Later, Pop sat me down to run down my tentative schedule. The highlight of my career was at hand. I had everything going for me. Child prodigies were in vogue, and the mayor of New York City was on my side. I also had Mr. Costello, a cardinal, an uncle who knew show business inside and out, and of course, Uncle

Frank, a powerhouse in the political community.

*****

Cousin Tony, Frank's black sheep son, always was in trouble. When he was thirteen and weighed two hundred fifty pounds, he hung a teacher by the back of his jacket in the closet and took his car keys for a joyride until the cops caught him. Needless to say, it was difficult for Frank to explain his son's actions, but he got him off the hook. Tony favored his Ukrainian mother with blond hair and blue eyes. I liked him, but he didn't want to truck with a younger kid like me.

During one holiday party at our house, Tony busted in full of coal dust. Behind him was a bull. "Frank, the Philly police handed him over to us. He was caught riding the railroad on an open coal car. I knew he was your kid, so I handled it before it went on the blotter."

Frank was furious, not over what Tony had done, but because he didn't want to owe this particular cop a favor, I later found out.

"Too bad he's your kid," Costello said. "I could use a Turk with his balls."

They laughed as Tony asked Mom if she had anything to eat. The men took out their instruments, just like Christmas. Dick played the meanest banjo, and I told him so.

"Did you ever hear Eddie Peabody play?" he asked.

"No."

"When you hear him, you'll know why I don't do this as a profession. He makes me sound like I'm in slow motion."

To top off the day, my cousin, Paul, came over, after the dinner Mom would allow friends to visit. My friends loved teasing him. He just had that kind of face and attitude. They would corner him in the hallway and make him feel uneasy. We didn't know it then, but Paul was some kind of genius, inherited from his inventor father.

"Hey, you guys, I just made a parachute. Want to try it out?"

"Where are we going to get an airplane to jump out of, stupid?"

Herman said.

"You don't need a plane with the way I designed it."

"I'll try it out," I said.

The next thing I knew, we were on the garage roof in view from our back kitchen window. From the kitchen window, you couldn't see the ground in front of the garage. If anyone fell from the roof, the viewer couldn't see him hit the ground.

Cousin Paul tested the wind by wetting his finger and holding it up. I had a black sack on my back. The parachute was made from an old umbrella and clothesline cord. I glanced back and saw Pop observing us. We waved at each other. I climbed on the ledge and jumped when Paul signaled me. Pop's last view of me was pulling the makeshift ripcord and plunging to the ground. Of course, the chute didn't open, and I hit concrete.

I was really hurting when I looked up at Pop's green complexion. He had run down the stairs, the worst thing he could do in his condition. The men, including Mr. Costello, followed Pop.

"I'm okay, just testing Paul's new invention, a low altitude chute," I said, shaking the bells out of my head while flat on my back. "The wind wasn't strong enough."

"Yeah, we have to find a higher place with more wind," Paul said.

Frank gave a clout off the back of Paul's head with his knuckles. Paul ran down the street dragging the chute and screaming, "Ma, Ma, Ma!" The men helped Pop by the elbows up the stairs. I had to answer to Mom.

*****

I did find a way to ease my stress. We bought a kite shaped like an owl for a penny. I asked Mom for a spool of her toughest black sewing thread. Tony and I attached a tail for balance and took it to Triborough Bridge. The kite flew so far that it looked like a dot on a typewriter. Could anyone imagine such pleasure for a penny?

Tony mentioned his ambitions of being in show business. He

told me he was going to march in a parade for Mayor LaGuardia and pulled out a piece of folded paper. I opened it and saw lyrics with the heading, "Marching Along Together." Tony sang the march and waited for my reaction. I could see this was important to him. He had a great voice. It was easy for me to boost his enthusiasm by praising him.

"Tony, this is great for a march, and I like the message it brings to us, about doing things together for the good of society. What a wonderful man La Guardia is. He loves people. His fight to upgrade the poor is relentless. He is admired for his accomplishments for the poor. It appears he chose Astoria as a role model."

Of course, it did cross my mind that Frank lived in Astoria and had contributed so much to the success of the mayoral election. In fact, Frank's effort was a political masterpiece. I was sure choosing Astoria was partly for Frank. Besides, it was the perfect location over the 59th Street Bridge, minutes from the city. It offered what the mayor needed: white and blue collar supporters. Many industries had settled across the bridge at Queens Plaza because of the geography, and for the plums the mayor offered to come to Astoria. Many old companies flourished through the years because Butch LaGuardia always gave them reasons to stay.

"You know, Tony, some canals will be built in the back with plans to connect into the ocean. And just past the bridge is a main freight junction that connects to all parts of the United States. This makes shipping less costly, and many of the large manufacturers are given railroad sidings into their property. Companies like Lofts Silver Cup, Ideal Toys, and many others."

The Little Flower also dedicated a community pool complex with acres of land and two pools. Olympic divers would perform for us. It was a long way from the tadpole-filled mud hole the previous mayor had offered us. This new LaGuardia facility had it all: lockers, dressing benches, and a foot disinfectant area before entering the pool.

THE SHADOW OF HIS SMILE

With the Triborough Bridge in place, industry deals were made, and new buildings were going up in Manhattan. We began to show signs of recovery, which could be credited to the little man they sometimes called Butch LaGuardia, a great administrator. I gazed at the river I'd grown so fond of, and each year would make my love affair with it stronger. It seemed to open my mind to see things more clearly.

"Giovanni, it's getting dark, and you know Mom, she'll let us have it if we're not home."

*****

Summer already was around the corner. I never dreamed I'd have to go upstate again. I became hysterical when I heard Mom and Pop planning to send Maria and I to Dominick. Hysteria didn't do me any good. Pop was not well enough to watch us for the summer, but Ninni would stay home again. Perhaps they felt we would have idle time filled with trouble.

The stay was even worse, for I was threatened every day because of the problems I caused the previous summer. This time, I picked cucumbers on Dominick's sharecropper farms, a backbreaking job.

With the Depression, it seemed Dominick was shylocking the farmers at his general store. Farmers would give up and come to the store with their deeds. Not being able to repay their loans, they lost their property. He couldn't care less if they all left. He had enough cash from store sales and bootlegging scotch during Prohibition to hold out while the farms gained equity.

A most unsettling day came On July 11, I spent the day envisioning Ninni singing and marching with LaGuardia for the opening of Triborough Bridge. I wished I could be there to cheer him on.

One day, it was nearly the end of our time at Uncle's when he got a long-distance call. I didn't know it was Pop until Dominick hung up.

"Well, I always thought your pop was nuts. Can you imagine

he called for money? Not a little money, a lot. He wants to open a grocery store. You know what I told him? I said, 'How can you go into business without money? How can anyone think money grows on trees?' To the back of the store, Giovanni, I have some tomatoes to be busheled. Huh, money, I'll give him money."

I couldn't help, even in my child's mind, analyzing; Pop sent him the money to come to this country, and to put him into business. My deep-rooted hate for him couldn't be described. Oh, how I detested him as my body ached throughout the summer, working from sun up to sun down with never a reward or kind word. I was upset, tired, confused, and prayed for all sorts of bad luck for him. This gave me no comfort or joy, though. I had no outlet for my despair. Maria and I never communicated, so I kept it all in. At thirteen, I swore I'd never see him again or accept any gifts. Dominick was dead to me. Dead.

I planned to tell Pop what I thought about him when I got back. I'd say he's a much better person than Dominick ever would be. That would make him feel good.

As we were about to board the train for home, I looked at Dominick with mature hate I know he recognized. He just snickered. For I was a child, what could I do? How could I hurt him?

He was wrong.

CHAPTER FOURTEEN

I was anxious on the trip home. We were returning earlier than planned because Pop was not feeling well, and somehow I felt he needed me after his phone call to Dominick. Once again, we arrived at a late hour. Much to my surprise, Tom was waiting for us. He was an early-to-bed man. I sensed something was wrong and clutched Maria's hand.

"Why isn't Mom or Pop here, Uncle Tom?"

For the first time, Tom didn't look into my eyes. "Well, Giovanni, look, your pop has taken a bad turn, and your mom asked me to pick you up. Now don't worry, he's had attacks before. He told me to make sure I told you not to worry."

"He must be pretty sick if Mom couldn't come."

"I won't lie to you, he's pretty sick, but as you know, he's been pretty sick before."

I quietly sobbed all the way home. Even as a child, I had an uncanny intuition. When we arrived home, I ran up the stairs. Most of our close relatives were there, which verified my suspicions. I ran into Mom's arms and noticed her eyes were red and puffy.

"Mom, Mom, can I see Pop? I want to see Pop."

"Yes, Giovanni, but you must be very quiet and not excite him. The doctor said he needs complete rest."

"I'll be quiet, Mom, I promise. I just want to see him."

I walked into his bedroom adjoining the front living room, divided by draw drapes that Mom had made. The religious candle flickered and the light danced on his pale complexion as he breathed heavily. He struggled to turn toward me and propped his right hand under his face for support. His mouth quivered into a faint smile. He was so weak he only could hold it a second or two.

"Hello, Giovanni, it's good to see you."

"It's good to see you too, Pop," I said, sobbing. "I missed you very much."

"I missed you very much too."

"Gee, Pop, you look good. Pretty soon you'll be out of this bed, huh?"

"Yes, pretty soon, Giovanni. Listen to me, let's just say if something happens to me, just for instance, you'll be the man in the family, and you'll be responsible for everybody."

"Yes, I know, Pop, but nothing is going to happen to you, nothing. I love you. We all love you, and you're going to be fine."

"I like the way you're talking. I think you're a man now, so I don't really have to worry. You've been such a good boy. I want you to know I'm proud of you."

Someone grabbed my shoulders. "That's enough for now, Giovanni, he must rest. He needs all the energy he can get."

As I knelt down to kiss him, my nostrils sensed the same odor Nonna had when I kissed her good-bye. I never could forget the odor, death. I swallowed my sobs so Pop wouldn't see my anguish and left the room looking back helplessly. *Pop won't die. He won't leave me. He loves me and knows how much I need him.* We sat in the kitchen for what seemed like hours. *Pop can't leave. He knows I'm not old enough to look after the family. Maybe I'll read the newspaper to Ninni, like Pop had done with me.*

"Ninni, would you like me to read the newspaper to you?"

"Oh, yes, Giovanni."

"Well, it appears we're in the middle of an election year. Roosevelt is running for presidential re-election. It says here, 'The president has moved Congress to agree to finally pay out the World War I bonuses to our soldiers, as much as $1,000, according to the amount of time they served and if they served in action overseas. The soldiers also will finally receive hospital and disability benefits, along with civil service preference at all levels of government. This is a monumental achievement for Roosevelt, given the tumultuous history of these bonuses for a war that ended seventeen years ago.'"

Mom ran out of Pop's room. "Frank, call an ambulance right away! I'm afraid he's giving up. Hurry, his breathing is like the last, and he stops for long intervals."

Frank ran out of the door, and an ambulance showed up shortly with lights flashing. Two attendants rushed up with a stretcher. In those days, they didn't carry equipment into the house. They covered Pop with a white sheet, and he kept his eyes closed and mouth open gasping for oxygen. I followed them down the stairs with the rest of the family and watched them slide him into the ambulance.

"What are you looking at?" I screamed at the crowd of curious neighbors who had gathered.

Frank clutched me. "Easy, Giovanni, at least he'll have the professional help he needs now more than anything."

This didn't comfort me. I hated everyone and everything. *This is Dominick's fault. I hope God takes him instead of Pop.* Mom and Frank followed the ambulance in his car, and everyone else stayed behind. For the first time, Maria was emotional. She cried and hugged Ninni, who had just turned ten four days before.

When Frank and Mom returned, they looked solemn.

"I don't know, it doesn't look good for John," Frank said, removing his hat. "They shoved a whole bunch of rubber tubes down his windpipe so they could drain his lungs. His heart is swelling, and they don't know how to correct it. If they had a medicine to bring down the swelling when these attacks happen, he would live to be a hundred, according to Dr. Fienberg, the heart specialist. So, they must try to suck the water out mechanically, which strains the heart. It's one of those damned-if-you-do or damned-if-you-don't situations."

Frank rubbed his chin with the back of his hand and looked at Mom. "You know, Ann, you must be prepared for the worst. With you going back and forth to the hospital, I think we should split the children among us until the crisis is over one way or the other."

I hoped this was a horrible dream that I'd wake up from. But then Aunt Millie volunteered to take me.

I didn't like her. She made me feel uncomfortable. I liked her daughter, Kitty, though, and I didn't mind her husband, Albert. He was an Italian immigrant, a rare one with a college education in art design. He owned a factory that made embroidery and appliqué for fancy dress lines. I recalled Uncle Frank saying he would do very well, for the Jews in the garment center farmed a lot of the dress work out to him. He got his financial start from my mother's sister, Mary, in the form of a dowry for marrying Millie. It was a hell of an opportunity for the family to marry her off because she was strange — beautiful, but strange, or nutty, as Albert aptly described her. I was to find out she had a vicious side too.

Their home was elegant for those times with centralized heat and furniture imported from all over the world. A Steinway baby grand sat proudly in the living room. Kitty was taking lessons. Millie figured Kitty would be part of my act someday, so she wanted me there so we could practice my arias together. Al was very private. He only seemed to tolerate his eccentric wife. After all, she was a beauty and could cook.

After Millie requested I sing while Kitty played the piano, I decided I'd find an excuse not to visit when this part of my life was over. Kitty had no sense of music. She played clumsily and mechanically, but she satisfied party guests who didn't know one note from another. I could just hear them saying to Millie, "My, what a talented daughter you have, and he sings good too." She had one of those private teachers who retained students by calling them geniuses.

I awoke late one morning around eleven o'clock and walked

down the wall-to-wall beige carpeted stairs. I could overhear Millie's voice quivering on the phone. She was wiping her eyes with a hanky. She put down the receiver, turned slowly, and noticed me on the stairs.

"You! You killed your father!" she yelled, pointing a finger at me. "Do you hear me, Giovanni? You killed him! He just died."

The blood rushed to my head, and my nose burst with blood as I screamed. I don't know how I managed to squeeze by her, for she was in front of the door. I ran. *Pop was   dead! He was gone. Why did she say I killed him? Maybe I did and didn't know how or why.* It started to rain, cold as ice on my body. I found a basement entrance to a stone house. A wrought-iron gate led to an apartment. I guess I just wanted to hide. She disturbed me so much that I didn't even think Mom needed me. I spent the whole night there crying. I didn't realize my family would call the police.

Early in the morning, I crawled out and looked around as though I were criminal. I was despondent and out of it. *Aunt Millie said I killed my Pop.* I staggered down the street, tired, wet, and cold. I wanted to die. I didn't get more than a block when a police car pulled over, hauled me into the car, and took me home.

"Is this your son, Mrs. Benedetto?"

"That's him."

"His Uncle Frank told us to bring him home if we found him."

I was sure I was going to get it. Mom looked at me in anger. "I'll take care of you later. I don't have time to find out why you did such a foolish thing. Your aunt told me she held you in her arms to tell you about your father, and you just hit her and ran. Is this any way to thank her for taking care of you?"

I couldn't believe it or understand. I felt paralyzed. I didn't have the sense of thinking my word against hers. I was like stone. I couldn't even answer.

I sat in a dark corner as visitors entered the house, thinking Pop wasn't really dead. He just wouldn't do that to me. I'll bet he just took a trip and he'll walk back through the door someday. What a wonderful day that would be.

The body hadn't arrived from the mortuary yet. The Moriscos were handling the funeral, as they did for the rest of the family. Uncle Frank took charge, as usual.

Mom was taking it as hard as expected. She loved him with a loyalty that rarely exists in our society anymore. She was almost twenty when the family arranged their wedding. She hadn't met Pop, although they were first cousins. Mom dressed in black from head to toe. With all of the deaths in our family, all she had to do was reach into the closet for her mourning clothes. She didn't even have to take in a seam.

I was tired, nervous, and Millie's voice still rang in my ear. I couldn't escape it, although I tried various ways to purge her hurt. It was to be a very long time, if at all, before I would get over it.

By this time, I was an old hand at the aspects of funerals. The familiar sick smell of flowers smothered the apartment, due to the competitive spirit of some of Pop's friends trying to outdo one another with oversize floral arrangements. The fancy coffin waiting for his body, fluffed in white, puffy satin material, and a kneeling board for visitors to pray beside the body. It all threw me back to Nonna's funeral, which further depressed me. The sadness was too much for a child to handle.

The body finally arrived. Mom flew into hysteria as her sisters comforted her and brought her glasses of water. I couldn't stand seeing Mom, the full strength of our family, so typically human, feminine. I realized I loved her very much, not the way I loved Pop, different.

Similar remarks from Nonna's funeral arose. "John looks so natural. They did such a good job on him. He looks well at rest. He doesn't have to suffer any longer." And they wore the same serious expressions, even the jokers. It was like a recurring nightmare.

Frank knelt over me in the corner, "The time has come for you to see your father. You must do it like a man, Giovanni. Come with me, I'll go with you."

He led me by the hand through the rooms to the casket in the front parlor. All of the theatrical weepers increased their wailing, remarking how sad it was I didn't have a father. I started to choke. Frank gripped my hand and looked down at me with a strength to steady me. At the coffin, I looked at the unnatural hulk, falsely made up with rouge, powder, and lipstick. It only assured me this was not Pop. *He would come to the door someday.* My eyes shifted to his crossed hands, bound with an ornate string of rosary beads, the crucifix between his knuckles. *This is a wax replica of Pop. He wouldn't do this to me.*

Millie walked over weeping and tried to put her arms around me. A cold sweat encased my body. "Don't touch me! Don't ever touch me! You lied to me. I don't ever want you to talk to me again."

"It's all right, Millie," Frank said. "He's distraught, he'll get over it."

"I don't understand. I was so good to him while his father was in the hospital, right until the minute he died. I guess that's what I get for being nice."

I raged into the deepest mania. I think if I'd had a weapon, I would have killed her. She was a witch, the devil's ambassador sent to harm me. Mom and I must stay away from her. "Get her out of here! Look at her she's evil! Won't someone listen to me? I don't want her here." I pushed her toward the door.

"Go to your room, Giovanni," Frank said. "You'll settle down and apologize to your aunt."

"I won't. I hate her! I'll never apologize."

I peered around the room, and everyone's expressions were as insane as my aunt's: looks of pity for my reaction to Pop's death. None of them knew she'd accused me of his death. I know now she was mentally sick. Proof came in time and my hate turned to pity, and I wondered what made her the way she was.

Mom entered the room, and I ran into her arms. She held me tightly for the first time. "I know how much you loved your father,

I know, Giovanni. You'll come to accept his death. You'll always miss him, but we all have to die, some before others."

Frank told Mom he had to take care of some business and he was leaving his son, Tony, behind to help. As soon as Frank left, an ambulance pulled up. Tony stretched an arm across the door, his wide body blocking the two attendants carrying a stretcher. "What do you guys want?"

"We have an order to pick up the corpse for a special autopsy."

Mom arrived at the door in time to hear the remark. She flew into a shocking frenzy of screams. It was amazing how Tony took control. "The only body going on that stretcher you're carrying is yours if you take one more step. We're having a funeral here. The body is already in the coffin, so beat it if you know what's good for you."

"Don't you understand? We have an official order from the city coroner's office. If you don't want to get into trouble, you'll move over and let us do our job."

"Maybe you don't hear good. One more step, and I'll cold-cock the two of you. Do you understand?"

Fear spread on the attendant's face, even though he was at least ten years older than Tony.

"Well, I'll have to go get a cop."

"Do that. Don't forget to tell him if he crosses this door, he'll be in the stretcher, cop or no cop."

The attendant turned to his coworker. "This is a new one on me. I've never had anyone defy a city coroner's order."

Tony's face tightened. "You never ran into me before, either. If you have a family, I suggest you retire from this job. You may run into me again. Next time, I won't be this nice."

They left as I beamed at my new hero. Cousin Tony was neat, tough, and my friend.

When Frank returned, Mom told him how Tony had handled the situation. She was worried they would return.

"Don't worry, Ann, I'll handle it right now. Just let me get to the phone."

I followed Frank to the phone. Evidently, he knew the head corner at the mortuary.

"Abe, what in the hell is going on?" Frank said. "Two of your goons came to my brother-in-law's funeral. They tried to yank his body, even though it had been embalmed."

Frank listened to his answer, then said, "Well, I'm not asking you, you son of a bitch. I'm telling you to kill the order. That was my son who stopped your men. He's all of fourteen, so imagine if one of us grown-ups gets involved." Frank listened again. "Okay, Abe, that's good enough for me. If I have your word, that's good enough. Remember who got you your appointment. I don't want these people having any more stress. They have enough to contend with."

Frank hung up and turned to Mom. "Don't worry, Ann, they wouldn't bother you again."

Mom forced the faintest smile. "It's good having a brother like you around, Frank. Thank you."

One of my bleakest moments came when Dominick arrived. His wife had stayed at home. He walked right up to the coffin and stared with his blunt, smoked-down cigar in his mouth while chewing it vigorously. He didn't kneel. He didn't close his eyes in prayer. He just stared at his brother. He turned and walked around the circle of seated relatives to shake their hands.

"Ann, I want to talk to you about something important," he said when he got to Mom.

Pop said I'm the responsible man of the house. "If you want to talk to Mom, then I'll sit with her," I said.

"That's okay. What I have to say is mostly concerning you, anyway."

The three of us retreated to my room and sat on the bed. I could tell this was a sell. Dominick was going to sell his head off.

"Now, Ann, as you know, we haven't been fortunate. We never had a child. I've done very well, and I could give Giovanni here all the education he could ever dream about. And don't forget someday all of the business will belong to him."

"Are you asking me to give you my son?" Mom asked with saddened eyes. "If so, this is out of the question. First of all, he's so deeply involved in a career here; he's at the threshold of stardom. No, your request is impossible."

"Well, you know, Ann, you're going to find it very hard watching three children, and the fact is, I don't want a girl. With Maria being the oldest, she'll watch Giovanni, so give me Ninni. Give him to me, and you'll never be sorry, I promise. He'll have everything a boy could desire."

Mom walked slowly to the portrait of Christ on the wall in front of the bed. She gazed at it for a time, then turned around. "We'll try it for a short time."

"No, no, Mom! Don't send Ninni away. Don't do it," I screamed.

"I know how you feel, Giovanni, but he's right. I have to work, and I promise it'll only be a trial. If I see it's not working out, I'll bring your brother back."

"You're young, Giovanni, and don't realize what your mamma has to go through," Dominick said. "You'll learn."

*****

The sound of Tony crying brings me back to the present. Even though he's never forgotten the resentment of being given away, he loved Mom deeply and took good care of her to the best of his ability.

Staring into his steel-gray eyes I can hear Pop saying, "Don't hit your brother so hard. See how frail he is? Remember, you'll be the man of the family soon. This means he'll be your responsibility, no matter your ages."

All I had to do was hear Pop's voice telling me how things had to be. It was law to me.

As I look deeper into Tony's eyes I remember how very thin and undernourished Ninni looked, though he was far from it. He ate like a horse and was very strong. I would never tell him this, in case he might fight back. As we grew older, we became closer and closer, bonding deeply. It was wonderful gaining confidence in each other's purpose. I would always take care of Ninni and believed he would always back me up, as I drifted from his eyes to Dominick's.

*****

Dominick didn't even stay for the funeral and gave a lame excuse about some business he had to take care of. I surmised later, that he wanted to leave before Mom had a chance to change her mind. At least one decent thing came out of it: Ninni didn't see the burial.

The Strega, Cousin Paul's mother, was at her peak as the lead player. She wailed stories about Pop from his childhood to the day of his death, inducing everyone in a trance. The worst part was her effect on Mom. Things were tough enough without her performance.

The last day of the wake, Mr. Costello showed up wearing a black band in respect of the mourning. He embraced me. "Giovanni, you must be brave. Now you're the man in the family. You are now responsible for the family. I know how you feel. Your pop was one of a kind, and I know you'll miss him. We'll all miss him very much. He was always a comfort. You know, I never told you, but if I ever had to make a moral judgment, I would meet with your father. And it's funny he never gave anyone the answer to anything. Somehow, he made you think for yourself."

I rested my head against his side and sobbed.

"It's all right, Giovanni. We men must cry at times. It's not unmanly. Get it all out of your system. Life is far from over for you, and your father is depending on you to take care of things. And you know something, Giovanni? He couldn't have made a better choice, believe me."

His words meant much to me in my sorrow. We sat together for a long time in silence. He knew he had made his point. I know

now he was a wise man.

On the day of the burial, the first two people I noticed that bleak morning were Rose and Cosmo. They finally had married. Rose gave into Cosmo's endless pleadings, even though they were first cousins. I knew Pop had much to do with it. He seemed to have touched so many lives. Cosmo was a nice man. He shook my hand in a most gentle manner.

Rose looked down at me and started to cry. "Oh, how I loved that man. He was so good."

"He loved you and Cosmo too. After all, you are his sister's child, his niece."

"My, Giovanni, you are all grown up, aren't you?"

Yes, I was. I had been through a lifetime in my youth.

It was a clear day at the burial site. The air smelled fresh while the priest gave his eulogy. No one raised a head until he finished. Then the performer, Strega Chico, attempted to jump into the grave. Uncles Dick and Jim stopped her as she screamed like a deranged person. Mom was wiped out and she stood stunned. Maria just cried, not knowing what was to come next. I took her hand as everyone filed away. All was quiet, astoundingly quiet.

After we arrived home in the limos, Mom's sisters started cooking spaghetti and sausage. Everyone ate heartily, even Mom. Some of the family broke the mood by making fun of some of the incidents during the funeral. I learned you always can find something to laugh about, even in deep tragedy, but I couldn't join the fun. I still didn't accept Pop's death, and it was a long time before I did.

It's strange how I recalled things I hadn't paid much attention to. Pop always hugged and kissed me good-bye when I left for a trip with the Met.

"You are close to being a man now, Giovanni, we don't have to do this anymore," Pop had said while hugging me before my last trip to Philadelphia.

I didn't think anything of it then, but now I know he was

preparing me for the task after he died. He knew the time was near. However, in my grief, I couldn't help but think he had cheated me.

In my heart I was certain nothing is forever and we all must face change.

CHAPTER FIFTEEN

Mrs. Quinlan arrived early one Saturday morning, waving a telegram with a big smile.

"This is it, believe me, Giovanni. You've been accepted to do the Al Jolson *Shell Châteaux* program on NBC. Do you realize what this means? Coast-to-coast hookup on national broadcasting."

We were stunned, especially Mom. "Wow, the big time! Giovanni, this will establish you once and for all. Do you know how big Al Jolson is?"

Excited, I asked all sorts of questions: Did they have a big band? What songs would I sing?

"All I know at the moment is the acceptance telegram," Mrs. Quinlan said. "This is as good as a contract. The money is good, and as soon as I hear more, you'll be the first to know."

My rehearsal was at the NBC 8H studio, the largest auditorium in the new Rockefeller Center, home of the National Broadcasting Company. Mr. Parado walked me in, and we met Art Jarrett, a socialite bandleader married to Eleanor Holm, the Olympic swimmer who was on the bill with me in this show.

The highlight was seeing my friend, Toto, the contortionist clown, again. He squeezed into a tiny taxi with eight dogs, fifteen balloons, and three suitcases. He captured me even without his clown makeup. I was disappointed Mr. Jolson was not there. He'd always been my idol. He had an aura with show people and was magnetic with audiences.

"La donna è mobile" from *Rigoletto* was chosen for the show the following night, and the thirty-piece band loaded with brass gave me a new high. I was handed some talking lines, including corny jokes. Ninni was so excited; he imitated Jolson all the time.

I was pleased Tom took me to the show because he was a great confidence builder and enjoyed being around celebrities. When we arrived backstage, I peeked at the vast audience from the wings. Mr. Parado was in his glory, for he was to lead the orchestra from the piano while Art Jarrett sat it out. Mrs. Quinlan arranged for the performance to be recorded on an aluminum disk.

I was getting stage fever. By this time, each stint seemed like the big one, and the adrenaline surged every time. We got news Al Jolson had fallen ill, and his replacement was one of the most prestigious acts on the stage and screen: the great actor and comic, Joe Cook. Even though he had incredible credentials, I was disappointed.

My anxiety built as I watched each act. For the first time, I worried I might forget my lines, until I heard my queue and walked on dazed. My heart was pounding down to my kidneys, but I started to calm down once I got into my lines. I went into my aria and finished before I even realized it, feeling the burst of applause. I took my bows, forgetting this was radio with a tight schedule, until they gently walked me off stage. I should have been embarrassed but didn't know better.

Mrs. Quinlan hugged and kissed me in the wings. "Bravo, bravo, Giovanni! It couldn't have been done any better. I'm so proud of you."

It was already past ten o'clock, and I was starving because I never ate before concerts. So Mrs. Quinlan took us to The St. Regis hotel for dinner.

"Boy, this is some fancy place," Tom said.

The maître d' seated us, and we were introduced to escargot. It was fun pulling the snails out of the shells.

"Giovanni, I have another surprise. While you were singing, I got a call from Vincent Lopez. He wants you to do a one-nighter in the Astor Grill Room with him."

The Astor was *the* place, and the Grill Room was the top of the mountain in show business.

"When?"

"Two days from now. You don't need to rehearse, because we have the charts of the aria you did tonight, and most of the boys in the studio band are in the Lopez band. It's a publicity stunt. You'll be in the audience as though a guest and will be called upon to do a number — a surprise guest artist. All of the biggest news men will be in, so the write-ups will follow."

The memory of that fulfilling night is as vivid today as that very night.

I hadn't worked a classy supper club before, so Dick clued me in on the differences between concerts and nightclubs. He said nightclubs are difficult to gain the audience's attention because people are eating and drinking. He told me to eyeball the audience first until I got their attention.

Tom and I entered the Astor's renowned show room and were seated where Lopez could see us. I heard a drum roll, and there was Vincent Lopez. He got everyone's attention pretty much as Dick had advised me. I felt more at ease.

"Ladies and gentlemen, we have an honored surprise guest in the audience who just finished a stint on Al Jolson's NBC *Shell Château* program," Lopez announced. "None other than our own Giovanni, known to us as the Little Caruso."

I learned the clout of coast-to-coast radio by the amazing reception. The performance went as planned, and the applause was better than expected. Walter Winchell, Ed Sullivan, Ed Zeltner, and Earl Wilson all picked it up. Much to my surprise, my manager handed me a three hundred dollar check, which was like thirty thousand to us. Mom almost fainted when I gave it to her. We had to get her a glass of water.

"We're going to invite all of the family for a dinner," Mom

said. "This is an occasion. It looks like you made it, Giovanni."

We had a real feast. All of the people I loved came to toast my success: my uncles, their wives, their children and Mr. Costello.

"Giovanni, I'm so proud of you and want you to know better things are coming," Mr. Costello said. "By the way, I want you to do me a favor. We're having the feast of San Juliana this Sunday. We raise all kinds of money for the underprivileged children of Italy. It's a charity, meaning no pay, but I'd like to depend on you to contribute your talent for an hour or so."

"I'd consider it an honor, Mr. Costello."

"Frank, did you hear that? He has your Midas touch for politics already. He said he'd be 'honored.' I like that kind of class, thirteen years old." Uncle Frank's smile bloomed. "You know, Frank, this is a crazy world. It seems LaGuardia is going to appoint Dewey as special prosecutor, and guess whose neck they're after?"

"I know all about it, Costello. No one will ever get your neck. However, Dewey is good, and he may cause you some discomfort before he's through."

"It's ironic, I save his life by stopping the crazy Jew from hitting him, and his way of thanking is trying to knock me off. If he were smart, he'd make sure I'm in the street if he wants to stay alive."

"Tom is very aware of that, and I must agree he's not showing good judgment, but you must understand he is a staunch right-winger. They have no cause other than what they consider Americanism, and according to them, Mafioso is un-American."

"Yeah, if I'm un-American, how come I create all these jobs, how come I elected a mayor, and how come the government calls me as a special consultant when they have a serious street problem?"

"I can tell you this, they're very upset about the new organization the Jew put together, the assassins group they call Murder Incorporated. They feel this organization may not stop business, but may be used to knock off political rivals."

"What? Are they crazy? They know I'd never stand for that."

"No, Costello, listen to me. They're not crazy, but they know Lepke's crazy, and the fact he's a Jew doesn't hold nicely to Dewey."

"My organization is growing in leaps and bounds. Before you know it, we'll be mostly legit, Frank. If they're smart, they'd let life take its course, and at some point, the problems will just go away."

"Be realistic, Costello. They know you won't live forever, and your philosophy may not be picked up. They're afraid of the unrest among the young Turks. You've seen some of the problems with them already. They want to move in on the whole ball of wax, including dope."

"Not as long as I'm alive, Frank."

"That's precisely my point, *compare*, as long as you're alive. In the meantime, stay on your toes. Don't ever do any of your own work anymore. You've grown beyond that."

"Frank, you know I always listen to you, but the party's getting rough. I'm being challenged every day by the young punks. They say I've grown soft with success. You know I really haven't. If I had to take the front tomorrow, I'd kill all of them with my bare hands and not feel one ounce of guilt. They don't understand my purpose. Without purpose, I never could've gone this far, and neither could they. If it were just for the money or power without purpose, everyone would lose. Enough of this, Frank, let's have a party."

Later in the afternoon my friends came into the festivity. Mom allowed me to invite them after we ate. Mr. Costello, laughingly said, "Oh look here, the angel, the devil, and St. Francis. What a ball team."

Mr. Costello came to me with Uncle Frank. "Giovanni, I fear you've outgrown Mr. Parado as a teacher. I'm going to find you a superior instructor."

Pop's death had changed my life. For one thing, my

performances felt robotic. No one noticed, but the thrill of being an artist and performing was mostly gone. I didn't lose the joy of listening, however. Chords still gave me a high and cured my headaches.

I realized no one invited me to a party unless they wanted me to perform. I guess I didn't have a lot of friends. I sunk into a long depression.

Mr. Castillo kept his word. He sent up an appointment for me with Mr. La Puma uptown on Riverside Drive near the musical art college. I rang the doorbell, and a short, elderly, rotund man appeared.

"Come in, Giovanni, you're right on time, a rarity among artists today."

He took me to a bright room with pictures of Caruso, Volpi, Gigli, Schipa, Pinza, and scads of others, all signed with warm regards to Giuseppe La Puma. "You like the collection of my friends, eh?"

"Oh, yes, they're all my favorite opera singers."

"You have good taste for a boy your age."

"I hope someday I could be half as good as they are."

"You know, Giovanni, greatness is more than the instrument God gave you. I was the baritone lead for Caruso for years. Apart from his wonderful voice, his greatness was in his character. I think I would've worked for nothing just to observe his audacity. He was a charming devil. He would do things that would get any singer thrown in the street, but he did it with a Caruso touch. That made it acceptable, and this made him the envy of artists. Many artists tried to copy his antics and lost careers before they ever started.

"I recall once in South America; he didn't like the theater manager. We were doing *Aida*. Caruso, to get even with the manager for mistreating the troupe, tied all of the scenery together. When the curtain went up, scenery was floating all over the stage. We laughed so hard the opera never went on, and the promoters didn't pay us. But Caruso paid us out of his own pocket."

I liked this man instantly. Initially I was concerned about leaving Mr. Prado, who had been coaching me for a long time. I now realized that change is inevitable if one is to grow. Mr. La Puma was exactly what I needed at this time.

"Come, let's go to the piano so I can see what I've got with you. Mr. Costello tells me you are quite a *cantatore*. We shall see." His pudgy fingers touched the keyboard mid-scale. "Let's test for range. We'll go down the scale first to loosen you up."

He turned to me when we finished. "You have a phenomenal range, three and a half octaves, yet no falsetto, and it's a mature, pure voice. I don't normally work with minors, but your voice is far from a child's. Very interesting, Giovanni. We're going to have a lot of fun working together."

*****

I hear a distant voice and feel someone poking my shoulder. "Uncle John, Uncle John, are you all right?"

It's Maria's adopted son, Tommy. I always loved him as my own.

"Uncle Tony asked me to come get you. He wants to talk to you."

I walk to a small room at the funeral parlor in a daze, and Tony is sitting alone, depressed.

"Where's your wife? I haven't seen her for a while."

"I had the driver take her back to the hotel. This kind of thing is not her bag, John."

"Well, Tony, it's not anybody's bag really. This ritual is so unnatural. The body on display is so pagan like to me. When I die, I want to be cremated and have my ashes scattered in the East River by the Tinsdale Lumberyard where Pop would take us swimming. Remember?"

Tony looks at me. "I don't remember Pop."

This is a clue he's harboring resentment. He was old enough to remember Pop in every way, but I don't challenge him. I ponder, *does he know I became a martyr to save his skin? Does he know the more successful he became, the more difficult it was for me?*

I close my eyes as though beckoning the past. As much as I loved Mom, I close my eyes tighter and tighter for an escape from this unbearable ritual.

*****

La Puma poked my chin. "Relax the bottom jaw, loose, loose, and, Giovanni, learn to breathe. If you breathe properly and get your voice placement correctly, you'll be able to sustain a singing note forever. Let me explain. First of all, you place your voice tones to the roof of your mouth. Get your voice out of your throat." He rammed his fingernail at the roof of my mouth. "This is where you want to direct your voice from. Now, Giovanni, I want you to breathe in slowly."

He placed his hand on my diaphragm. "The diaphragm must come out as you breathe in. You're not on the beach showing your chest, you're breathing for as much air as you can hold. You see, Giovanni, apart from being able to hold notes at length, you'll have a reservoir. If you have the thought to change or create new phrasing, you'll have the ability, not needing to take frantic breaths in the wrong place. . . . My daughter, Giuseppina, will take you for an hour on solfeggio (sight reading). Then I'll take you on voice coaching."

"That may be too much money for Mom."

"Mr. Costello said he had arranged for Mayor LaGuardia's city program to take care of part of it, and the rest is on me. I owe Mr. Costello a favor, and it'll be my pleasure to pay it back this way. Don't tell him, but I would have taken you on as my student for nothing."

He renewed my confidence as I gazed at the masters on the wall. I couldn't wait to tell my brother about this.

Back at home, I busted through the door as Ninni was drawing a masterpiece at the table. I grabbed his arm. "Come, Ninni, let me show you what I learned today."

We ran through the railroad rooms to the front room. For most of the afternoon, I repeated word for word what La Puma had taught me. Ninni's attention was more than a signal of wanting to be involved. In fact, he picked it up in one afternoon.

Gee, I wish Pop were here. Ninni sings so much like him and better now. I couldn't believe the beautiful head tones coming from his mouth.

*****

The time had come to do the Steinway private concert. I found myself blasé, not eager. I didn't know it then, but I was heading for an early burnout.

Believe it or not, my formal attire and tails still fit. Mrs. Quinlan picked me up in her snappy Lincoln-Zephyr. Its midnight blue color looked black at night. The interior seemed like a much better place to live in than our low-rent apartment. I still was questioning why so few in the world were wealthy while so many people were poor.

As usual, entering the driveway and driving up to the house was as breathtaking as ever. I couldn't help but notice the awesome semblance of wealth in the form of concrete and expensive niceties in the furniture, silverware, and extravagant amount of space. The maid's quarters looked like mansions. I gazed at the grandiose chandelier in the front vestibule. All of these money jocks seemed in competition over their entrance chandeliers. I was brought to the performer's room.

"You must be our Little Caruso," a man said in a course tone.

We walked to the Steinway grand to get acquainted and do a run-through. I finished my first aria in falsetto, a usual practice for singers to save their throat for the performance. The accompanist paused with his hands on the keys and turned to me. "Give me a C, now give me an F sharp."

We went through this for ten minutes until he placed his hands on his knees. "You gave me all of these notes without a lead-in from me," he said in a heavy voice.

I smiled. "Yes, I know."

"Do you read?"

"Yes, I graduated from solfeggio at eleven."

He asked who was coaching me and looked impressed when I mentioned La Puma.

"My name is Lorenzo Capriccio."

I recognized the name. He had a fine reputation for working with the most renowned vocalists, such as Marian Anderson, who suffered at the hands of influential prejudiced people. Now, my second such experience with censorship of the arts. Although I didn't understand the reason I had been asked to change my music selection for the cardinal years earlier, it became more evident over time, people in high positions did have the power to allow or disallow an artist's work.

I felt secure with Mr. Capriccio as I performed my Italian arias and ended with one from *Lohengrin*. Everyone stood to applaud. I turned to my accompanist and addressed the audience. "Bravo, bravo, *al mio* maestro." (Praise to my teacher). The audience went wild for quite a while before I retreated to the performer's room to dry off.

"I owe you an apology, Giovanni," Lorenzo said. "I thought you were going to be just another fresh kid. But I must say, I found you professional. You are a well-schooled musician and a fine artist. I bow to you."

I blushed. "In all of my years, I've never had anyone play for me as you did, and I shall never forget this monumental event."

He extended his hand, then pointed at the door. "You know, part of the deal is to mingle with those people out there."

We strutted out in a most jovial manner. I'd made a friend. Everyone was telling us how they enjoyed our performance, and I'd hand them Mrs. Quinlan's card when they asked if I would do a concert for them.

A tall, handsome man, dressed immaculately, approached me. "My name is Henry Steinway, and I want to thank you for your great performance. It was most enjoyable."

"I thank you, sir. It was my pleasure, and your friends here seem to be very nice."

He chuckled quietly. "Giovanni, let's go out in the garden where two men can talk freely."

It seemed we talked for hours. He told me his family came from Germany, where they still had a factory. I told him about Pop and how Mom had struggled for years, working so hard to ensure we got the education we deserved.

When I got to Frank, he said, "Frank Suraci is your uncle? What a small world. I know him very well. Please give him my best regards. And oh, yes, please tell him I think of his kindness each and every day. Now, Giovanni, I must get back to my guests. I want you to know if you ever need anything or any favor from me, here is my private number where you can reach me most any time."

I thanked him with obvious affection, which I'm sure he noticed.

Mrs. Quinlan walked over, and I told her about handing several people her card. "You did a splendid job, Giovanni."

We chatted all the way home. As I climbed the stairs, a fast depression came over me. I knew Pop wouldn't be there, but I boosted my spirits by remembering our conversations. Mom was waiting for me in the kitchen.

"Mom, why don't you go to sleep when I'm at a concert? You have to get up so early, and you work so hard."

"Listen to him. Now he's telling his mama what to do."

She looked so tired, and I felt guilty.

"Good night, Mom, I'm going to bed."

"Good night, Giovanni."

When I got to my room, I thought about Pop again. Maybe I was missing him more than usual. I spent most of the night pondering his pearls of wisdom.

"Whenever you feel you're getting depressed, just think of

your mind as a mirror," he said once. "You know your mind reflects everything you think and feel. So if you think of one good thing each and every morning, you'll be a very happy man by the end of your life."

CHAPTER SIXTEEN

One more defeat was at hand following my fourteenth birthday. I was to headline a concert on Long Island. Mrs. Quinlan had been informed the Vanderbilts would be there. Any affair they attended was newsworthy, so we expected cameramen to take pictures for the society page. I was more equipped than ever from Mr. La Puma building my confidence. A compliment from him was worth ten curtain calls.

I felt kind of peculiar the evening of the concert, and I drank a glass of ice water just before it went on. This was not usually a good practice, but my throat felt dry and tight. I had gotten through more than half of my act when I cracked on the last note of the big one, "Celeste Aida." This didn't mar the performance, according to the audience reaction, but I felt I had failed for the first time. After the show and the usual compliments, the Vanderbilts came backstage to take pictures for the press.

Afterward, Mrs. Quinlan invited Mom and I out for a late dinner. I know Mom liked this, mostly because her life consisted of work and no pleasure. She couldn't afford the good life, and she wouldn't date.

"It must be very difficult for you, Ann, working and caring for the children," Mrs. Quinlan said. "I don't know how you do it."

"Let me give you the answer, Lillian: love and prayer. I pray a lot, and I believe in Jesus Christ. Something tells me he'll help in his infinite wisdom, to take care of all my children, as I love them dearly. They are my life."

"Ann, I've observed you for a long time. I envy your courage, your devotion, your tenacity. Maybe some of it will rub off on me. God bless you."

"I'm praying he does, Lillian."

I thought, *Mom loved me, she wanted me, and it made me feel so good.* I started to view her differently. What I had perceived as meanness started to shape into authority. Her commands began to take a different meaning. I thought back about her and Pop and started to see through her frustration. She must have felt cheated, knowing he was to die and having the responsibility of the breadwinner. Yet, her strength of conviction, her religion, and her vows made the sacrifice an act of love.

Her life was forged, and she was determined to give it the effort expected of her as a widowed mother. She was doing this and much more, more than she ever knew. Her capacity was that of a champion.

*****

Days became dark for my friend and benefactor, Mr. Costello, as Frank had anticipated. The energetic Dewey sharpened his ax and went hunting. Frank threw all things aside to protect his *compare*. When it finally came down, Frank only could get him off with a sacrificial lamb., someone to take the fall for him.

"It goes with the work, Costello. It's something we must accept. Think of all of the judges sentencing these guys, who cut money with them the day before."

"You're right, Frank. I just get tired once in a while. This has been a bitter fight. You know, I could have run. I have enough money to live anywhere, anywhere they have no extradition. I stayed for two reasons: to protect my friends and the cause for which I've sacrificed my legitimacy. No matter what I do the rest of my life, I'm a hood, according to the average guy in the street. It's ironic, especially when most of the bread on their table comes from me."

"Costello, you have a couple of weeks. Why don't you go to Greenwood Lake to rest? You're going to need your senses. You can't afford to be emotional, not for a minute."

"Right again, Frank. I'd like to do something for you, but you embarrass me by turning me down all the time. Someday you'll need and I'll give."

Costello turned to me. "Giovanni, I hear you're doing great things, but I got some news that may disturb you. La Puma tells me you're beginning a voice change. That's why you cracked the night at the end of the concert. Now, he's an expert, and he knows what he's talking about. This doesn't mean you'll never sing again, but he says it's best not to strain the voice box during this period. You'll continue your music theory. It'll give you a chance to get ahead of the game."

This development never had crossed my mind. I felt an emptiness, a loss. What would I do? It was like taking half of my life away. I knew it would take time to adjust to what I viewed as nature's cruelty.

Costello continued, "And while you're waiting to sing, your Uncle Dick has arranged for you to study acting, drama, comedy, and dance with a friend of his, Ms. May Homer. I also know her. She works with some of the best talents. You should take this opportunity to become well-rounded in the entertainment field."

Ms. Homer and I became fast friends, and I met great talents like Eddie Bracken, Nancy Kelly, and her brother Jack Kelly. I was fortunate to work and study on this level.

The year 1937 was not starting off great: voice cracking, hiatus on performing, Mr. Costello's right-hand man going away for ten years, and Dewey chosen as district attorney of New York County, Manhattan, just as Frank had predicted.

I was fourteen, but my manager was advertising my age as eleven, which was easy because I was small as a result of the mumps. They wanted to bill me as Little Caruso a bit longer. This was my first exposure to the fantasies of show business.

The following months were sort of like suspended happiness. I lacked drive but was happy with Mr. La Puma. Each session became an interesting memory. He told me inside stories about the great artists. It didn't take long for me to accept what had to be. In fact, my frame of mind improved once the pressure was off.

I became involved with athletics, taking the boxing team more seriously and playing goalie for the Astoria Maple Leaves. Hockey on roller skates was a popular sport, so much so that the bookmakers took bets. Our biggest rival was the Bengal Tigers from the Ravenswood section. They were tough, and I think the fights drew more crowds than the games themselves.

I was also hung on flying kites. We built our own mostly and flew them for days at a time by securing the cord to something overnight. I was finding pleasure in becoming more of a normal boy, doing what boys do.

We were living in the age of the zeppelins, with Germany as the leader with the *Hindenburg*[3] and the *Graf Zeppelin*[4]. One day, I was flying my kite by LaGuardia's Triborough Bridge[5] when the enormous *Hindenburg* appeared overhead. I knew its destination was Lakehurst, New Jersey, because I had picked up Pop's habit of reading the newspaper front to back. To my horror, I watched this great craft sink into the west as it caught fire while trying to dock. By the time I got home, the newspaper extras were in the street with the headline, "The fatal crash of the *Hindenburg*."

I recalled Pop telling me the Germans were using hydrogen, which was unstable but cheaper than helium. I couldn't conceive men could be so shallow to let money cost the lives of all those people. Unfortunately, several tragedies occurred with zeppelins, but airplanes were making strides. Companies such as Grumman, Fairchild, Lockheed, and Ford were competing to design faster,

---

[3] The Von Hindenburg crashed May 6, 1937.

[4] The Graf made its first long distance journey in mid-October 1928 with a crossing of the Atlantic to the United States, crash 1936.

[5] La Guardia's Triborough Bridge was opened to traffic on July 11, 1936.

larger, and safer aircraft. This industry infatuated me, and I spent many hours designing and building model planes.

*****

Mom was reading a letter from Dominick, written by his friend, Scarfone. Dominic still hadn't learned to read or write. It seemed Ninni was in all sorts of trouble.

Each age group in school was in one large room because the town was so small. Kindergarten to eighth grade only amounted to thirty students. Ninni, at age ten, had orchestrated all of the kids to write excuse notes for each other, which resulted in the whole school being absent one fine day. Another time when Ninni got caught whistling behind the teacher's back, she ordered him to whistle in front of the class to punish him. Instead of being embarrassed, he turned it into a comic act, which enraged the teacher. When she came at him, he ran out of the class and hid in the woods for two days.

Mom clutched the letter in her lap. "Why is he behaving so badly? He has all the things he wants, yet he's being so bad."

I looked at Mom. "He doesn't have us, his family. He thinks we don't want him."

"Don't be silly, Giovanni. I explained the advantages to him. He knew I sent him there for a better life."

"He's a little boy. He wants his mother and family. Things are useless to him."

Mom's eyes filled with tears. "Are you sure, Giovanni?"

"I'm sure. But not only that, I never told you, Dominick hates us. He hated Pop. He worked me to death, and if I complained, he would tell me I was lazy just like Pop. I used to cry the whole summer. Honest, Mom."

She walked to the phone and made two reservations with the railroad to Canton, New York. She turned to me. "Thank you. I want you to come with me. Perhaps if you explain it to Ninni, he may come back with us."

It was my first recognition of being the head of the family, and

I considered it an accomplishment. She had understood me, and she acted upon it.

We arrived in Canton during the latter part of the winter. It was bitter cold, and the snow was piled as high as some of the houses. The sky was a bleak gray and the snow a blinding white, so bright that it hurt my eyes. We arrived unannounced, so we took a taxi. Nothing seemed to have changed much, except I wasn't used to seeing the river across the road frozen in ice or the landscape pure white.

Dominic emerged from the general store. "What in the hell are you doing here? Why didn't you tell us you were coming?"

"I was concerned about Ninni," Mom said as she entered the store. "His behavior has been so bad by your letters: I thought I'd surprise him. You see, if he was at home, I wouldn't allow him to get away with these antics, and I didn't want him to burden you."

"It really isn't that bad, Ann, nothing we couldn't handle."

"He's my son, and if I feel his behavior isn't to my expectations, then I have the right as his mother to decide how good or bad he's getting along."

We went upstairs for warm drinks. Dominick was overly polite. I wasn't allowed to drink coffee, so Aunt Maggie made me hot chocolate. They were treating me far better than ever, although Maggie stared at me threateningly.

Ninni finally returned from school and was shocked to see us. I was taken with his expensive clothing: a corduroy jacket with a full zipper and leather elbows, and knickers to match. His schoolbag was leather. He looked confused, like he didn't know what to say, so he just stared.

Mom looked at me, and I said, "Ninni, let's take a walk."

"This is homework time for him," Dominick said.

"It's all right, Dominick, they haven't seen each other in a long time," Mom said. "I'm sure they have a lot to talk about. Go ahead, boys, it's all right."

Uncle's face tightened the way it did before he killed a calf, which frightened me as I remembered his temper and reprisals. But Mom's determination on her face made my fears fade as quickly as they'd arisen. Ninni and I walked out and stood outside the door, studying each other for changes after nearly a year.

"Are you still singing opera?" he asked.

"Didn't you get my letters?"

"I never got any letters."

"That's funny, I wrote at least ten, Ninni. I wondered why I never got one from you. I thought you were mad at us, or maybe you forgot all about us."

He gritted his teeth. "I *never* forgot about you."

I sensed not to push yet. I knew he was bitter and sad, not like a child glad to see his family.

"You know, let's walk across the river. It's frozen hard right now," he said.

We picked our way across so we wouldn't slip. When we reached the other side, the store was well up river, almost a mile.

"Hey, Ninni, how come we started by the store, walked straight across, yet the store is far from where we started?"

"I'll show you."

We walked down about a quarter of a mile, where he pointed at ice going over the dam. "The river is moving. That's why we ended up where we did."

His casual attitude didn't stop my spine from tingling. It was a dangerous walk. We started our hike through the woods as Ninni snapped branches from young birch trees. We both wanted to talk but didn't know where or how to start.

"How's Maria?" Ninni finally asked. "I hardly remember what she looks like."

"That figures, 'cause I sent you pictures with my letters. I'll bet Uncle hid them."

"Could be. I don't like him. Why did Mom give me away?" he said as quickly as that.

"She didn't give you away. She loves you, and because she

loves you, she thought you would have a better life. Good clothes, a better education, all those things. Besides, she was upset because you were so young when Pop died, she didn't know how she would take care of you."

He started to cry. "She sent me away, and I don't think she wants me."

"Why do you think she's here? She loves you and thinks maybe you're not happy. After all, you were only sent here on a trial. That means if you're not happy, you could ask to come home."

"You mean if I ask her to come home, she'll take me back?"

"Yes, Ninni, we miss you just as much as you miss us."

"Will you ask her?"

"It would be better if you ask her."

"You're sure she'll take me home with her right away?"

"I'm sure. You know what? I don't like Dominick either."

We laughed and worked our way back across the river to the general store. The day passed quickly with a lot of idle chatter. I was getting worried Ninni hadn't talked to Mom yet. I could tell my shrewd uncle knew something was up. He wanted to hold on to Ninni and had long-range plans for him. He was paranoid about not having children, and Ninni was the closest he could get.

We sat down for supper. The snowstorm was intensifying, and the windows looked whitewashed. Ninni couldn't have thrown out his line at a more dramatic time.

"Mom, I want to come home with you," he said in the loudest possible voice in the middle of the quiet dinner.

"What in the hell are you saying?" Dominick shouted. "This has become your home. What do you mean you want to go home? Your mama can't take care of you. She has too much on her mind."

"Mom, will you take me home with you?" Ninni repeated in the same loud voice. "I miss you and everybody."

"Don't listen to him. He's only a child. Besides, look at all I've invested in him, the clothes and all."

227

"Well, if it's such a sacrifice or burden for you, Dominick, keep in mind our deal was a trial," Mom said. "I'll gladly relieve you of the burden."

She turned to Ninni. "If you want to come home, then home it is."

"Who said it was a burden?" Dominick said. "I didn't say it was."

"My son is not an investment like all of the things around here. He's a human being with feelings. He'd better know now he's loved. I have the feeling, for whatever reason, he thinks he's not loved. Besides, my son told me he never got the letters or pictures we sent him."

"I didn't want him to get homesick, Ann, you know."

"He's returning with me, Dominick, and I regret the day you talked me into this. It'll take a long time for him to understand my motives. I only hope it's not too late."

I got a certain satisfaction out of this, but it was just a down payment on the misery he caused Pop and me. I found a sense of power. If a person plans, he can move things, ideas, and conditions. I intended to use this discovery against him again at my first opportunity. *Yes, this was the first step toward evening the score, Uncle.* His eyes met mine with hate. I smiled.

*****

Now Tony's eyes are the ones meeting mine. I think of him as my brother, yet he's acclaimed as the greatest entertainer of our time. He has an inhuman drive. His dedication comes through in his work, resulting in mass hypnosis all over the world. I wonder, *does his drive have anything to do with feeling rejected by Mom? Hadn't all the love Tony received after he came home overcome her mistake?*

*****

Life at home certainly wasn't the same without Pop. Ninni was developing quickly with a flair for art. He could copy sophisticated cartoons with professional authenticity at eleven. His personality was one of a relentless teaser. He claimed to remember nothing about Pop as though he'd never existed. Maybe that was a blessing, because I still mourned for Pop and hoped he would come home.

Maria was left in charge while Mom worked. Ninni and I tortured her no end. Looking back, her life for a girl her age was miserable and was to get worse.

Mom made us wear starched collars and a tie every day. After working all day, she'd hand-launder our shirts, then starch and ironed them. The collars were so stiff, they would irritate my neck.

One Saturday morning, Manny's mom came to the house hysterical. When she finally calmed down, she said Manny had been shot in an attempted holdup this morning and she wanted to get in touch with Frank. Manny was in critical condition at Bellevue Hospital. Apparently, he and some friend from the city planned the holdup of a loan office on 52nd Street without being armed. After the police ordered him to halt, they shot him in the chest when he kept running. The bullet severed an artery and touched the main valve into the heart. Back then, heart surgery was the least successful next to brain surgery, so Manny's mom wanted to be sure he got the finest care and wouldn't be used as a guinea pig.

In fact, the new media had nicknamed this hospital the slaughterhouse. It wasn't fancy, but it actually had a fine staff of surgeons who oversaw the interns. Mom took us to the hospital with his mother by subway, and Frank met us there. Vinnie and Herman were waiting in the hallway.

"They don't know whether he'll pull through," Herman said.

"He's got to pull through. He's tough. He'll be all right," I said. "Can I see him?"

"I don't know if they'll allow it," his mom said. "He's in intensive care."

After Frank got him a private room, we were all allowed in as long as we were absolutely quiet. I wished I'd stayed in the hallway. Manny was lying on his back with tubes attached to him from every direction, and an oxygen tent covered his head. His face was as pale as chalk, and he was taking long, deep breaths. He was fighting for his life. I made the sign of the cross and said one act of contrition after another. The doctor, a close friend of Frank's, came in. He announced they would chance surgery if Manny's pressure stabilized. The bullet had to come out.

The tears poured as I loved and hated Manny. *C'mon, Manny, pull out of it. We want you to live. Why did you do such a fool thing? Always trying to play tough guy, you really got the chance this time. I swear, if you live, I'll beat the hell out of you for being such a fool, you dumb head.*

We waited in the corridor for hours. Finally, an intern approached us. "It looks as though your friend is tougher than we thought. He beat the crisis. We're going in for emergency surgery, it's the only chance the boy has. Frankly, we don't see how he survived the shock at his age. I want donors to stand by. We're going to need blood."

Manny's mom sobbed while Mom rubbed her back and assured her he would be all right. We children were sent home. The surgery took five hours. All of my uncles gave blood, and God had it Manny would pull through. I was so relieved.

Today, though, I think: *The coming years of the butchery he was to inflict on mankind would make one wonder if God had anything to do with saving him.*

*****

Frank's deal or trade worked. Headlines read, "Underworld figure indictment works. Haymes found guilty on all counts. Ten-year sentence."

Costello wouldn't tolerate drugs. His one requisite was firm: None of them were to deal in this traffic. Yet, some of them were on the fence, for millions of dollars were passing them by. It took a great amount of confidence, persuasion, and guts for him to hold them together on this sensitive issue. Costello had to live with the fact that some of his confidants would be asked to assassinate him. The assassins had a strong selling pitch: the highest profits ever realized in the organization. So, Costello, despite his suspicious nature, had to rely on loyalty more than ever. It was a living nightmare for him.

He tightened his security and only visited places he felt safe, such as a handful on Manhattan Island and one on Long Island. He sent emissaries when business had to be done in Jersey. The two brothers controlling the area were notorious for doing their own bidding, feared no one, and were cold, cruel killers. Not as bright as Costello, they had to second-guess him, for he was never present. They created all sorts of problems to draw him face-to-face, but Costello was too smart for that.

At one point, they monitored Costello's brother. They knew the goon was prone to making mistakes. When they caught him in a bad situation, they sent word to Costello for a meet, or they would kill his brother. Costello sent a message back, "One must do what they have to do. If you must kill my brother, then kill him. Then I'll do what I have to do."

They released Ed, and Costello once more proved his masterful talent for chess and his image was stronger than ever.

*****

I'd been exercising my vocal chords by Mr. La Puma's instruction. He told me it was time to vocalize mildly, not push too hard, or I may damage my vocal chords. I followed his instructions to the letter, and the results were great. The best part: It appeared I'd remain in the tenor range and only lost a couple of high notes I didn't need anyway.

"Giovanni, if things keep going this way, you'll be able to perform in three months, and I can assure you better than you've ever performed before."

Mr. Petri called to ask me to come to the Met studios at four sharp on Saturday. He was sitting at his nine-foot Steinway piano.

"Giovanni, it's so good to see you," he said, opening his arms.

"You know; I'm having a devil of a time with the boys' chorus. I don't have enough strong tenors to lead the rest of them. They all sound like sick oboes." I laughed and Mr. Petri smiled. "I was talking to your maestro, La Puma. He informs me your voice transition has been just fine, and it wouldn't hurt your voice to do a few performances. Let's do some scales."

When we finished, he looked at me with a glint in his eye. He said they usually let all boys go at age thirteen, but he might make an exception in my case for two reasons: the quality of my voice and my short height. My depression seemed to lighten. I couldn't wait to tell everyone.

*****

When Manny returned home from the hospital, we visited him. He spoke quietly with much effort, like an old man on his way out.

"It's great to see you guys. What have you been up to?" he said.

We were told he couldn't stand any excitement, but Herman let loose at him.

"Manny, why did you get mixed up in such a fool thing? Are you crazy?"

"You're right, it was dumb. Look at me. . . . From now on, I'll do my own work by myself. If I had done the job alone, I wouldn't have gotten in this fix. I'll plan the jobs so no one will suspect what's coming. Someone was tipped off, and we can't determine who because too many people were involved. Someone chickened out."

I could not hold back either. "Manny, don't you know if it weren't for your uncle and mine, you would have gone to the can? Are you crazy or something? Bug off on this shit, man. You're gonna get killed."

"Listen, Giovanni, you take care of your singing, and I'll take care of my thing. Do I ever tell you how to sing?"

"That's stupid, Manny. I can't get killed singing."

"That's what you think. I could think of a couple guys who

232

would kill you if you sang opera for them."

"C'mon, Manny," Herman said. "You're talking like an idiot. Knock it off, will you?"

Manny folded his hands and breathed deep. "I'm tired. I'm gonna get some sleep."

Herman and I left shaking our heads. We knew Manny would get in trouble again the first chance he got. He was tough and stubborn. All he wanted to be was his uncle, his idol. Manny's life was set.

CHAPTER SEVENTEEN

My morale was being battered. The Metropolitan had dropped me at fifteen, and I still was depressed from Pop's death.

I sensed things were not right with Maria either. She was losing a lot of weight and was jumpy. She would graduate in a few months from an all-girls school with honors. Mom wanted her only with girls and didn't allow her to date.

Her fragile state didn't stop Ninni and me from teasing her, though. I borrowed a stage knife from the May Homer studios, and Ninni applied some Mercurochrome around my heart. I inserted the knife under my armpit so it looked like I was stabbed. When Maria saw me, I held my hand under the knife so she would be sure to see it. She passed out on the floor. We were frantic, but Ninni's response surprised me: He dampened a towel with cold water and filled a glass. I patted her face with the towel, and Ninni lifted her head so she could drink the water as she came around. She began to scream.

"It's all right. It's only a joke, Maria. We didn't think it would frighten you so," I said.

She pushed us away and got up. "You two were born of the devil. I, for the life of me, can't see, in my wildest imagination, how this might be even near funny. It's a pure sadistic act. You can bet I'll tell Mom tonight."

Ninni and I offered to do her chores for a couple of weeks. We tried just about everything, but she didn't waver. I truly felt guilty.

Maria finally agreed not to tell Mom.

Ninni celebrated by singing some Jolson songs and doing some soft-shoe. I told him about the May Homer studio. "Ninni, how would you like to come to the studio and learn some tap dancing and acting? Of course, you'll have to take an audition, but I can't see where you'd have a problem. You have a very fine voice and good rhythm." I could tell he was becoming anxious, and at the same time we were becoming better friends.

"Ninni, I'm going up Friday. You're welcome to come with me after school. I can take off from school because I have special dispensation from the mayor's office."

"Can I get the same thing, Giovanni?"

"Well, I don't know. I think you have to be a professional artist with a track record and belong to Variety. That's the union."

The following afternoon, Mom beckoned us to the kitchen. "Boys, we have a serious problem with Maria. I have to go to the hospital now, and I want you to behave like the gentlemen I know you are. Your sister's in St. John's hospital."

"What is the matter with her, Mom?" I asked.

"I don't know. She's having a nervous breakdown, they tell me."

Mom started to cry when we handed her a note for Maria saying we loved her and wished she'd be home soon. We felt responsible.

During our time alone, Ninni asked profound questions about my experience in the business. I could tell by the way his eyes sparkled that he was married to the idea of show business.

I don't recall falling asleep that night. I guess sleep was some kind of escape mechanism. I'd never been so depressed before. I woke up the next morning thinking of how I wasn't enjoying concert work anymore, and might aspire to science if it weren't for Mom and Pop's sacrifices for my music.

After school, I ran all the way home hoping Mom would be in the kitchen to tell me about Maria. When I arrived, she was sitting with Maria. I saw a tender side of Mom I never knew before. My respect for her was growing deeper and deeper. I had made up my mind I'd do all I could to make her happy. Of course, I didn't know life could take so many strange turns.

We were never much for kissing and hugging, but I think Maria knew how I felt about her. She was eating again and gaining back some weight. Before, she had looked like a skeleton, all eyeballs and bones.

*****

I hear Irene's voice and think it's in the distance, like an echo chamber. I turn to my dear friend and cousin.

"Are you okay, Johnny?" she asks.

Patricia is asking the same question on my other side.

"Whoa, I'm just fine. I have my best friend on one side and my wonderful wife on the other —the most beautiful girls here — and you guys ask if I'm okay?"

They look relieved.

"Let's go for a cup of coffee," I say.

Irene gets that humorous look about her as we chat.

"I have a dandy to tell you," she says. "I called Aunt Nettie's house the other day, and guess how she answered the phone?"

Patricia and I could use a laugh. Irene's eyes twinkle. "She answered, 'Tony Bennett's aunt speaking.'"

We burst into laughter. "Well, Irene, I've heard it all now. I know why the masses have idols."

Irene still has the wide, beautiful eyes she had as a kid. She always gave me motivation concerning anything I attempted to accomplish. She was the catalyst. She stood by me in some of my darkest moments, and I had many. Always up, always positive. She has her father's blood. Her sister, Jesse, has many of the same qualities but is introverted. Does Irene know how close her father and I were? He didn't mention much to his family about me, but they knew he would take me fishing. It seemed Irene's husband, Peter, and I shared the rare pleasure of being allowed to go with

Frank.

"You're staring, Johnny," Irene says.

"I know, I was just recalling all the wonderful things you did for me growing up and want you to know it was very appreciated. I shall love you forever. The sin of life is, we rarely see the ones we love most until it's too late. . . . You realize we've never had an argument in all of our years?"

I can sense Patricia is beginning to see the love for family between us. I've told her stories about our culture and how we celebrated the holidays. Irene's husband, Peter, fell right into the mold as though he'd been part of our family from the beginning. Frank treasured him, and Frank was not easy to reach. Peter and I'd become close as brothers.

"Life has treated you well," my dear cousin says.

"You mean to say the scars aren't showing? If they're not, I owe it to Patricia. She's been a great friend, and like you, Irene, has given me strength, at least until this minute anyway."

Irene smiles. "She's got my vote, Johnny, and a looker too."

It isn't easy to embarrass Patricia, but this time she blushes. Irene tells Patricia about some of our fun times and some of my accomplishments. Then we exchange stories about our grandchildren.

After returning Irene to the funeral parlor, I take Patricia to the river I learned to love so much. Of course, I can't expect her to see what I saw. It's the kind of river that takes years of observation, gives you respect for it, and turns into love. I think the word I have used so many times is *character*. This river has character, and each time I look at it, I see something different about it. I drive to the end of the street perpendicular to the river, on the left side of the community pool toward the Triborough Bridge. I'm in awe. She looks truly magnificent and majestic as we walk toward Hell Gate Bridge. I wanted to save that for last, mostly because of the defined currents under this antique bridge, the well-named Hell Gate. I once took a forty-foot boat under her, and the currents pulled me into a circle before I could straighten out the powerful diesel. So, I know firsthand the awesome character of this part of the river.

Patricia isn't patronizing for anyone or any reason, and she seems to be taken by the East River. I thought the tales and descriptions I'd given her all these years might have given her a longing to see it If you look to the east, you can see the monstrous skyline of New York City with the Empire State Building, the Chrysler, and some additions I don't recognize. Closer to us are the four bridges I so loved as a child: the old Brooklyn Bridge, 59th Street Bridge, the Triborough, and Hell Gate.

Across the river is Blackwell's Island[6], which holds all sorts of legends, from secret government experiment buildings to insane asylum. Beyond Hell Gate is the prison on an island that housed everything from hard-core criminals to drug addicts and wife abusers. You name it, this prison had it. I recall thousands of pheasants would fly over to the Long Island side at sunrise.

Patricia takes out her faithful Minolta and waits for some compositions to take shape. A beautiful old tug passes by, green with red trim, fighting the tides, and Patricia nails a hell of a shot. Patricia is a better photographer than she gives herself credit for. She has an eye for composition, especially for stills. We stay until the sun sets behind the bridges.

We collapse when we get to the hotel. I regret the next day for the rest of my life. I was supposed to go to Port Washington to see one of my dearest friends but don't make it. I have no excuse other than depression and exhaustion. Ralph Herman, one of the most formidable composer arrangers in the world, the president of Avant-Garde Records, recorded me. We gained affection for each other, which grew to brotherhood in every sense of the word. I can barely find the strength to call him. Thank God we were blessed to

---

[6] Blackwell Island today it is called Roosevelt Island and worth a visit. It has been an insane asylum, a prison, a hospital. It is a tram ride from Manhattan, with a compelling memorial park to Franklin D. Roosevelt.

spend time together the next year.

Patricia and I eat at Patsy's, a longtime favorite continental Italian restaurant. Joe and Rose gave me their secret recipe for Patsy's shrimp scampi and swore me to secrecy. They knew I was a chef buff and lived three thousand miles away. And I have honored their secret to this day.

*****

It was a Friday afternoon, and I took Ninni to the May Homer studios, as promised.

"So, this is Ninni," May said. "What a handsome boy. His coloring is so light with grayish hazel eyes."

"I know, Miss Homer, like Pop and Mom's mother. She was called The German."

"And his hair is dark blond and straight," May said as Ninni fluttered his big eyes.

Although Ninni hadn't sung formally, I wasn't worried because, at only twelve years old he had such rhythm and fine pitch. He also had a broad range, mostly in the upper register. May introduced us to her accompanist, Ada.

"What song would you like to sing?" Ada asked.

"Al Jolson's 'Sonny Boy,'" Ninni said.

"Do you know your key?"

"He's never sung with an accompanist," I said.

Ada moved Ninni to the piano. "Let's see, Ninni, we'll find the right key for you." Her finger hit a middle C. "Can you sing this note?"

Ninni took a deep breath, and this went on until she reached a G above high C.

"My, my, you have a wonderful voice and range."

Just before he began to sing, Eddie Bracken entered the room. "Hi, everybody. And who's this good-looking young man?"

"It's my little brother, Ninni, and he's going to sing for us."

We settled back to listen. What a surprise! Ninni left me breathless. His voice was golden like Pop's. His delivery sounded like someone who had studied for years. Everyone stood up to applaud.

"Ninni, can you do something with a beat? You know, rah tah tah," Eddie said.

I laughed when he turned to the piano and asked for "Tootsie."

When Ninni began "Toot, toot, Tootsie, good-bye," I fell on the floor in laughter and appreciation for his talent. He had all the right moves. He synched with the piano player as if they'd worked together for years. I knew he was going to be something to be reckoned with. Yes, he had the talent of a seasoned pro.

Eddie Bracken gave me some slapstick material to read, and he played the straight man.

Eddie: "How come you're afraid of flying?"

Me: "Because I believe in Terra."

Eddie: "I don't understand. What is terra?"

Me: "All I know is the more terra there is, the firma I am."

The devastatingly corny line cracked me up. Then he did his famous baseball act. This seasoned actor was truly talented, so much more than a comic. He said a comic wasn't well-rounded until he could make people laugh or cry. He thanked me and asked if I'd like to go over some things next Friday. Of course!

Ninni jabbered all the way home in excitement. "You know what Eddie Bracken told me? Did you hear him? He said I had a great sense of comedy, and he'd like to work with me anytime I want."

Ninni was hooked. I smiled as I hoped this enthusiasm would never leave him.

*****

I took all sorts of odd jobs to bring home money, from working in the drugstore, vegetable store on Saturday, to delivering customized curtains for a decorator. My bicycle made it fairly easy to get delivery work.

Finally, Mr. La Puma informed Mrs. Quinlan I was ready, so

she set up a radio date for me. The performance went well, but everyone was concerned about the hair on my face. My age could take the edge off my image of a young boy with a mature voice. No one seemed to care that I had a great voice, of course. They still were selling child opera.

But they were right in a sense. Great singers were plentiful. What went wrong? Whose fault was it? I hadn't thought in these terms before, I just did what I was told, but now I was being forced into the mechanics of show business. I realized the artist was not the only one responsible. Why did the manager get a percentage? Was it the manager's job to get the artist exposure, hire a promotion man if necessary, or get out and beat the bushes for me? If I flubbed a performance, I was sure to catch hell. What about the manager's performance? Was I entitled to give the manager hell? But my youth and respect for elders held me back. I was beginning to learn how it was wired, though. I would talk to Dick about it. He knew the whole ball game.

After Dick recognized my concern, he talked with Mrs. Quinlan, who got me another chance at a screen test within four days, this time with Paramount. All I had to do was walk about a mile from our house to the Paramount base. I thought I was dreaming when I arrived, because the director and makeup artist were a blueprint of the men at Warner Bros. They talked the same, acted the same, wore their hair the same. It was weird.

Everyone seemed to get fairly excited about my test. In fact, they wanted me to sign a contract in two weeks. Of course, Mom had to be the one to sign.

"You're not signing anything until I read it," Dick said when he found out. "You tell Mrs. Quinlan I'm requesting a copy in the mail for my edification."

I trusted Dick's judgment and believed he would protect me. All of us were subject to making mistakes out of innocence, and it was much wiser to seek counsel from those whose judgment you trusted.

CHAPTER EIGHTEEN

Dick flew into the house one day in a rage with the contracts in his hand.

"Ann, these guys want blood. They want to own Giovanni lock, stock, and barrel, power of attorney, all until he is eighteen. Then at legal age, he'll renegotiate the contract, and the money is not great either. If it were up to me, I'd say we should take the chance and give them some counterproposals. Mrs. Quinlan is coming here any minute to discuss this."

When Mrs. Quinlan arrived, Dick told her how he felt.

"Dick, if you're sure, then I must agree. We should go in with one thing in mind: sink or swim. If we get a negotiation, fine. If we don't, then let's wait for a better opportunity. I'm for it."

Dick studied me after she left. "Did you get the point, Giovanni? I want you to understand because your future is involved."

"I wouldn't be disappointed if it doesn't work out. As you said, I can wait."

"You're a real trooper, Giovanni. You behave as though you were born in the trunk, as they used to say in vaudeville. I'm proud of you."

"Thank you, Dick."

"How are things going for you, Ann? Are you all right? Do you need anything?"

"I'm all right, Dick. I can take care of myself, so don't worry about me."

"I'll say one thing, Ann: You're tough. You have the Suraci blood in you. I was just thinking the other day of how different your life would have been if Pop had let you go to college. You always wanted to be a schoolteacher."

"Dick, I do believe I've had a good life. Looking and behaving like a woman is an art, one that should be practiced by ladies. I remember a compliment John gave me time and time again. He used to say, 'You look like a lady, you smell like a lady, you behave like a lady, so you must be a lady. I'm a very lucky man.'"

Mom sort of shocked us; she hadn't talked about Pop in a long time. Her sadness was very private. She never shared her grief, not even with close friends, which really concerned us. We couldn't tell how she was coping or truly felt. She quietly worked her tail off to provide us an education and clothes. I didn't know how she was surviving mentally. It wasn't natural.

Mom's eyes filled with tears, and her voice broke slightly. "Dick, the only regret I have is I'm falling deeper in love with him now after death from memory. Mostly, because I was detoured by the problems of his illness, and I really wasn't listening to him at the time. I was just taking him for granted. But now, his words are coming to me, and they're making so much sense. He was a beautiful human being. Yes, Dick, I was lucky to have known him, had him, have his children. I'll never have the need for another man."

Even as she said this, I still hoped he'd return. I couldn't accept his death and drew out the fantasy.

I began considering leaving school and getting a job so I could help Mom, but she blew a fuse when I mentioned it.

"What the hell do you think I've worked for all these years? So you could become illiterate?" she said. "By the way, Giovanni, we have a wedding to attend, and they want you to be the pillow boy again."

Oh no, not again. I'd been a pillow boy more than five times and hated it. "Mom, why me? I'm fifteen years old. What they want is a little boy; even Ninni is too old."

"Decco is the one getting married, and he wants you. And whatever Decco wants, Decco gets. Don't fight it. The wedding is next Friday."

"Mom, I can't do this wedding anyway. I don't have a George Washington suit to wear. In fact, I don't have anything I could wear as a pillow boy."

Mom smiled. "I already thought of that. You can wear your formal suit, the one you wear when you give a concert."

"I can't wear that. It's not for this kind of occasion."

"I thought of that too. This wedding is going to be in the evening, and the suit is formal evening wear, so you'll wear it."

Talking to her was hopeless.

"Giovanni, come to the table. I want to tell you a few things about this wedding. You know this part of the family is involved in the organization. So you'll refer to yourself as Giovanni if anyone asks your name. You'll notice the groom is old enough to get married, yet he is referred to as Decco, when his name is Dick. This is their way, so we'll respect it. You'll be witnessing much wealth in gowns, diamonds, and the children will be dressed like *Vogue* magazine. Just take this all in stride, Giovanni. All you'll see is blood money. These men live on the edge. They don't know whether they'll be alive the next day."

My head was swimming. I was so confused.

"Let's try the suit on and make sure it doesn't need repair, Giovanni."

The suit fit perfectly, as though I hadn't grown at all since I got the mumps two years ago. I could close my eyes now and remember the pain from the mumps.

"Do you think I'll ever grow any more, Mom?"

"I don't think so. The reason why I'm so short is because of a childhood illness. As a matter of fact, one time a friend of the family came back from Florida, and I was on the front stoop. He asked me who I was. I said Anna Suraci. He looked at me in surprise and said, 'You can't be Anna. The last time I saw her, she was pronounced dead.' Well, the rest is history. I'm still here, and the only thing I have wrong with me now is a devastating allergy to nuts."

All but one of Mom's sisters and brothers were tall, which showed how an illness could affect you. Mom was about four feet, eight inches, but proportionate. She never looked very short unless you stood beside her. Maria was tall, and it appeared Ninni would be fairly tall, so I had to resign myself to being shorter than five foot.

"You know, Giovanni, the Lord moves in mysterious ways. Just think, you might not have gotten all your recent work if you had grown normally."

This didn't console me because I would have sacrificed my voice at this point for a normal height.

On Friday night, we were dressed to kill, as they say. Ninni wore our communion suit, and Maria was stunning. I was beginning to realize she was a knockout. Mom was as beautiful as ever, of course. We had to go to church early, because I was part of the bridal group. I was a bit surprised when introduced to Decco in the waiting hall. He was bald and didn't look right for a young man. His *fiancée* looked like a glamorous movie star who Decco wasn't supposed to be with, but I began to realize he made his own rules. You could tell he was in complete command at all times. I cringed when I noticed the best man's gun under his jacket when he bent over to tie his shoe. *Why would anyone wear a gun to a wedding?*

Decco's face warmed up a bit, but he straightened into a military stance. "So, you're Giovanni, the great singer. You know, I've been told we met some time ago through our fathers, but I think we were too young to remember. I'm honored you have accepted our imposition on you."

Strange language. The beautiful bride bent down to kiss my

cheek. They gave me the ring pillow, and I couldn't believe it: The bride's wedding band was a cluster of large diamonds in a gold setting. Decco detected my awe.

"Like that, Giovanni? You should. Most people could buy a house for what it cost. That's what I think of Anita. Nothing is too much for her. What she wants, she'll get."

What a pompous guy, I thought as the evening proceeded.

At the reception hall, elaborate settings with gold utensils adorned the tables, unlike the football weddings. Bottles of Scotch, rye, wine, and Champagne stood in the center of each table. It looked more like the parties on Long Island where I gave concerts. The orchestra played soft Neapolitan music while we waited for the meal to be served.

An entourage walked through the door, and the music stopped as the leader, a man about seventy years old, walked to the dais. Decco kissed his ring, and they embraced. Everyone treated this man like royalty. You could hear a pin drop. Then the band resumed with a waltz, and the old man led the bride for a dance.

Tom walked over. "Do you know who that is, Giovanni?"

"No, Uncle Tom, I've never seen him before."

"Well, just between pals, he's the *capo dei capi*, the boss over all Italians, even in Italy. Giovanni, let me give you a tip: Stay away from the arias if they call you up to sing. Do you remember Carlo Buti's 'Parlami D'amore, Mariu?' Well, if they ask you to sing, do it for the old man. I assure you he'll never forget your voice or your song choice."

"Of course, Uncle Tom."

This wasn't like Tom. He wasn't a hero worshipper, and usually he'd be critical of leadership.

After an hour, Decco walked to the microphone. "Friends, we have the pleasure of having with us tonight Giovanni Benedetto, also known as the Little Caruso. He has given concerts all over the country. And if you put your hands together, I'm sure he would bless us with a song."

This was a strange group. I hoped I could satisfy them. I approached the mike. "Thank you, Decco. For you and your wonderful guests, I would like to do Carlo Buti's rendition of 'Parlami D'amore, Mariu.'"

Decco pulled the mike from me. "Now, I want all of you to be quiet. If I catch anyone making noise, *a ciappato* (you'll catch it)."

The crowd settled down. I directed my song first to the bride, then moved to the old man, whose eyes were watering. As I moved on to Tom, he flashed me a big okay sign.

When I finished, the crowd called for *Pagliacci*. The piano player nodded at me that he knew it. I was the highlight of the evening. Mom, Ninni, and Maria looked proud, which made me happy. After I returned to our table, the old man summoned me. Tom accompanied me and kissed his ring.

"I was told this young man is Suraci's nephew," the old man said. Tom nodded. "*Figlio mio*, (my son), you've been blessed with a wonderful talent. I want you to know you've contributed to my having a wonderful evening, and my wife, Maria, is forever grateful."

I thanked him warmly. "Keep an eye on that boy, he's going to be important for the Italians and for business," I overheard him say as I walked away.

What looked like his bodyguard said, "Costello has shown much interest in him."

"If that's the case, we don't have to worry. But I don't like these little secrets he keeps from me."

I couldn't believe the white-glove service and the food: filet mignon, baked potato, string beans, mushrooms in a savory sauce, fruit cocktail, and Italian ice smothered with crème de menthe. I was stuffed.

"Now I know how you get those strong lungs of yours," the waiter said when he picked up my plates, smiling.

I later found out Frank had used the excuse of attending rallies to explain his absence at the wedding. I knew it was because too many wise guys were there, and it could have hurt his chances even further. All the way home, Tom chattered about me becoming the greatest Italian-American singer in the country.

However, I knew in my heart that show business was not my calling. Yet, I plodded on for Mom's sake and disliked her for it at times, I must admit. I lay in bed thinking about it most of the night.

CHAPTER NINETEEN

Frank didn't look well when he paid us a rare visit one morning. The campaign was taking its toll. He drank coffee and talked with Mom. Then the door sprung back open as he left. "Giovanni, walk me to my car, I want to talk to you."

On the way downstairs, he asked me if I'd like to go fishing with him.

"Boy, would I, Uncle Frank! I love to fish."

"Are you scared of the water?"

"No, Uncle Frank."

"By the way, do you have a rod and reel?"

"Gee, no, Uncle Frank."

"Okay, I'll start you off with your first rod and reel. It's just a boat rod, but it'll do. There's a place called Cold Spring Harbor out on the North Shore of Long Island. I have to tell you, it's one of the most beautiful sights you'll ever see. We'll take a rowboat from the harbor out to the lighthouse and fish for blacks. You'll like catching blackfish. They're tough and don't give up easily. . . . Oh yeah, I heard about your stint at Decco's wedding. Good going, the old man is a very important force in this country, and it's good to have him on your side. You'll know what I mean someday."

I ran upstairs. "Mom, Uncle Frank asked me to go fishing with him!" I was so excited because I'd always been told I was too young to fish.

Mom looked quite surprised. "He did?"

You see, I found out much later in life that Uncle Frank was a voracious womanizer, and the family knew he used fishing as an excuse to get away.

Early the next morning, I answered the phone.

"Giovanni, are you ready to go this morning?"

My heart beat harder and harder. "Yes, yes, Uncle Frank."

"Well, the tide is right. We should hit about two hours before flood tide if we leave in a half hour. Could you be ready?"

"I'm ready."

He chuckled.

It was a beautiful ride. Back then, anything past Whitestone was the country. Cold Spring Harbor was like fairyland. The squat trees stretched to the water, and the white New England-style houses dotted the horizon. I fell in love with the ocean smell. Though this was part of Long Island Sound, it was still ocean water. I could see clear to the bottom. The water moved gently, and Uncle Frank looked pleased. We parked in an area with seafood restaurants.

"Have you ever had raw clams on the half shell, Giovanni?"

"No."

"Let's go in this one. They have the best fresh clams on this water. First, Giovanni, don't eat the popular cherrystone clams. They are fishy and sometimes bitter." We walked along the glass showcase. "What we want is middle necks. They are as sweet as they are tiny. Give us a dozen each of the very pink middle neck clams." Then he walked me to the condiments. "See here, the very hot sauce. First, you put some on all your clams, then you squeeze lemon on them lavishly. Now, pick one up with your index, middle finger, and thumb. Peel off the clam with your upper front teeth. Roll it around your tongue, chew, and swallow."

Uncle Frank opened his eyes. "Now, Giovanni, the moment the heaviest taste of the clam lightens in your mouth, you're ready for the next one."

I followed his instructions, and I liked the sauce even though it was a bit hot.

"You see, Giovanni, you picked the next one in just about the right time. Most people who haven't tried this usually don't get it right for a time. The main thing is, Giovanni, you are now a connoisseur and can pass it on to anyone you like."

I felt so adult. Uncle Frank never treated me as a child. He always made me feel as though we were on the same level, and little did I know I would pass this on throughout my life. He rented a rowboat with a modest outboard motor and bought some bait, a crustacean mutation called a fiddler crab.

"You know, if we had time, all we had to do was go over to the beach and catch them," Uncle Frank said. "You find a hole in the sand and dig deep in one sweep with a gardening fork, then lift the sand. And there you have it. However, you must keep in mind the only ones that seem to work are called china backs."

Frank pulled one out of the bait basket. The light bluish symmetrical design on its back was amazing. It looked as perfect as Mom's delicate chinaware. Frank took out a different one. "See, Giovanni, this one is all black, and the fish don't want it for whatever reason. I'll prove it to you by putting one of the blacks on my extra hook. You'll notice the fish will hit the china backs instead."

I was in a trance, fascinated. "Hey, Uncle Frank, I remember Pop saying, "If you want to learn how to fish, find the oldest fisherman on the beach, and he'll teach you."

He smiled nostalgically. We walked to the lighthouse on grayish-green rocks, just about the bedrock color in the East River. The lighthouse wasn't huge, but had an elegant white with red trim. Frank noticed me staring at it.

"This lighthouse has been here since the colonial days. Actually, it was put here to signal other shore towns if any British ship might be in the area. This was a perfect disguise, for the British thought it was just a lighthouse."

I was so happy being with Uncle, learning, smelling the

mussels on the rocks and salt air. I never wanted it to end. "When do we start fishing?"

"Just about now, Giovanni. Let me show you your new pole and reel, and how to bait up. First, you grab a crab like this from the back of his claw." All of them had one claw for some reason. "Hold the claw close to the crab's body and remove it. Don't worry, it won't hurt them as much as when a blackfish attacks him. Now, face your hook toward you and push it into the hole from the claw you removed. Don't kill the crab. These fish aren't stupid. If the crab is dead, they'll get spooked. Now drop your line on the side of the boat closest to the rocks. Blackfish hang around rocks all the time."

I dropped a line with a two-ounce sinker where Frank had instructed. When I caught my first black, I couldn't believe the fight. Uncle Frank looked more pleased than I did.

"He's a big one, Giovanni. Keep his head away from the rocks, or he'll go between two of them and swell his body, and you'll never get him out. If that happens, just loosen your line, give him a lot of slack, and sometimes he'll swim free."

My fish looked pretty big when he surfaced.

"Grab him under his gill and move him into the boat!" Frank said.

"How much do you think he weighs? Huh, how much?"

"About eight pounds. Wait until you tie into a big one, Giovanni. You can imagine the kind of fight he'll give you after catching this one."

I ended up catching five fish, and Uncle Frank boated at least ten. He was a master. Then he showed me how to gut the fish.

"The reason why you must gut a blackfish is because they're very fatty, and they'll have an impossible odor by the time you get back home if you don't gut them. As a matter of fact, they have so much fatty tissue, they must be skinned too."

"Hey, neat! Can I try that?" I said as he showed me an easy way to skin them.

"Of course, but keep in mind the knives are very, very sharp. If they weren't, you couldn't clean a blackfish. . . . You know, Giovanni, the Indians named this fish tautog, so if you hear this name, they're talking about the fighting fool blackfish."

I gutted and skinned one. It wasn't pretty, but at least I tried. I was sure I would become an expert in time.

"Giovanni, have you noticed the teeth the blackfish have?"

They resembled human teeth, perfect in shape and not one tooth out of line.

*****

We found our way home, and Aunt Emma, Frank's wife, was waiting for us at the door. "Did you have a good day, boys?"

"Fantastic, and Giovanni is going to be quite a fisherman."

I hugged and thanked him before I left. I ran all the way home with my rod and reel, proud and happy.

"Here's some fish for you," I said to Mom. "This is the rod and reel Uncle Frank gave me as a present."

Mom stared at it and knew it wasn't cheap. "Did you thank your uncle for this wonderful, expensive present?"

"That's the first thing I did just before I came home. And Aunt Emma said you can marinate these fillets in cold milk and garlic all night."

I began to feel dizzy and fainted. The next thing I recall was lying on the couch while Mom patted my forehead with a cold compress. I threw up most of the night. By morning, my temperature was hovering around 105, so Mom called the doctor.

"Annie, whatever he has is not the normal childlike diseases or any virus I know of. He's all alone on this one."

I still hadn't eaten two days later, and I asked for some black olives when Mom came into the room that morning. She grinned for the first time since I'd been ill. Mom took my temperature, and it was down to a hundred. I'd never seen Mom so happy. She hugged and kissed me.

"Giovanni, you've broken the fever. It's almost gone. Let me see, I must call the doctor, and it just so happens I have a couple of cans of black olives just the way you like them with the pits."

Mom watched me eat a whole can. By evening, the fever was gone with not a trace of pain. I tried to jump out of bed and fell down.

The next morning, Mom came in with my robe. "The doctor said you can carefully get out of bed and eat in the kitchen today."

Mom helped me up, and I found myself looking down at her. Yes, she was looking up! I had grown an unbelievable amount. It was like a miracle.

"Giovanni, you're much taller than I am. I can't believe it."

I was still wobbly, but not too wobbly for humor. "They won't be able to book me as Little Caruso any longer. They'll have to think of a new angle. I hobbled to the kitchen with my arm on Mom's shoulder. *Nothing is forever.*

Ninni and Maria were in the kitchen, and Ninni flipped out. "Hey, can I call you stretch now?" he asked. We laughed.

While we were sitting at the breakfast table, the doctor arrived.

"I've called every medical center in research about Giovanni's symptoms, and only one doctor in South Africa had a similar case," he said. "It's extremely rare. The simplest way I can describe what happened to his body is that he had an explosion of genes. Let's say they might have been bottled in and due to come around some time ago, but they decided to make their moves at once. This could cause these symptoms and his results, by the way."

*****

Spring was forcing itself in, chasing away winter. Dogwoods were budding, and all the birds were singing. I loved this time of year. It felt like being reborn.

My friends noticed I had grown, of course. My friend, Micky O'Brian, had brought me schoolwork so I could keep up with the class. It also helped to keep my head straight. Like Maria, Micky was an egghead. He carried a straight-A report card and was a fine athlete.

"When are you coming back to school, Giovanni?"

"Next week, and thanks for all the help you've been. I would've been lost without all these notes."

"Forget it, you're not a bad guy for a wop, and smart too."

Micky was one of the few people I'd let get away with that remark, for I knew he wasn't prejudiced. Our rapport developed when I started calling him Mick for short. If anyone else called him Mick, it wouldn't sit well with him. His father, a wonderful man who was an ex-priest, was on the police force.

Mom decided our neighborhood was not fit for us to grow up in. Murders were still an everyday occurrence. In fact, a chain of bowling alleys found a way to profit from them. They offered locker service for guns used in a homicide for two hundred dollars a month, so the police couldn't produce the weapon in evidence. The lockers at all ten locations were full.

After working all day, Mom would go out in the evening to look for apartments. Finally, one night at the dinner table, she folded her napkin and made an announcement. "Kids, we're moving Saturday, and I want you to know the rules before we move. It'll be in a two-story house, and the owners will live under us. Now this means you boys can't romp around the apartment and make all sorts of noise."

Her brow furrowed, and she spoke quietly. "I can't wait to get out of here. It has sad memories, and it's a lousy neighborhood. Just today, iceman, Carbone was found in his truck with an ice pick in his head. He always complained to me about men pressing him for protection money. He told me once, 'Over my dead body.' Well, he predicted right. He left a wife and seven children. I want out of here: the faster, the better. It's no place for children to grow up."

We moved from Clark Street to 23rd Street in Astoria, a more desirable part of town closer to our grandparents with better schools, nicer parks, and prettier houses. To our surprise, we had steam heat. I wouldn't have to start the fire every morning anymore, or steal coal from the rail yards. No more waking up in the morning freezing to death.

Mom made us all dress as soon as we unpacked. "You're going to meet the landlord, the people downstairs. Now mind your manners, if you know what's good for you."

We filed down the stairs, and I was shocked as we entered the apartment. The woman was the witch who performed the ceremony on me to chase away the evil eye. Her husband's face was strong and mean, and they had three children, Matt, Pete, and Lorraine. Matt and I hit it off, and he showed me his drawings. He was quite an artist. His work intrigued Ninni too.

Things seemed to be working out fine, and even Maria had someone her age. She and Lorraine took to each other. Matt and I would talk for hours about my music and his artwork techniques. Ninni and I would draw with him and compare notes. Matt and Ninni truly had a great gift. I could draw, but not to Ninni's level. It was amazing how his caricatures captured people's souls with just a few lines. I was envious but proud of him. Matt was more of a detail artist. Everything he did was like a photograph. No doubt he was a technician.

I almost had forgotten about my friends until I started telling Matt about them. I realized I missed my three buddies, so we decided to meet up with Matt by the Tinsdale Lumberyard by the East River. The East River was a veritable work of nature's art. It had color, shape, rough banks, and so many currents. I could sit and watch the squalls lathering the water for hours.

"What does your Pop do?" Vinnie asked Matt.

"Oh, Pop is a contractor in cement, and we own our house on 23rd Street."

"Whatta ya gonna be when you grow up?" Manny asked.

"A commercial artist."

"How do you know?"

"Because I'm learning all about art now, and I'll be one if I keep practicing."

"I'm gonna be a racket guy. Do you want to see my bullet wound?" Manny lifted his shirt. "It's still raw."

"Wow, how did you get that?"

"Aw, just in a holdup across the river."

"Gee, it looks like the cops got you right in the heart."

"Yeah, I was supposed to die, but I'm tough, just like my Uncle Frank Costello."

"Costello is your uncle? Holy Toledo. Is he as tough as they say he is?"

"Tougher, believe me. He plays it down for the papers."

Matt just gawked, then turned to Herman. "Hey, Herman, what are you going to be?"

"I'm going to be a priest, and Manny and I are going to be partners."

"How can a priest and a hood be partners? Are you kidding?"

"That's our secret," Manny said. "We got plans that will turn this city upside down."

Matt backed off and turned to Vinnie. "Hey, I've seen you around. Where you come from?"

"I think I've seen you too. Have you ever been to Mount Carmel Church?"

"Yeah, my cousin, Renaldo, was baptized in Mount Carmel."

"Well, I live just around the corner."

Manny announced he had some business to take care of, but he'd be back. He returned with ice cream, soda pop, and paper cups for us.

"Gee, it was nice of you to spend all of this money," Matt said as he finished his last drop of pop.

"Naw, I just cop it. I told old man Schultz someone was beating up on his son. We do it all the time, and he falls for it. So he ran out to protect his little boy, and I grabbed a brown bag, helped myself to the goodies, and here I am."

"Hey, you got a lotta guts, Manny."

"You have to in our woods. Visit more often and you'll get all the guts you need."

I realized we were running late and reminded Matt, who turned pale.

"Let's get out of here," he said. "My old man will kill me if I'm one minute late."

I soon was to find out why Matt was worried. His old man was waiting at the front of the house.

"*You!* Get in the house right now. Understand?"

I followed them into their basement apartment, which was partially below street level. He pushed Matt against the kitchen wall and slipped off his thick leather belt with a heavy brass buckle.

"Now, you know the rules. If you move either way, if you even close your eyes for a second, you get another five."

He looped the leather around his hand. His face tightened, and his coal-black eyes seemed to shine. He looked like a mad dog as he pulled back the belt and struck Matt across the face. I don't know how Matt didn't flinch. He took five across the face until it bled.

"Now, Matt, let this be a lesson. I told you, when I say something, you obey."

I started to cry, which seemed to infuriate him. "And you! If I catch you leaving the gate open one more time, I'll dispossess your mother right out of the apartment. Now, get the hell out of here!"

I ran five steps at a time to my room. I sat for hours feeling for Matt. How does he stand having a father like that? Does he get punished like that often? We were only a half hour late. I was to find out, yes, Matt went through this pretty often. It was sinful, for Matt was a sensitive child with a refined talent, and these beatings were to take their toll. Matt was turning bitter with a resentment that would shake a whole city one day.

I would discuss my social objections with my science teacher, Dr. Weirda. I could tell he was evaluating my intellect when I spoke. I mentioned my belief that language was a harmful tool. As language became more sophisticated, it enabled humans to say one thing but mean another. We had evolved into semantics. I believed deviates took advantage of the use of words to deceive people. In fact, I felt language was man's bitter enemy.

Dr. Weirda leaned back in his large Napoleon chair, wiped his glasses, and cleared his throat. "You know, Giovanni, I've been reviewing the idea of a program on the student level to teach a class innovated solely by the student. I offered your papers as an example, and all agreed your approach was just as good as a professional."

Over the weekend, I worked very hard on my first class. I tried to simmer down, but I couldn't. Would I be facing friends and enemies, and would they give me the chance to present this to the class? It was tough enough for adult teachers, much less a student.

I felt cold when I stood behind the desk in front of the room. My knees shook and my heart drummed as I addressed the class. "Ladies and gentlemen, I have created a class I think is most important for our age level. It's not English or grammar. It's about the history of oral communication of man."

My confidence began to build after I didn't get a jeer. "Have you ever thought of how language came about, or what forms of communication the prehistoric man had? How simple must it have been for primitive man, who expressed himself with motion and grunts? And now, language is so delicate, man can deceive his fellow man by clouding what he really thinks, by toying in the art of semantics."

*****

I come out of that memory thinking *how true that is even today*. Language constantly leads us or misleads us every day. We're living in the age of deception. Crackpots are writing advice books, some even promoted by government agencies if they benefit the reigning politico and using "national security" to promote their selfish motives. Dianetics moves the masses into an enigma of not being responsible for anyone, thoughts of loving anyone being shallow, or some sort of mental manifestation.

I know Tony is into a lot of these pseudo-intellectual books, mostly because of the pressures and vast problems thrown at him every day. He needs some crutches, I'm sure. Sometimes when he gets into one of these publications, he calls me to discuss it and to suggest I read it, not realizing he's asking for the recognition of the phony facts thrown together by the writer.

I questioned, does he love me as a brother, or does he fall into the social, literary trap written by those who have nothing but money to gain and nothing to lose? Even the finely written books are on trial in my mind, because no one on Earth can interpret what some skilled scientist has written without personally questioning the author on the matter.

I do know one thing: I'm not ashamed to love my brother or sister, and no one could talk me out of it. Much more than that, loving or caring for anyone entails a natural feeling for their happiness. It's not a sacrifice and doesn't hang me up in any way, for anything I do for the ones I love is a natural reaction, like blinking my eyelids.

Tony seems to read my thoughts. He smiles ever so faintly, then changes his expression, bows his head, and leaves the room.

I think of Mom. How could God make this magnificent woman suffer so? For even during those grand moments of conquests watching us perform so well, she suffered a pain no human should endure and managed to survive many more years than she should have. I believe the thought that we needed her kept her alive, and we did.

CHAPTER TWENTY

Uncle Frank was being installed as a Master Mason. A chauffeur drove me to The Plaza Hotel next to Central Park. I liked to dress in tails for this kind of occasion. To my surprise, Mrs. Quinlan was there with a photographer.

"Giovanni, how nice to see you. We're going to shoot some pictures because I'm certain we'll get some AP attention for this."

These meetings were secret, but they let me sit through the ceremony because I was to perform afterward. The candles and the procession intrigued me. I was proud as Uncle Frank received the famed silver gavel. He would be in a smooth position to twist arms here and there for political favor.

I sang "E lucevan le stelle" ("When the stars were brightly shining") from *Tosca* and closed with "Invictus" by Bruno Huhn. Frank introduced me to Congressman Sol Bloom, who was kind looking with an enormous torso.

"Shake hands with Sol Bloom, Giovanni. He's a good guy to know, he's running for reelection."

"How do you do, sir? I wish you all the luck in the world, and if I can help in any way, please don't hesitate."

"What did I tell you? A real trooper," Frank said.

"He has your blood, Frank. What do you expect?"

"You'll make it all right, Sol, a Jew in New York State with the gift of blarney and an honest, impeccable track record. How can you miss?"

I enjoyed this kind of chatter, even though I didn't always understand what they were saying. It made me feel involved and grown up.

When dinner was served, I had seconds. The artificial coloring in foods at these functions enchanted me. I didn't get steak and pineapple for dessert filled with all kinds of dyed green fruit very often.

Uncle Frank drove me home and informed me Mr. Costello had requested to see me the next day. I ran up the stairs for bed. It was after one o'clock, and tomorrow was a school day. Everyone was asleep except Ninni with his eyes wide open. "How did it go?"

"Well, everyone told me it was great, so I guess it went well."

Ninni looked quite serious. "Gee, do you know how lucky you are? I wish it was me. I would be happy."

I smiled. "It's possible to be happy and tired at the same time."

He smiled with me.

The next afternoon, I rode my bicycle to Frank's house. Mr. Costello greeted me in the study.

"Sit down, Giovanni. What I have to say is very important for you. You know I'm getting so much adverse publicity it would be bad for me to associate with you in public. Now you must understand you're not the only one involved. For the benefit of all the very talented people I know, Giovanni, my effort and concern always will be present. It's just that we won't see each other anymore, at least not until the world has some sort of change."

Uncle Frank looked surprised, and I started to tear up.

"Now, now, Giovanni, let's not have any of this. After all, we'll always be friends. And that's what counts. . . . Frank, I know what I must do. Things are going to get rough. Let's face it, even though the agencies leave me alone, I could get my head blown off, or a bomb, or whatever. We can't take the chance of risking this boy's life or image, and I think he's old enough to know the score."

"I agree, Costello, we do have some problems, and the Turks

are restless. They want your seat."

"I know. So why risk one of the real important parts of our thrust that I want to establish while I'm alive? Our creative people shouldn't be involved in risk under any circumstances. They're not like us, and they are valuable to our cause."

"You know somehow, Costello, you always give me a reason for admiring you. It's a pity no one knows what you're really like, the kind of class you move with. It worries me to think of the day someone may have to fill those large shoes of yours."

"Giovanni, let's embrace now, for it may be never that we'll talk or see each other. Just try to remember me kindly, and don't believe everything you read in the paper, okay?"

I hugged him. "I think I know what you mean, but you'll be my friend always, forever. I promise."

Frank half smiled at me. "Run along now, Giovanni, I'll be in touch. How is your mother? Does she need anything?"

"She's all right. We're getting along fine."

"Good, I'm glad to hear it. Now run along."

I turned the doorknob slowly, wanting to say more, wanting Costello to feel my friendship. As I turned to look at him, his expression let me know enough had been said.

*****

Once more, it was the feast of San Juliana and I performed every year at Costello's request. I didn't have to be asked again. As I watched the parade down Astoria Boulevard, I remembered Pop saying, "We'll always have wars as long as men march in a parade." I didn't know the significance then, but I did as I matured.

The parade included a brass band, local politicians holding banners, and an embroidered picture of the patron saint. Throngs would run to the banner as it was lowered to pin dollar bills to it, along with a smattering of fives and tens. The head of the parade recognized me as the entertainer and motioned me to join their march to the picnic site. At the rear, ten men carried a heavy pole on their shoulders as they grunted and perspired. The name over the gate on 23rd Avenue was still the same: Volkets Hall. I always found it odd that an Italian feast was held at a Polish pavilion.

The grounds were small but nice with tall trees dressing the earth, a few barbecue pits, and a beer hall. The men greased the fifty-foot long pole and attached goodies, such as Italian salamis, provolone, prosciutto, ricotta, and gallons of olive oil, to the top. The men lifted the pole, and it sank about five feet into the ground. For a dollar, anyone could try to reach the top to pluck the treasure and carry it down. I couldn't wait until I was old enough and had enough money to gamble. I dreamed of bringing the surprise home to Mom.

The first man tarred up the inside of his knees with some dirt, but he only made it one third up. One man after another failed, and the crowds seemed to root for the contestant to lose. Next up was a rowdy cousin of mine. He was Aunt Mary's son, Jim. He had a reputation as a thief, liar, and cheat. Aunt Mary could handle him, but his meek father couldn't.

"C'mon, Jim, get the goods!" I yelled.

Not only did he reach the top, but he also grabbed an extraordinary amount of goods. I waited at the bottom to congratulate him. "Boy, that was really neat, Jimmy. I don't think I've seen anyone do it with such skill."

"I've been practicing all week on the telephone pole in front of my father's store. I knew I'd make it," he said, trying to catch his breath.

I admired his spoils. "Boy, will your mom be proud of you when you get home with all this stuff."

"How would you like to surprise your mom and bring home this provolone cheese?"

"Gosh, you'd give this to me?"

"Why not? Your pop kept me out of more trouble. In fact, he hid me from the cops in your house. You're too young to remember, but I lived in your house for a week."

"Gee, thanks, Jim. Mom will flip when she gets this, especially when I tell her how you won it."

"Yeah, be sure and tell everyone how I won it, because they're going to think I stole it. So you are my star witness, right?"

"Boy, I sure am." I helped him load his car with the prizes.

"Hey, I hear you're going to sing today. I've never heard you sing. Can you beat that? Tell you what, why don't we go back in and feast on some of the good food at the concessions?"

"I don't have any money, Jim."

"Don't worry about money. Just come with me."

I had such a good time going from one booth to the next with sausage and peppers, meatballs, and Italian-style kebabs with veal and dreamy spices. The smells drove me wild. The best all: Italian coffee ice. My day got even better when he took me to the game machines. One of them measured the thrust of a punch with ratings such as pansy, weak, normal, and champ. Jimmy was surprised when I rated a champ. We played the roulette wheel and visited the weight guesser, who never missed.

A leashed monkey perched on the shoulder of an organ-grinder. The monkey would crawl to the organ and tip his hat when someone gave him a coin. To make the crowds laugh, he would put each coin between his teeth and attempt to bend them to ensure they were real.

An Italian puppet show was about to go on. The authenticity of the dolls was beyond belief. The sculpting and richness of the costumes were matched only by the fine actors voicing them. The story of the day was an all-time Italian favorite, Pinocchio. We watched to the end while jeering and cheering with the crowd.

I was glad to get to know the real Jimmy, not the stories I'd heard about him. I learned you rarely get the truth or the true person when you listen to gossip. Now I know why Uncle Dick would say, "Always get it from the horse's mouth." This attitude proved to be the right way to go in my life.

I was called to the bandstand. As I sang, I glimpsed the figure of the man I loved so much, Mr. Costello, in the shade of a distant tree. Our eyes met, and he nodded with a smile. My day was complete. I carried a prize for Mom, a five-pound ball of imported provolone, and fond memories.

*****

It was June and hot. When I arrived home from work, Mom and Maria were together, a rarity given everyone's schedules. I cut an inch slice of round Italian bread, soaked it in olive oil, sprinkled it with Romano cheese and fresh, chopped basil, and slid it into the oven. Things always tasted better in the old gas stove. I asked Mom why she was at home.

"Well, Uncle Frank has gotten Maria a job as a librarian. You know, the beautiful one on Hopkins Hill."

"Wow, that's great, Maria. When you graduated with honors, I knew you'd end up in a high-level job."

Maria didn't look happy. "The pay is ridiculous, and I have to decide if I want to do it or not."

"Well, how much do they want to pay you?"

"Nineteen dollars a week."

"That's very good money, especially for a first job, you know, considering most women make half that."

"Well, my main concern is there's not much chance for advancement. The library is run by grants and donations. As a matter of fact, when Uncle Frank was the president of Queens Library, he did it for prestige only. The job paid a dollar a year."

"Maria, give it a try. If you don't like it, quit. But don't forget to tell Uncle Frank your intentions first."

"Giovanni is right, you know," Mom said. "Nothing ventured, nothing gained."

Maria knew her potential, but Mom couldn't send her to college, not even with a full scholarship. Mom needed the income from Maria's job. I knew Mom was agonizing over this.

Mom had told us many times that she wanted us to go to college, but women in those days knew it was out of the question unless they were debutantes who could afford Vassar. Life was so painful then; so many dreams never got off the ground.

As for myself, the slowdown of my career disturbed me. Uncle Dick advised me not to sign Paramount's contract, and I accepted this without question, of course. Club dates became slim, and I gave a concert or radio show only now and then. I was farmed between three stations: WNYC, WBNX, and NBC.

NBC commissioned me to do a special as a Christmas doll. I had to freeze in place until the master of ceremony wound me up so I could walk in rigid, spring-like steps to the center of the stage to perform an Italian aria. Rehearsals lasted from the summer of 1938 until November. I was the only artist to get glowing mentions in Variety.

As I grew older, it became more and more difficult to captivate audiences. Even though I was only fifteen, I didn't have the same impact as when I was eight or nine. I had to work much harder, which frustrated me. My only consolation was Mr. La Puma's kindness and understanding. He reminded me most child entertainers became has-beens by thirteen.

I filled the main stem of my life working very hard to understand music. Prokofiev was my favorite ultra-modern composer, Debussy my favorite impressionist composer, Tchaikovsky my favorite romantic . . . until Rachmaninoff came along. His "The Isle of the Dead" blew my mind. Even though he was a contemporary, he wrote in the tradition of true romantic. He was dynamite and one of the great concert pianists of our time. I never missed his concerts at Carnegie Hall. He played most of my favorite piano compositions by Chopin, my favorite instrumental composer.

I could take Richard Wagner's music any time, but not for voice. I thought he was cruel to singers. His politics came out in his feeling for mankind. He was a profile of Adolf Hitler and became Hitler's favorite composer. In fact, Hitler made a national shrine out of Wagner's music and bypassed greater German composers such as Beethoven and Bach.

*****

One day when Dick was visiting, Ninni came out of his room singing Al Jolson's "Sonny Boy." We laughed, and it felt like the world had been lifted from our shoulders. Mom brought Dick his favorite nectar.

Dick undid his tie, slid it to one end, put the glass of whiskey on the long end, and slid it up to his neck like a conveyor belt. I never failed to laugh because he would change the pacing each time.

Dick still looked as though he just stepped out of a style magazine. Everything was so right: his skin, his graying hair, and his impeccable clothes.

"How's your career coming along, Giovanni?"

"Kind of slow, Uncle Dick. I'm doing things here and there but nothing consistent."

"Things will pick up, Giovanni. I can recall great names staying out of work, sometimes if the part wasn't right, other times because the salary offer was less than the last gig. Once you come down on your price, it's like committing suicide in show business."

"Why, Uncle Dick? Isn't it better to work than stay idle?"

"You can do benefits and so on. You're better off working for nothing. It's amazing how it gets around when you come down in price."

*****

The pressure wasn't letting up on Mom. She had befriended a family who owned a candy store, and the woman offered me an afternoon job while Mom worked. I would sweep and clean, and Mrs. Melnick would serve me a two cents plain with Middle Eastern halvah, one of my favorite treats. She had two sons and one daughter: Irving, the oldest at twenty-eight, Herbie, the youngest, and their sister, Sylvia. Herbie was studying piano and music theory at The Juilliard School of Music. We had a lot in common, and we'd listen to the masters by the hour.

I learned much about the Hebrew culture, dietary laws, and

religious holidays. And I really learned to love Mrs. Melnick. She treated me as a son, and she had reason to love me. Many of the prejudiced boys would pick on Herbie, who was no fighter. He was afraid of bruising his hands, and I didn't blame him, so I took on being his protector. On a few occasions, I needed protection myself. Some of these guys were no slouches, but they gained a respect for me. They knew I was a street fighter, and I wouldn't chicken on them.

*****

Manny was always in trouble with the police and was not about to give up his ambition of being public enemy number one. His uncle, Costello, was being accused of controlling unions and meddling with extortion in the garment district.

I needed a job, so I went to Uncle Albert, who had a factory in the garment district. Mom made sure I paid respects to Aunt Millie.

"I tell you what, Giovanni, I have a place for a hard-working boy to deliver rush orders to contractors. Then, if you show you have some feeling for the business, I'll start you off burning buckram off the material after it's embroidered. You come to my place at four o'clock every day and work until seven, all day Saturday, and sometimes Sunday when we have a special rush on an order. I'll start you at thirteen dollars a week. How about that?"

Of course, I didn't know what buckram was, but I soon was to find out. After putting stencils over dress material, they used a blackboard-like eraser saturated with white chalk to brush over the stencil. This imprinted the design on the material for the three embroidery operators at the machines. Two of the operatives were relatives. Albert had adopted Jimmy from Albert's brother. I surmised his father was not fit to raise him, so Albert took him in. He slept in the small basement of Albert's fine new home.

Bessie and Theresa did needlework by hand on special jobs, and the comical Odessa did odd jobs, from porter work and buying lunches to burning off the buckram in a controlled heat oven.

Buckram was a stiff cloth used as a base to keep the material straight on sharp, delicate turns on the machine.

After the sewing was completed, the only way to get the Buckram off was to burn it with heat and an acid. Odessa taught me the system. It was brutal, especially in the summer with no air-conditioning and a 300-degree oven. I had to put my upper body into the oven to pull out the hanging garments. The embroidered material had to come out at the precise time so the material wouldn't fade. This was critical, for if it did fade, that portion of the garment wouldn't match the rest of it. It didn't take me long to get bored and annoyed with it. I liked the delivery end, though, with fresh air and visits to various factories.

On my way back from a delivery, an ape-like man pulled me into an alley and dangled me in the air by my shirt. "What's your name?" he asked.

"Giovanni."

"Where do you work, punk?"

"I work for Albert Ianone around the corner."

"You belong to the union?"

"Of course not, I work for my uncle."

"Mind your tongue, or I'll cut it right out of your head."

I went to Frank's house Sunday and told him what happened.

"First of all, Johnny, you're a minor, and you're not eligible or liable in any binding contract. What I want from you is a description of this man and where he's working."

After I gave him the details, he dialed the phone.

"Hello, I want to speak to Johnny. No, not that one, the other guy, Dee, get it? I want this goon here in fifteen minutes. I know who he is, and he doesn't live far from here. . . . No, I won't call him, you call him, and I'm letting you know out of respect, I'm going to give him a hard time. Thank you."

Uncle Frank and I chatted until there was a loud knock. When Uncle Frank opened the door, I wanted to hide under the chair. The big hulk was taken by surprise when he saw me.

"You recognize this boy, Rocco?"

"Yeah, Frank. I didn't know he was a friend of years."

"He happens to be my nephew and well favored by Costello, you fathead. What the hell do you think you're doing picking on a minor anyway?"

"Frank, I knew what I was doing. We found out he was a relative of Ianone, and we thought he might spring for a contract if we intimidated the kid. We knew the kid couldn't sign a legal contract."

"First of all, punk, Ianone is my brother-in-law, and you're going to answer for that too."

"Listen, Frank, this guy Ianone brags around the circuit he has connections to keep him out of the union. Now he's still operating a scab shop. It makes us look bad, so we got orders to nail him. So I tried what I thought was the easiest way in."

"Rocco, apologize to my nephew, then we'll discuss my dumb brother-in-law."

"I'm sorry, kid. If I had known you were Frank's nephew, I never would've bothered you."

Boy, this big goon was really scared. I was so proud of Frank. He could do anything. By the end of the day, he managed to take care of my problem and Rocco's. He called Albert to give him the riot act about bragging about his connections and made him promise to join the union, assuring him it would be a friendly contract. Rocco left bowing, excusing himself, and apologizing out the door.

The work at the factory got heavier with labor and more responsibility. Albert was so tough that I began to brainstorm ways to get fired. When I was working the oven, I would leave the garments in too long so they would fade. It took three lots of two hundred dresses before Albert called me into his office.

"Giovanni, I don't like to hurt your feelings, but I think you're a better singer than an embroidery man. I hate to tell you this, but I'll have to let you go. I know you work very hard, but I almost lost some accounts because of faded garments. I can't afford this. So, just tell your mom I said you're not suited for this business."

I tried to look sad, but I felt victorious. I didn't have to be pushed around anymore. I prayed he couldn't read me. I sang all the way home on the subway. Explaining this to Mom wasn't easy, but I got away with it, apparently because she had no love for Uncle Albert. In fact, he reminded her of Dominick.

"Don't worry, Giovanni, I know it's not your fault. After all, you've never been fired before, and I know he's hard to work for. In fact, I knew a lot of operators who worked for him, and they never had a nice thing to say about him. He is a chiseler from way back. I'm glad you're out of there. We'll do it on our own. I don't need him reminding me every time he sees me that he's doing us a favor, especially when I know he would suck the blood out of a person for a penny."

Mom's stand was admirable. I went to bed happy. She was a real Mom.

*****

Cousin Kitty brings me back to the present. How can she look so attractive with the ugly marriage she went through? I can't help but think of the sadness her father and mother brought to my childhood and the injustice her father did to my mother. I've learned to deal with it, knowing how the conservative mind works. Yet, I still harbor some bitterness.

I look at her, though somewhat still in my trance. "How are you, Kitty?"

She doesn't hesitate telling me about her awful marriage, everything from her husband physically abusing her to him stealing her mother's money.

"Would you like me to pay him a visit?"

Evidently, her upbringing stuck. "What makes you think you can deal with my doctor husband?" she asks as if I'm still the poor cousin from her youth.

"Well, Kitty, you know I always like a challenge. After all, your situation can't get any worse, can it?"

I actually could have helped her, but her brash attitude makes me slough it off.

CHAPTER TWENTY-ONE

Herman was now attending prep school to realize his dream of becoming a priest, and he visited me during the week off before exams. His hair was cut Marine style with sidewalls, and he looked fit from the physical education programs. In fact, he had won the state title on the boxing team. He described his better understanding of God through his training and Mass.

Manny showed up and signaled us to join him outside. We slinked into a dark alley.

"Hey, you guys, want to see something neat?" he said as he lifted his shirt and pulled a shiny steel-blue German Luger out of his belt.

I gripped it. "Wow, where in the hell did you get this, Manny?"

"Don't point that thing at me. Never point a gun unless you mean it."

Herman took it from me and butted the handle against Manny's shoulder. "Have you blown your mind, Manny? What in God's name do you need with this? It'll only lead to disaster. If a cop knows you're armed, he'll plug you sure as shit."

"No cop is going to get the chance, Herman. I've learned when to pull it and when not to."

"Yeah, that's why so many dead crooks are in the morgue."

"What in the hell are they teaching you in school, Herman? You know damn well what I have to do, I have to accept the risks and punishments, and no cop is going to shoot at me again. I'll shoot first."

"I'll pray for you, Manny," Herman said with a hopeless expression.

"Thanks, Herman, I'll take help anywhere I can get it."

*****

What every young man longs for had come upon me. It was March 18, 1939, my sixteenth birthday. I was hoping for a surprise party, but the day dragged on as each minute felt like a century.

"Giovanni, I forgot I need some Romano cheese. Will you go over to Mr. Jarrett's and get me a pound?" Mom asked around six o'clock.

"Okay, Mom. Can I get some black olives?"

"Not this week, Giovanni, we can't afford it."

Mr. Jarrett greeted me at the store. "Well, Giovanni Benedetto, Anna's oldest son." He turned to address his patrons, "Hey, we have a celebrity in our midst. This is the Little Caruso. Did any of you hear him on the Al Jolson *Shell Château* program on NBC?"

I wanted to crawl into one of the pasta bins. As I ran home, I noticed a figure running from our window when I turned the corner, and the lights went out. It was pitch black when I opened the door. My heart stopped when the lights switched on.

"Happy birthday, Giovanni! Happy birthday!" everyone screamed. "Happy sweet sixteen, Caruso, happy sixteenth!" Uncle Jim's voice boomed.

I was in shock as my eyes swept the room. I couldn't believe so many friends could fit into our apartment, everyone I loved: the Melnicks, my two best friends I hadn't seen for a while, Dr. Weirda, Dr. Watson, Giuseppe La Puma, and my local relatives. Gifts were piled a mile high on the kitchen table. Tears came to my eyes.

My heart was pounding like a bass drum. My uncles had brought their guitars, mandolins, and concertina. Dick's favorite banjo rested on his knee. My happiness was mixed with guilt. Despite how hard Mom had to work, she always managed those little things to make us feel the force of family. Mom had fixed a table of Italian hors d'oeuvres: meatballs pastries, and candy, plus four gallons of white and red wine from Grandpa's cellar.

The wine began to take effect, and the music became louder and burst into the *stornelli,* one melody with improvised storytelling, like a folk song, some comical, sad, or off-color. They roasted people in the room to a jaunting melody, all in good fun. My uncles took a break to drink more of Nonno's wine.

My favorite uncle put his gentle hands on my shoulder. He was like Pop, a deep philosopher, loved his fellow man, and the only one in the family who had the nerve to be a Democrat. "Giovanni, would you do your uncle Tom a favor? Would you sing 'Una furtiva lagrima' from *L'Elisir d'Amore?*"

Everyone applauded. I thought of Pop and sang it with such feeling.

Time to open presents. Manny and Herman stepped forward, and Herman handed me the most beautiful prayer beads I'd ever seen. "These are from Rome, Giovanni," he whispered. "They keep you safe, blessed by the Pope." We embraced.

Manny presented me with a fancy briefcase. "This is to carry your music. It's real alligator skin, but don't worry, it won't bite you." Everyone laughed.

My godfather showed up with his driver, Pete, and kissed both my cheeks. "Giovanni, now you're a man, and every man should have an impressive pen and pencil so they can do business." He opened a velvet box to reveal my name engraved on the pen and pencil. "That is the highest grade platinum, very expensive, so make sure you don't lose them, eh? And here's an envelope, some money to help in the house."

He kissed Mom's hand. "You know, Anna, Giovanni is a very good boy. I keep tabs on him. You should be very proud of your whole family. And, you know you can call on me anytime if you ever need anything. Don't forget."

*****

I hear loud murmurs as Tony sits down next to me. He's asking me something as time transports me from 1939 to 1977.

"John, what's the hunchback doing here with the hooker?"

"I don't know, Tony. He couldn't get in unless someone in the family invited him, and his brother, who was here yesterday."

"I know who it was, he and the hunchback were doing some business together. This is a mockery of a church event, my mother's church event!"

Tony begins to cry and we embrace. "I know, Tony, we shall miss her, and the best way to show our respect is to love her in death as we did in life."

I take a long look at Tony. I always feel his pain, always. Winning in his game is costly.

I'm furious anyone, let alone a family member, could so disrespect our mother. But objecting only would make it worse.

Imagine being extremely poor and struggling for many years until someone waves a magic wand and you're not only famous, but also earning more money in one night than you've made in two years. People had criticized you, called you a lazy bum, and said you'd never make it with your big nose. Then, like snapping on a light, the same people cling to you, praise you, and say, "I always knew you'd make it, Tony." It's disturbing, to say the least, especially coupled with the tense responsibility of performing to vast audiences all over the world.

I never forgot that Pop asked me to take care of Tony. I was the first to recognize his greatness, so I made a pact with myself to protect him, appeasing him when necessary, and help anyway I could. Tony had what I didn't: dedication to any craft he endeavored. To make it, as they say, you marry your craft as a priest would marry the church. I'm immensely proud of him, and I've used Al Jolson's quote to tell him and the world, "They ain't seen nothin' yet."

Exhausted, I stand to leave the room. I know I can't say anything to make him feel better. "Get some rest, Tony."

"I have a date coming up right after the funeral. Do you think I should cancel? Would it be appropriate?"

"I think it would do you a world of good. Do it, and if anyone criticizes you, in the words of the great Confucius, 'Fuck 'em.'"

Tony smiles meekly. "Thanks, babe, I'll see you later."

Patricia and I go back to the hotel to freshen up. As I lie down for a minute, I find myself back at my sixteenth party.

*****

As the music played on, Tom whispered to me, "Giovanni, please sing 'M'appari' from *Martha*."

"Gee, Uncle Tom, everyone seems to be having such a good time dancing and singing. I hate to impose on their fun."

Tom signaled for the music to stop. "Quiet, everyone. Giovanni is going to sing 'M'appari' from *Martha*."

This drew applause. When I finished, one of my newer friends, Rudy de Harak, walked over. "You're a fine artist, Giovanni. Stay with it."

Rudy was a fine art painter. His work hung in exclusive high-end establishments and homes. He also had a flair for commercial arts, a rare combination. His works graced the most respected buildings in Manhattan, starting with the Met.

As the party broke up, the guests came to congratulate me. It was the best high ever.

Little brother rubbed his eyes. "Here's a birthday hug for you, Giovanni. I'm tired. Good night."

Maria hugged me and told me how happy she was for me. My scrawny sister was growing into such a beautiful woman.

Mom looked content. "Giovanni, I'm so proud to see how much my children love each other."

"I swear to God, someday people won't say 'poor little Annie.' I don't know how, but we'll make you the proudest mom who ever lived."

A tear trickled down her cheek.

*****

We still had some snow on the ground. March seemed to be going out like a roaring lion. Mom wouldn't allow me to go outside, so I was bored until Ninni walked into the bedroom.

"Hey, Giovanni, would you like to try our ESP one more time?"

"Yeah, good idea, Ninni." We each held a piece of paper, and Ninni went into the next room. I thought for a moment. "Ninni, would you like to try single numbers this time instead of shapes, say one to ten?"

"Let's go for it, Giovanni."

Afterward, I felt compelled to call Dr. Weirda with our results, a 98 percent success rate. He said he would send them to a professor friend at Duke University and request a profile test at the university, which would rank our potential.

Not only was Dr. Weirda very kind, but he also was extremely talented. I was to find out he was foremost in his field. You wouldn't have known it. He wasn't interested in money.

*****

Uncle Frank called. "Giovanni, the Masons are having a national convention and are being hosted by the Foresters. Ethel Merman will be there, your friend, Eddie Bracken, and a host of other celebrities. This will be a good one for you, Giovanni. It'll be getting national and international press, and Mr. Costello would be very happy if you'd do a show as his protégé."

"Anything for you, Uncle Frank."

"Okay, Giovanni. It'll be in about three weeks in Boston. I'll get all the details and call you back. By the way, Uncle Tom will be taking you to this one."

"All right, Uncle Frank, I'll be waiting for your call."

The phone rang again soon after, and Mom answered it. "Mrs. Melnick, how good to hear from you. How is everything? . . . What? Oh, my God! I'm so sorry, and he was only twenty-seven years old."

Tears flowed down Mom's face as she hung up.

"What's the matter, Mom?"

"Irving died this morning at nine o'clock. Just a mere boy. I feel so sorry for the Melnicks. Giovanni, we'll have to go and sit Shiva this afternoon, and I want you to help the family in whatever way they may need. Do you understand?"

"Yes, Mom."

"Oh, and you'll have to wear a dark suit out of respect."

I sat at the Melnicks' without remorse. I'd built a resistance to becoming emotional when someone died. However, I was sinking into a depression, perhaps from my struggle to leave school to help Mom with money. School wasn't fun anymore.

When we got home, I sat in an armchair in the living room and stared at the ceiling. Pop's wisdom kept returning to me. I loved him more than ever and still needed him. "Thanks, Pop. Thanks for all your help." I smiled and fell asleep.

While it was an uneasy time for the Melnicks, it was an uneasy time in the world too. Hitler was stirring up a storm with his bible of hate. Evidence began to creep into our newspapers of crimes against Catholics and other minorities. However, Hitler couldn't gain power without doing his German populace some good deeds. First, he pulled Germany out of its worst recession. Then he broke up chains and divided neighborhoods into zones for stores. Each zone was allotted a certain number of stores so they could thrive without competition.

The media reported a British government official visited Hitler, thinking he would be listening to his pageant of peace, but Hitler was stalling to amass a formidable military force. All of this was happening as Roosevelt was slowly bringing the United States back on its feet. I was not to forget the lesson.

It looked as though Mussolini was going to bed with Hitler. Most of the people were behind Italy's leader nicknamed Il Dolce, but I saw him as a clown, a buffoon to be ridiculed. How could Italians align themselves with this animal? This devastated me because of my heritage. The Italy I knew was art, music, farming, and exotic flowers.

How would I explain to the Melnicks that I did not support the Mussolini regime? However, I came to find I had underestimated their depth. They knew I never could give myself to fascist thinking. "Giovanni, we know you," Mrs. Melnick said.

June arrived, and I was off to Boston to perform at the Mason convention. This proved to be much different and larger than Uncle Frank's local installation. I met Joseph Earl Perry, re-elected Grand Master.

CHAPTER TWENTY-TWO

September 1, 1939, added a word to Webster's dictionary: blitzkrieg. I was still sixteen when the headlines read, "German army attacks Poland," "Cities bombed, port blockaded," "Danzig is accepted into Reich." Hitler conquered the country overnight by air. The rest of Europe was nervous about the ambitions of this vicious dictator. It was like a mad dream. It took me back to the previous year when Orson Welles did a mock invasion of outer space creatures, an adaptation of H.G. Wells' novel, *The War of the Worlds*, from 1898. The brilliantly directed radio show propelled Orson Welles into national fame overnight.

It didn't take long for the reality of this insane German head of state to infiltrate every mind in the world. His cruel acts would go down in history as the most infamous of all time. He committed genocide on those he felt were not of pure origin, and he proclaimed the Aryan race as the supreme supermen of the world.

He directed most of his hate at Jews, which created our own haters here, some of whom joined the American Nazi Party. Propaganda defamed Jews, blacks, and Catholics. Thankfully, most Americans were not of this mindset.

I couldn't believe how one man could perpetrate so much misery throughout the world, and the United States was doing everything it could to stay out of the fight, even though its allies were being subjected to punishment beyond belief.

The Melnicks developed a venomous hate for this man. They

had run out of Russia under another dictatorship, so they knew the path of this madman.

*****

I was already a senior in high school in 1939, being ahead by almost two years. I organized a fine swing band, and many of the members later became famous. We bought stock arrangements, and I was influenced by Benny Goodman and Tommy Dorsey, so I patterned the instrumentation after them. I carefully chose my musicians, and the outstanding ones were Louis Graw on drums, Sonny Sasso on tenor sax, Danny Martucci on base, Pete Chandais on lead trumpet, and Al Cremin, a dynamite guitar player. I chose a school chum named Johnny Vekassy as the leader, even though he was square and in love with himself, he had the knowledge of music and arrangements.

May Homer donated her studio for our rehearsals four nights a week. I landed a gig for the 18-man band at a large community hall, and the pay was ten dollars each except for twenty for the leader. I forwent commissions to hold the band together.

The band impressed Uncle Dick, and Herbie tailored some of the stock charts to the lead men's abilities, which gave us a distinct style. Dick arranged a free bus for us, which boosted our morale.

Our gig ended up being an overwhelming success. We had all the sound and poise of any professional band in the country. I began celebrating.

We played the same center for the next month, but scouts started snatching the lead men for the big-time swing bands. I was happy for them, but also frustrated, because it was next to impossible to replace their caliber. After much deliberation, I dismantled the band but didn't feel defeated. The learning experience had been a revelation, touching on problems of organization, etc.

Big bands were the rage with Tommy Dorsey, his brother, Jimmy Dorsey, Glen Miller, and many more. One of my dearest friends, Bobby Hackett, a true one of a kind admired by millions, was asked to catch a new singer named Frank Sinatra at the Astor Roof. He was singing with the Tommy Dorsey Orchestra. When Frank finished his act, he walked over to chat with Bobby. It was not every day a new singer had the opportunity to sit with the master.

"K-kid, i-if y-you knew wa-what was g-going t-to ha-happen t-to y-you i-n the n-next t-twenty y-y-years, y-y-you would b-be s-s-scared t-to d-d-death," Bobby stuttered at Frank.

*****

As early as 1940, the trauma of a possible war was on everyone's mind. Incidents like the Japanese attack on the *USS Panay* led everyone to believe Japan would join the Axis powers. The Japanese ambassadors were doing the most skillful public relations ever known with apologies galore, and they baited our naïve officials into one of the most incredulous betrayals. We were shipping arms to our pre-allies, our factories were producing, more and more jobs were being created, and the scars from the long Depression slowly faded, as if the misery of poverty never had happened.

Stories of Hitler's atrocities were becoming more common, and vivid pictures of the massive slaughters were appearing in the newspapers. It was almost as though Hitler was scoffing at the world by allowing these pictures out of the country.

It was a presidential year, and Thomas Dewey threw his hat in the Republican nomination ring against a formidable opponent, Wendell Willkie, who won the nomination. Roosevelt, who had proved not only to be a great president, but also a skillful politician and a great orator, found himself in a fight. Willkie blew the election, and Uncle Frank was furious; he hated losing. Willkie later wrote *One World*, urging a unified world government. He was certainly not the first, nor the last to believe in this for world peace, as I remembered Uncle Patsy was sent to the asylum when he made what he called the United World Flag.

Roosevelt's camp was stronger than ever, and Uncle Frank's

prediction he would be our country's first dictator was beginning to loom. Those who had laughed at Frank's analysis became quiet.

My endeavors had become quiet too, so Uncle Frank gave me a chance to make some money. As Republican Party leader, he had access to a building belonging to the Party, and he offered it to me Tuesday nights to run bingo games. This mild gambling game was taking hold, and churches were the forerunning exponents of the game, for it raised money to supplement their collections. Frank also gave me the supplies, such as bingo cards and the numbers cage. I agreed to split a percentage with the Melnicks across the street for supplying soft drinks. That way, I didn't need capital up front. We had some dandy prizes: toasters, mixers, dinnerware sets, and portable radios. The admission was a dollar and fifty-cents per card.

When I mounted the podium to start the game, I discovered my aunts and cousins smiling in the two wings of the front row. I was pleased until the nightmare started. They won the first six prizes — the most expensive ones — and most of the neighbors knew they were my family. Grunts, groans, and angry expressions filled the room. It was the first and last bingo game I ran in Astoria. Everybody accused me of cheating, and I could find no way to vindicate myself. I considered this my first political defeat.

*****

One of the major streets in Astoria was named after the Steinways. The family had moved a plant from Germany that provided industry for our town. I knew the Steinways from my concerts. They were planning to convert the plant into a defense operation to make military gliders for the government.

This great company was an expert on wood and the stress factor, which enabled it to build these grand gliders to handle the strain of war. The Steinways hired the most illustrious wood carver in the world, Albert Stewart. In fact, one of the sculptor's credits was the White House's Steinway grand. He had sculpted three American eagles to support the piano instead of conventional legs.

*****

One Sunday, John Vekassy, Frank Rose, and I were invited to Herbie's house to listen to some Toscanini efforts and sight-read as though we were conducting. How exciting!

I arrived at Herbie's house at nine sharp in the morning. Mrs. Melnick answered the door and hugged me. "Come on in, Giovanni. Herbie is doing his finger exercises."

I sat in awe as Herbie played some Chopin. He was truly a creative musician. When he finished, he smiled at me. "I have Toscanini Verdi's Requiem with Jussi Bjorling and Nicola Moscona."

This sent chills up my spine, for they were my favorites, and this requiem was the finest interpretation.

Herbie walked over with the book. "Are you ready, maestro?"

I bowed as he handed me the baton. He put on the record, and he seemed to forget Frank and John were to join us. Then I realized Herbie never wasted one second of joy when it came to music.

He would stop the recording without warning and ask me to point out the spot of the lead trumpet. "I'm sorry, Giovanni, but I lost concentration."

"Herbie, I really know how to sight-read; you don't have to check me."

Herbie smiled meekly and apologized. I told him I didn't want to compete, but he would lose if we did. Herbie went back to the book as if he didn't hear me. The wonderful chords of Verdi captured my soul, and I knew Herbie was on the same high.

Our two friends finally arrived. Frank, who had a deep love for opera, played the accordion while John played the violin. John had completed his studies in solfeggio, which gave us something in common.

John posed, as though he were a movie star. I could tell he worked out a lot and that Frank was an idol worshiper, as he asked me many questions about the opera stars I had worked with. He said he got stopped on the street frequently because of his resemblance to George Raft. I didn't want to deflate him, but I didn't agree.

So, here we were, Herbie suffering from deep-rooted hang-ups, John thinking he was God's gift to women, and Frank being stranger than fiction. I wondered, *what did they think of me?*

CHAPTER TWENTY-THREE

I was in dire need of work, so I asked the Steinways for a job. The timing was perfect. The factory officially had been closed for two years with only a small staff. But now they were adding back workers, and I was one of them.

I made the great sum of seventy-five cents an hour in the action department, which dealt with the mechanism that throws the hammer to the string when a note is hit. I met the personnel, which were mostly Italian, German, and Hungarian. Our foreman, Mr. Peterson, was a grand old man of seventy. In fact, most of the highly skilled men were older than sixty.

Mr. Peterson's responsibility had nothing to do with pianos, though. He was designing templates per government specs for parts of the glider project, and the stress demand dictated the types of wood. This was a monumental job, and I went to his office to watch the genius every chance I got.

The action department was fascinating. Most of the parts were hand carved, assembled, and hand glued. This was one of the many reasons their products were expensive. The factory of five buildings looked as though it were from another country with dark, antique brick against the cobblestone streets. One of the most important buildings was where they seasoned wood. Some wood was in the kilns for as much as twenty years. Seasoned wood was used on the larger areas, so the piano tops wouldn't bend or warp when the mahogany veneer was applied to the base wood.

The two boys born of William Steinway's second marriage worked in Steinway & Sons. William and Theodore saw major growth and expansion. The facility had a new Steinway — Henry's great-grandson, Henry Ziegler Steinway — who had been there three years following his graduation from Harvard. He was the same Henry I had met three years ago when I performed at the Steinway concert.

One day, young Henry approached me. "Giovanni, how would you like a firsthand tour through the plant? It'll be a long time before we make pianos again, and I'm sure you won't have the opportunity to see this again. Production on pianos will stop in seven months. Even though the glider work is mechanically similar, the finished product is as different as day and night."

First was the pressing room, where they veneered the hull of the piano by sizing the wood, then placing the cut pieces that matched the wood base. Two men ran the pieces through two huge rollers dripping with hot glue. The rollers resembled old-fashioned washing machine wringers rolling in opposite directions and sucking in the wood. The panels were stacked in front of heat-controlled fans to dry.

The tour made it more and more obvious why this family produced the finest piano in the world. The soundboards were made to perfection, and the stringers' job was dangerous. A deep scar could result if one of the strings snapped.

The damper area really captivated me. Those shiny black shapes of wood with felt glued on their bases smothered the sound of the strings when a pianist pressed a pedal. They started wider at one end for the heavier strings and became narrower as the strings got thinner.

The beautiful black finish, called French polishing, a thing of beauty. The workers, called rubbers, applied the base paint twenty-eight times. Each time they rubbed the paint deep into the wood until the surface became so saturated, it appeared as though the surface paint were baked right into the wood and couldn't be scratched off.

In the final assembly room, a piano tuner was in constant concert as each piano came off the production line.

It took a whole day to absorb the masterfulness of this great factory. Now I knew more about this instrument than any concert player.

When the big boss came through the plant, he paid special attention to me. He was well liked, and the older men accepted the fact we were acquainted. At first, they asked me how I knew him, but I just said he knew my uncle, and he probably did, being a Republican.

Even though he came from a staunch German family, the government must have highly regarded him because they entrusted him with a project requiring stiff national security.

The conversion was progressing smoothly. There were rumors of fifth columnists within the ranks, and the owners were given the authority to bring in a security force. All defense projects worked the same way: The government paid 10 percent over the total cost, and profit was guaranteed with the owner facing no risk.

The security contract was given to John Shields Detective Agency. Shields was a pro. Key army men belonging to either Hitler or Mussolini were arrested at the factory. Talks with Lieutenant Shields fueled my fantasy of being an avenging American spy seeking out these traitors. He showed his prejudice, though, when he told me stories of working in Harlem. It was those like him who caused Roosevelt to create his Fair Employment Practices Committee, and it was those like Philip Randolph, speaking up for the porters on railroads, such as Grand Central, who got it done.

The conversion proved to be an education beyond belief. They produced pianos up until the last day before switching to the glider project. The factory was ordered to stockpile as many pianos as it could to meet sales demands for perhaps as long as the war lasted.

*****

Growing up as a talented Italian American wasn't easy. I stare at Ninni, now called Tony, again and again during the funeral ceremony at the church. I think about the war. What would have been the outcome if they had assigned me to the USO rather than the clandestine activity I requested? What if I had dodged bullets rather than fired them? Was I so burnt out that I refused entertainment and accepted combat? So many loved ones tried to protect me from this.

*****

Our armed forces were building up.

One day, I met Dick in the street, and he told me he was offered a job as a road manager for USO 1941 through a friend related to Barney Baruch. The new government agency was a group of entertainers whose job was to keep up the morale of the soldiers.

Dick met him through a man named Perry Wolf, who owned a pool hall in Astoria. "Come with me, Johnny. I want you to meet a great guy, a real gent."

Perry taught me billiards, and we became close friends.

On the way home, Uncle Dick and I stopped by Uncle Frank's. A man in the den was introduced as Vito Marcantonio, a two-year elected official to the House of Representatives.

"Look, Vito, even though you're in the opposite party, we're close friends, and you know my basic philosophy is similar to yours," Frank said. "But the way you're operating and the public statements you're making are going to get you a hatchet you never dreamed of."

"What in the hell are you talking about, Frank? What hatchet? All I did was get up in the middle of the night to help one of my poor constituents out of being evicted. So what do I see? A whole bunch of cameras. They catch me in my pajamas with an overcoat on, and for the life of me, I don't see why it rates front-page pictures in the *Daily Mirror*."

I recalled Pop telling me about a vicious newspaper magnate

called Hearst who sold papers with all sorts of sensationalism: bloody crime, bribery, vice, scandal, the defamation of public officials, especially if they were Democrats.

"Yeah, Vito, but you didn't have to scowl at the reporters and tell them they should be taking pictures of the louse, capitalist landowners who were causing this kind of scene, instead of you."

"It was the truth, Frank. What's wrong with the truth?"

"The truth is a matter of interpretation, Vito. They're going to chew you up alive. You'll be called a left-wing communist."

"Frank, I appreciate your warm, friendly concern, but I must say you're not in my district, and I must react to the needs of the people. You take care of your velvet glove area, and I'll take care of my people who are oppressed, poor, and feel defeated. It's just politics as usual. Now, if I get voted out because of caring for them, then the next guy who does the same will be booted too. So, you see, we are at an impasse. Listen, Frank, thank you, but I must run. Nice meeting you all."

They embraced in the traditional Italian manner before the great Marcantonio left.

*****

Ninni, now fifteen, was deep into his appetite for art. Even though his work was traditional realism, it seemed to radiate much passion for a boy his age. He never ceased to amaze me. Looking back now, I realize his personality had two fierce sides. One was focus. He continued to mimic my practicing scales, and he had a voice quality I'd never heard before. It was not only exciting, but bewitching.

The other side of his personality: He appeared to will what he wanted. One Thanksgiving week, Ninni asked for a nickel to go to the movies even though we had no money for turkey dinner. He pleaded with Mom, telling her there would be a ticket drawing for a turkey and he would win it. She gave in, and he returned with the turkey he won!

Dick would sit both of us down to preach the entertainer's

bible. Ninni was enchanted by his lessons of how show business was wired, the ups, and the pitfalls. Quite frankly, I was bored with it and looking to get out, but Ninni soaked up every word.

I wasn't bored with the Steinway conversion, though. I became more enthralled with each passing day. I asked questions in every department, but I didn't get a total answer. So I decided to ask for an audience with Henry Steinway.

"What can I do for you, Giovanni?" he asked.

"I've been watching the conversion with interest, Mr. Steinway, and quite frankly, I have no complete picture of what the glider really is, or how big it is. I know conveyor means carrier, but I have no idea what these gliders would carry."

"Well, Giovanni, knowing you and your background all these years, and knowing your uncle Frank so well, I can't see why I can't explain some of it. A lot of it is unclassified, except certain pertinent facts are held back in the plant, because we still suspect the chance of sabotage."

He opened a giant folder to reveal the first picture I'd seen of the glider. The glider dwarfed a ten-ton truck beside it.

"Wow, it's huge."

"Yes, Giovanni, the GC-4A troop transport gliders are huge, and it's easy to deduce why we've been chosen to engineer the stress on the various woods. It has to be capable of hauling trucks, tanks, ammunition, and a platoon of fully armed men, air-landing paratroopers on point, and towed by giant planes over enemy territory wherever landings aren't possible. So the ship has to be so stable. Chances of it disintegrating will be impossible, and the wood stress is only as important as the glue we've perfected. We use glue and nails. If the glue doesn't hold, failure is inevitable."

I was wide-eyed, enchanted and felt important. Very few knew what I had been shown, and I wouldn't betray the trust.

"We had the glue, the same glue we used on the pianos, but we couldn't afford the long dry time for this project. So our engineers developed a way of utilizing air hoses to speed the drying process.

Then our genius resident, John Bogyos, revolutionized the glue process by utilizing high-frequency radio waves. It was taking us four hours to dry, but now it takes two minutes. We've even beaten out Ford's time. Many parts require glue, so this has enabled us to reduce our assembly time by half."

*****

I had to ask for a day off. I received word from Lillian Quinlan that I had the chance for a Broadway part in a play called *Brother Rat*. I was ready for this. I'd been taking acting lessons for about two years with the great Henry Travers.[7]

George Abbott was producing it, and he had a track record a mile long of successful Broadway shows. When I met with him, he liked my style and the way I read my lines. Unfortunately, he said I was a bit too young looking for the part and about four inches too short. But, he said he would use me at the first opportunity. I knew he was sincere and not the kind of phony who would be polite for the sake of elegance. In fact, he was notorious for telling actors to quit the business if he thought they had no talent.

Mrs. Quinlan said it was only a matter of time before I broke through the magic circle. I continued learning with Professor La Puma, or Maestro, as he was called. He told me he was working on a part for me with the Mascagni Organization. They were rated second to the Metropolitan and had a stable of fine artists, so this maintained my interest and dedication. But, frankly, my desire to perform every time I was invited to a party was wearing thin. I was awfully busy with my work at the plant, my lessons with La Puma, and fun at the Homer studio.

*****

The newspapers were full of antics by the Japanese ambassadors toying with our heads of state. Our cynical senior

---

[7] Henry Travers at age 72 played Horace P. Bogardus in the 1945 movie Bells of St Mary's with Bing Crosby and Ingrid Bergman and Angel Clarence Odbody, in the 1946 movie It's a Wonderful Life, with Jimmy Stewart and Donna Reed.

senators were called warmongers for shouting their resentment of it. No one would listen to them.

It was a cold Sunday morning, considering it had been mild the past ten days since Thanksgiving. By mid-afternoon, I was in Perry Wolf's pool parlor playing a game with friends. Even in my deep concentration, I heard a newscaster say the Japanese air force had attacked our Navy at Pearl Harbor and killed 2,400 people.

Everyone put their cues down and listened in shock. We knew it was only a matter of time before we entered the war, but we didn't expect this stab in the back. At this very moment, the Japanese envoys were apologizing to our government. As "Remember the Alamo" had been born, now so was "Remember Pearl Harbor," another time, another inspiration for the proud American to fight. And so they did. Thousands crowded the induction centers to volunteer.

I faced the greatest decision of my life. I could claim exemption with a widowed mother. Plus, I had an essential war job. Mom thought I was safe at home, but my conscience was struggling. Unbeknownst to her, several friends and I proceeded to Grand Central Palace to volunteer. I got into one of two lines, and my friends got into the other. I went through the physical and mental tests and became a proud member of the great U.S. Army Air Force.

I knew this would blow her mind, for all she talked about was how I was exempt because she was a widow and how easy it would be for me to obtain a letter from Steinway claiming my job was sensitive for the war effort.

My order read I had to report to a place that would take me to Camp Upton for basic training and placement after some tests.

My friends decided to throw a bash for our departure. Mom was waiting for me when I arrived home at seven in the morning.

"Where have you been, Johnny?"

"Out, Mom."

"A brilliant, fulfilling, descriptive statement. Now tell me where in the hell have you been?"

"I told you, Mom, I was out, out with friends. You can ask them. Herman, Manny, Vinnie, and Matt. We had a party."

"What kind of party lasts all night? Is that how I brought you up?"

"Well, some of the guys are going away, so we had a blowout for them."

"Do the guys wear lipstick, Johnny?"

I looked down at my white shirt, and there was blood-red lipstick all the way down to my belt buckle. I felt so ashamed I said nothing.

Party we did all week long. A group of us went to a night club, the Latin Quarter, owned by Lou Walters. The best headliner acts played there. It was a swinging club. None of us were into the drug scene, but everyone knew, if you were, just check the garter on the goat.

I felt like the proverbial man of infidelity when the cheating husband is spotted by all but his wife. Everyone knew I was leaving home for the service except Mom. I asked Uncle Dick for his advice.

"Johnny, there's no right time or place to tell your mom. She's going to blow her steam no matter how you handle it. And by the way, you are the only one to tell her."

On the bleak, drizzly morning of my departure, my heart pounded heavier. Mom hadn't turn on any lights, so it was quite dark in the house. She appeared more like a silhouette, something surreal. I held my orders as I felt her staring at me.

"What's on your mind, Johnny? You were never able to play a good game of poker with me, so let's have it."

I handed her my orders. She read them slowly as I retrieved my packed bag with all of Army's suggested items. When I returned, Mom was staring at the wall with the papers hanging as though she was about to drop them on the floor. I looked into her sad face. The explosion never came. She did something much more effective that

I carried all through the war.

"First, go say good-bye to your brother and sister," she said.

When I returned from their rooms, she handed me the papers. "How could you do this to me, Johnny? How?" she said in a low monotone voice without quivering. She embraced me and simply repeated, "How could you do this to me, Johnny? How?"

I heard her over and over again as my new adventure unfolded. I knew I had done Mom a great disservice.

CHAPTER TWENTY-FOUR

The service was an indignity to man. I felt the shame of thousands of men losing their identities, wearing the same clothes, being conditioned for the kill.

Basic training was in Miami, Florida. It was amazing how little our citizens knew how close the German wolf packs were to our shorelines. We often would witness a German submarine blowing up one of our merchant ships in the late evenings. I must say the morale was high, and our president's fireside chats kept the country in high spirits. He was truly a master orator, and I don't think we would've survived without him.

Advanced training was in Atlantic City. I was called to Captain Shonegan's office two days after testing. He was reading a form that cited my civilian background and test grades. I saluted him and stood at attention.

"At ease, Private Benedetto."

I was shocked to hear my name pronounced properly.

"After reviewing your form twenty, it seems to me you are a natural for special service."

"What does that mean, sir?"

He smiled. "It means with your show business background, you should be entertaining your buddies. I might add, this is a badly needed contribution during wartime."

"All due respect, sir, I volunteered for two reasons. The first was to help get Hitler, and the second was to get out of the field of entertainment. I would appreciate it if you would forget the entertainment and place me where I could be useful in combat."

Captain stared at me until he spoke in quiet tones, as though he seemed upset. "Well, your patriotism deserves the service's appreciation. Your testing does show us you would be very successful in intelligence. Your aptitude shows us you have much ability to be trained in clandestine activity."

I knew what this meant, for I used to fantasize about getting Hitler myself. Of course, I didn't realize how immature I was. "I would like this very much, sir. That is, if it's possible."

He saluted me. "Well, let's see how your advanced training goes, then I'll make a judgment."

It was our misfortune that we were having a devil of a winter, particularly with our forced marches with full packs for twelve- to twenty-mile hikes every day. I received a marksman's medal and was named a sharpshooter. It was an honor at my young age, mostly because it was so far removed from my civilian experience.

The next morning when it was snowing heavily, we were awakened by our friend, Drill Sergeant Shickle Gruber, nicknamed for his bigotry. "Put on your full packs, men. We're going to force march before breakfast. Before you come out for formation, I want you to strip your beds and roll your blankets toward the wall."

When we fell into formation, Shickle Gruber began roll call as the snowstorm intensified. Halfway through the march, I began to feel nauseous and was in pain. By the time we returned to our hotel, I broke ranks.

"Hey, wop, you haven't been dismissed!" our precious sergeant screamed. "Get back in formation, or I'll write you up."

I felt numb, yet I still had the presence of mind to find my room. The next thing I recall was being shaken by a ninety-day wonder shavetail (second lieutenant).

"Stand up, soldier. Get off your ass, now!"

I couldn't move. I felt paralyzed. He shook my shoulder vigorously, and I fell over to one side, my body frozen stiff.

The shavetail put his hand on my neck and boomed to the sergeant, "You dummy, this is a very sick soldier, get an ambulance at once."

I vaguely recall being wheeled into the hospital on a stretcher. A doctor tried to move my chin to my chest, but I was too rigid.

"Oh, my God, we have another case of spinal meningitis on our hands," the doctor said. "Take him to quarantine at once."

The next thing I remembered was waking up as a nurse pulled a sheet over the head of the patient next to me. "You're a tough one, soldier. You are going to pull through." It was then she informed me that I had been in a coma for four and a half days.

When I arrived back to my outfit I was surprised to find them in front of our billet with their gear.

"Okay, wop, your buddies put all your gear together for you, and you are to embark for destinations unknown on her Majesty's ship, the Queen Elizabeth," Shickle Gruber boomed,

The ship was of awesome size, and we had more than fifteen thousand personnel on the ship, including five thousand nurses.

CHAPTER TWENTY-FIVE

I had a sharpshooters' medal, good conduct medal, and four campaigns under my belt. I studied Sperry gunsights and Norton bombsights. With the Royal Air Force, I studied Vickers unit, the energy thrust for the airplane's gun turrets. After being stationed in Blackpool, England with the Army Air Corp 599th Bombardment Squad, 397th Bombardment Group, I was transferred to an elite intelligence unit. There were many stories I couldn't or wouldn't relate with the Office of Strategic Services. My most interesting time was spent in Stalingrad training Soviet troops. I taught Russian personnel our techniques and trained them in our high-tech equipment for six weeks before being transferred to clandestine activity.

I learned Nonno died in 1943. I had such fond memories of him that it made his death easier to take. Still, I loved him dearly, and I missed him terribly.

I sunk into a deep depression. The war was lasting much longer than anyone expected. I wanted to go home. I fell madly in love, though, and married a fine lady, Greta, who worked for the British foreign office. I loved spending time with her great family. Within a short time, she gave me a beautiful daughter, Ann. To date, she had been the greatest blessing in my confused life. I was elated, and life seemed precious again.

The 397th Bombardment Group received the Presidential Unit Citation for conspicuous action against the enemy on December

23, 1944.

Germany surrendered May 7, 1945, and I was honorably discharged on Christmas Day with two medals and a Presidential Citation. I was a mixed-up G.I., like so many others. I wasn't stable and didn't know what I wanted to do. I didn't know how to transition from war zone OSS into civilized society. How does one make the transition from war zone OSS into civilized society? Similar to the transition from Opera Singer, Patron of the Arts, to government issued killer?

Tony had left for the service in February 1945, ten months before I got home, and was mustered out almost eight months after me in August 1946. We hadn't seen each other since I left home in December 1942 when he was sixteen. It was difficult to imagine a mature man of twenty now. It was only a short time before I left that we had begun to call him by his given name, Anthony, or Tony. He saw the worst times with General Patton's army.

When Tony returned, we talked all night. It was amazing how close our social thinking aligned.

"You know, John, after the war, I did a lot of singing in the service," Tony finally said around three o'clock in the morning. "I entertained grave detail troops. Would you like to hear a tape of one of my performances?"

"Yeah, Tony, that would be great. But what about your art career?"

"I'm still working with it, but I want to entertain. I love it."

I dragged out an old Webcor tape-recording machine that weighed over twenty pounds, when I saw he had a reel-to-reel tape. Tony looked tense. "This was done with a sixty-piece jazz band in the field."

The orchestra was top-notch, and I was stunned when Tony sang "St. James Infirmary." He had voice, complete phrasing, but most of all, a unique sound and style. I knew it was his calling.

"Gee, Tony, this is fantastic! You are truly an artist."

He looked relieved. "I was concerned you wouldn't like it. You

THE SHADOW OF HIS SMILE

know, with your background in the classics. I thought you might not grasp this kind of music."

"Look up the definition of musician. It'll read, 'One who has a full appreciation and understanding of music.' I love any medium done with dignity. You have that, Tony, and you'll knock 'em dead if you follow up with some serious voice and drama training."

I hadn't told him yet I'd lost my drive for the business.

"Hey, Tony, I have an idea. I've been singing with a great trio at the Flora Dora Club in Sunnyside. I have Al Cremin on guitar, Louis Graw on drums, and Danny Martucci on bass. And, visiting is Gene DiNovi on piano. Why not sit in for a few tunes?"

Tony accompanied me to the club the next evening. I asked one of the Flora Dora girls if my brother could do a few tunes with the band.

"If he sings anything like you, he's on," she said.

Tony got up and did thirty-two tunes with crowds cheering at the end of each. I was proud of him.

"Tony, I was just messing around here. You have to start somewhere. Why don't you take this gig? Important newsmen stop here for an eye-opener, and I know you'll get some press. Hey, if I get press, you'll get a novel."

That night, I felt good as I remembered my promise to Pop. I was following through in his footsteps, watching over little Ninni.

Having achieved the status of a booked entertainer, he felt he needed a stage name, not something as difficult as Anthony Benedetto. He chose Joe Bari.

Tony had found a great voice coach, Fred Katz, an accomplished musician and composer. Tony lived with my family as he suffered the pains of an artist looking to be recognized. I tried my best to boost his morale, but he didn't need it. He was possessed and convinced he would make it, and nothing would shatter his drive. Meanwhile, I had been working feverishly to keep busy and regain the sanity to function in society again.

Mom was still working in the garment district with her sisters.

After I returned from the service, I had trouble adjusting to civilian life. My therapist advised me to study a trade that used my hands, so I chose hairdressing from a roster of training schools,

I found myself back in show business performing at conventions and trade show all over the county, along with conducting classes for Clairol, Roux, Helene Curtis, Nestles, Esca. I quickly earned a reputation, and was featured in trade magazines.

I eventually ended up working at Rosalier, the finest salon in the country. I worked with the blue bloods and Hollywood stars and was given the stars with hyper ego problems. With huge successes in the beauty field I found myself on TV again on shows such as Maggi McNellis's weekly *Crystal Room,* which was broadcast live on ABC. Lifelong friendships developed with notable people in the industry; Rose Meta and Joe Louis.

The following year, a second blessing and miracle arrived, a perfect, pink bundle of joy and love. We thanked God for our little one, Lynn. Big sister, Ann, was almost two at the time.

I took a hand in teaching. I was hired at the school I graduated from, Vogue Institute, and formed an advanced wing, wrote and illustrated the manuals, and taught the classes. I gained a reputation with high marks from Veterans Affairs, handling returning soldiers like myself unable to cope and adapt to social living, and in need of rehabilitation. I met some lasting friends who I was able to help adapt well, such as Tony Curtis.

I had a salon over Billy Rose's Diamond Horseshoe taking care of his chorus line, a bevy of the most beautiful girls in the world — Joan Brandon and Pat Siri, the Swedish beauty. One day, a huge Indian-looking woman walked into the salon.

"Mr. Benedetto, I'm Arianna, a folk singer, and work at Number One Fifth Ave."

This got my attention because it was the top of the line in the village.

"I would like to offer you a deal," she said. "I'll act as

receptionist for you at no pay. I would just like to use your phones during the day to promote my career. I can give you references. In fact, Ted Mack is one of my benefactors."

"Okay, when do you want to start?"

"How about right now?"

I walked her to the desk and gave her a rundown on how to book appointments. She was great.

One day, I overheard Arianna talking to Ted Mack. "Ted, I need special material for my opener at the club. Might you know some creative writer? . . . Okay, call me back as soon as you can."

I stared at her six-foot frame, her high cheekbones, and slanted doe eyes. Her silky, straight black hair flowed below her waist. "Arianna, I happen to know an accomplished composer who just wrote a tune that would fit you like a glove. It's called 'Satan Wears A Satin Gown.' "

She gulped. "What a great title."

I called Fred, described Arianna, and handed her the phone.

"Hello, Fred. I've heard such glowing things about your work. Yes, I need special material, a song to open my act. The title is great, but I'd like to hear the song and lyrics."

"I can save us a lot of time," Fred said on the loudspeaker. "I have one of my students here, Joe Bari. He'll sing it for you."

While she is waiting, I whispered to Arianna that Joe Bari was my brother.

Upon hearing the song, she turns to John. "I want the song, but I have a meeting with Frankie Lane and a heavy promoter. I'd like to take Fred, Joe Bari, and you to the meeting."

We met Fred the next day at Columbia 30th Street Studio, where they were recording one of his singers. Fred introduced Tony and me to the promoter, Ray Muscarella. Little did I know this meeting would launch one of the most prestigious careers in show business, for everyone flipped over Tony singing "Boulevard of Broken Dreams." Yet, there's a downside to every upside.

"He has a great style and unbelievable voice, but his hair is thinning, and his nose! He would have to get a nose job," one of the promoter's cronies said.

The promoter turned to his crony. "You're not paid to evaluate talent. See that kid with the big nose over there? I'm going to make him a star!"

Good or bad, Tony had a manager.

"What a stroke of luck," Arianna said. "Your brother is in. Ray is the number-one gun in promoting vocalists. He rarely misses."

Ray walked over. "Tony, do you know Brooklyn?"

"He knows France, Germany, Austria, Astoria, Long Island, and Broadway, but I know Brooklyn," I said.

"Well, you're his brother. I want Tony over at Carroll Street in Monte's restaurant tomorrow night at seven sharp, and we'll discuss contracts."

In those days, I owned a '41 Plymouth which might or might not run. I said, "We'll be there."

When we entered Monte's, I noticed wall-to-wall heavyweight city fathers and wise guys. Ray had a round table and with him were eight or nine men. He stood as we approached. "Boys, this is my new find, Joe Bari, and this is his brother, Johnny. They are Frank's nephews. You know the Republican leader of Queens."

They chuckled, but not a friendly chorus.

*****

In 1949, we were thrilled when God sent us another bundle. We chose the regal name of Patricia. She had two big sisters to help look after her: Lynn, age two, and Ann, four.

Tony's manger, Ray Muscarella, got Bob Hope to come to the quaint little neighborhood in Manhattan called the Village and watch Joe Bari and Pearl Bailey perform. The result? Bob took Tony on tour.

Bob told him he didn't like Tony's stage name though.

"Well, I chose Joe as a typical American name and Bari after a region in Italy," Tony said. "My birth name is Anthony Dominic Benedetto."

"Oh, too long for the marquee. We'll call you Tony Bennett."

Within a short period of time Tony Bennett had a recording out, "Fascinating Rhythm" and then "Boulevard of Broken Dreams."

*****

A year later, nine days before Thanksgiving, we gave thanks for a healthy son, John. How lucky he was to have three doting sisters. They would pamper and spoil him his whole life, no doubt. My capacity for love seemed to increase with every child.

I enjoyed every minute of opening and operating my chain of salons to support the four little ones. I had met such interesting people, such as Leonardo Rizzuto, who was making magnificent hair rollers in his garage. We did business together, and he became a lifelong friend. His little garage company became Conair Corporation, run by his son, Lee, a great businessman who grew the corporation.

Ray wasn't happy when Tony married Patricia Beech on February 2, 1952. Ray and Patricia didn't hit it off after Tony met her about seven months earlier in Cleveland. For the next three years, it seemed the two fought for control of Tony. Tony just wanted to perform.

*****

I was quite tense preparing for a meeting with Tony's manager, Ray. He had called the meeting using a rift between me and Jack as an excuse. Jack Wilson, a childhood friend of my cousin, was not one of my favorite people, even when we were kids. I never had respect for anyone who would deny their heritage and culture. Much of how Pop brought me up clicked in. I felt shame for Jack.

"What's the matter with you, Johnny? You look nervous," Ray said.

I looked into Ray's steel eyes. His mouth would smile, but his eyes always remained penetrating and cold. I got the feeling I was going to be on the hot seat, and I was.

Tony recently had bought out his contract from this man, Ray,

who had made him a star. However, I never forgot there wouldn't
be a sustaining star without my brother's genius talent. Being
familiar with Ray's background, I knew this was going to be big
trouble for Tony. I feared Ray would take this as a personal insult,
a slap in the face, and wouldn't tolerate it. I had become very close
to Ray from working as a liaison on Tony's career. I remembered
the fun we had arranging a parade and the massive traffic jams
with the trucks playing Tony's recordings four years ago. I had to
laugh, as it reminded me of 1933 when Costello had trucks rolling
with music and dancing in the streets to celebrate the end of
Prohibition.

Ray folded his hands, looked at the table, and lifted his head
ever so slowly. His eyes glared on his Neanderthal-like face. He
spoke softly "You know things are not right with me and your
brother. I'm certain you're aware he just bought his contract out
with me." He slammed his fist on the table. "Johnny, you realize
this is all her doing, that wife of his. I warn you, she'll somehow
separate all of us, even you and your brother. She wants to always
be the one in control."

"Ray, what in the hell are you talking about? What does she
have to do with your business with Tony? You two have been
biting at each other for years now. You had to get along, or this
was bound to happen."

"I can't face my people with a punk broad and a young punk
singer taking me down. Maybe I'll kill them both," he said so
casually.

I waited for Ray to rant and then calm down. I knew Tony's
wife, Sandy was difficult and tried to remove persuasive people
from Tony's life. I also knew Ray would do anything to preserve
his profile and position. The mob culture had a possessive trait.
They loved to say, "My fighter, my horse, my mistress, my actor,
my singer," etc. Like all wise guys, he had to retain his
possessions. But he was suffering the loss of an important one. He
wasn't stupid, and he'd find a way to come out on top.

I finally spoke. "For me to promise I could straighten it out, well, I could try, but I know it will be next too impossible. However, I'll say this to you, Ray. With all due respect, if anyone harms one hair on my brother's head, it'll take an army of ten thousand of you to stop me from getting even."

He obviously thought I was in a position to bring Tony back into the fold, but I had no intention of even mentioning this to Tony. He was my younger brother, and I always would protect him, no matter the cost.

Ray's face broadened to a smile as he cupped his meaty hand. Even though he considered it gentle, he gave me a few clouts on the side of my face. It felt like an atom bomb going off in my head. I wondered what would happen if he took a serious swing?

"Johnny, I want to thank you for your sincere confidence in me. I would never hurt you physically. As for your brother, we do have many ways to put pressure on people without violence, so you don't have to worry about him."

Pressure, pressure, I felt a pressure on my shoulder. I stared at him and got the feeling Tony and I weren't safe. I said my good-bye.

Ray's remarks tormented me the next few days. *We have ways to put pressure on people.* Although difficult to concentrate, business matters needed to be addressed. I was waiting for my public relations man, George Douris, to arrive in the reception room of my largest salon, which I had designed and termed "open concept." Major trade magazines had raved about the cutting-edge design. My name was painted on the double window, which had an entrance door in the middle.

George, who also was a columnist for a Newhouse publication, arrived. In the middle of our meeting, a bullet shattered through the *J* on one window, and another bullet smashed through the *B* in the second window. George panicked.

I grabbed his hand as he ran toward the phone. "What in the hell are you doing, George?"

"Calling the cops. What the hell do you think I'm doing?"

I tightened my grip on his fat arm. "George, have you noticed the accuracy of the two shots? One in the middle of the *J*, the other directly in the middle of the *B*, and we know they were shot from a moving car. If they meant bodily harm, either I, or both of us, would be dead."

George's sweaty body fell into a chair. "I'm not sure your account is worth it. This is too dangerous," he said, wiping his face.

"George, I release you. I do most of the work I pay you for anyway."

George stomped out of the salon.

What would be next? This was just a prelude of what was to come.

CHAPTER TWENTY-SIX

I hear music in the distance, an organ softly playing. It falls silent, and the priest speaks. As I sit in St. Francis Church, I can't believe my mother's funeral is so circus like. The priest's words are shallow, even though he was a lifelong friend of Mom's. He can't say anything that would reach the depths of her life's adventure, her loyalty to her children, and of course, her Puritan nature. I try to hide my anger as my eyes wander to my brother. I never imagined my promise to Pop would so scar my life.

Perhaps on the day I left for Boston so many years ago, Pop was thinking the same thing I was: *Suppose he dies while I'm gone.*

Seeking refuge, I slip back into my trance, back to *the* darkest day of my life, back to when I received *the* phone call.

*****

"John Bennett, you'll appreciate my not identifying myself," the caller said on the morning before Tony's performance at The Copa. "We're going to bust up your brother's opening and destroy his performance. You'll see it in the papers the morning after. When we get through with him, he'll be running an elevator for the rest of his life."

"Wait a minute. Can we meet somewhere and talk this over?"

"Yeah, so you could have the law waiting for us?"

"Call Ray Muscarella. He'll verify I would never do anything of the kind."

"Let me call you back in fifteen minutes."

I knew Tony's ex-manager, a button man, was behind this. I called Ray, acted innocent, and asked his advice.

"My advice to you is to keep calm and try to reason with them. You can use my name if you care to."

"Gee, thanks, Ray. I knew I could count on you."

It was then and there I knew what had to be done. The phone rang. I picked it up and didn't say a word.

"I guess you know who this is. One condition: You come alone."

"Are you going to be alone?"

He laughed. "Like hell, Bennett."

"If that's the case, then I pick the place and the time."

"Sure, but early enough so we still have time to get to the first show if we don't come to an understanding."

It was winter, so it would be dark by six-thirty, and no one would be in the park because it was snowing. "How about six-thirty at Rainey Park across from the restaurant? You know the one."

"We'll be waiting."

My hands turned cold and sweaty. These were the worst of men who would hurt for pleasure. I visualized the terrain. A lavatory building faced the skyline across the East River. If I stayed in the shadows of the building after turning off the lights in the area, I could hide behind the tile wall and watch the men. But they, of course, would hesitate to walk there. I visualized and rehashed the possibilities for hours. I was soaking wet with perspiration.

I pulled my 9 mm Parabellum from its case, carefully took it apart, cleaned it, and examined it. It felt like a century of waiting. I knew from my OSS training that I would make mistakes if I couldn't force myself to stay calm.

The time had arrived. I left my office, got into my car, checked my piece again, inserted thirteen slugs into the clip, pushed the clip into the gun, and pulled back on the loader, which placed one bullet in the chamber, ready to fire. At the park, I placed my car in an escape position. A stretch black limo arrived at six-thirty sharp, and six men got out. There were probably at least two more in the limo for backup. Luckily, the limo doors were in my sight.

I'll never tell how we settled our differences, but let's say I now had a reputation with the boys. I got a call within minutes of returning to my office.

"John, this is Ray. I see you settled things. I want you to know, for one, I'm proud of you. I like to see brothers stick up for each other." He promptly hung up.

Obviously, I feared his next move. Two weeks later, all hell broke loose. The union picketed in front of my shops. They poured white mice through mail slots into one salon. Another day, it was swarms of wasps. I knew the play: They thought I'd run to my kid brother, and convince him to go back to Ray. I didn't. Did Ray forget the Italian way? My role was the protector. I knew the worst was yet to come.

****

In church, I look at Tony, who had become the top of the heap. I can't help but feel good that he didn't know what transpired until this very day. A mass of mixed emotions comes over me. I'm so proud of his successes and dedication to his craft, but I resent my martyr role. I did some things I can't possibly explain as rational.

Having such vast experience, I knew the political pitfalls Tony would face. I also knew he wouldn't be able to handle most of them, for he was an artist in every sense, engrossed in his craft. He wouldn't understand the evils that accompany the sudden wealth of a successful artist. My mission was to keep him clean and away from *those*, whether they were family, agents, or synthetic friends, full of shallow advice that could lead to a bitter end — something I had witnessed for so many artists before him.

The service concludes, and people file out. Mom will lie a bit longer than usual because so many people from all over the country are coming to say good-bye. Outside, the news media invades. They are not about to respect our sadness, nor our privacy. I ask a pushy photographer to back off when Tony walks out, and the photographer makes a slur. I don't know where I get the strength, but I pick him up and throw him over the hood of a car. His camera goes flying. He gets up and appears he might charge me.

"If you want more, punk, just take one more step," I say.

He brushes himself off and limps away.

"What a punch you have, Giovanni, you could be a champion," Uncle Tom says.

My wife looks at me in surprise, "Chill out, John. Remember this is your mother's funeral." With her remark she displayed a look of amusement. She's that kind of gal.

My punch sends me back to a beloved friend, Rocky Graziano.

*****

I was getting lots of press coverage at the grand opening of one of my salons, thanks to George, who was covering a new salon opening for the newspaper.

Rocky, a famous boxer, walked in. "Johnny, I'm here to help out with your publicity. What can I do?"

"Well, Rocky, you can stand behind this model with a comb and scissors and pretend to cut her hair. That'll make a great shot for the papers."

Rocky stepped behind the beautiful model, lifted a bit of her hair with the big comb, and brought scissors up to meet the comb. He paused for the photo, and-Oh no, Rocky closed the scissors and cut her hair! Now someone had to fix that and convince her she liked it.

Another time, I was doing platform work at a national hairstyling convention, and Rocky appeared. "Hey, Johno, I'm here to help you out."

"No, Rocky, I don't need you cutting my models' hair!"

"No, I thought I could be your model today."

"Wow, what a PR event."

We had a blast kidding around, or I should say, "cutting up."

*****

It was now the 1960s and *Change* was the order of the day. I sold my beauty salon chain and moved on. John Kennedy was elected President. Jackie Kennedy set the world on fire with fashion. The Beatles invaded the US.

Given my connections and background, I was asked to arrange housing for a foreign dignitary's visit to the United Nations and to watch over him. Cuban President Fidel Castro apparently didn't want to stay at one of our upscale Manhattan hotels with our government guards. No, he wanted to stay in Harlem. It was stressful because Fidel met with groups our government considered subversive.

I needed a break to collapse and relax, so I spent time on the boat of a dear old friend, John Kluge. John didn't take the boat out. He enjoyed just sitting in the marina, relaxing, reading the paper, and thinking in solitude.

That year I even did a recording with my dear, supportive friend and composer, Ralph Herman. We recorded the two "contemporary" songs Mr. Parado and I had chosen in 1933 — "Prisoner of Love" and "More Than You Know." I soon realized what I had suspected all along: The money jocks - the wise guys again - were impossible to deal with. It was impossible to communicate on an artistic level. They wanted to own you.

The Money Jocks, mostly Jewish Mob ran the industry. Wise Guys, Italian Mob got the play on radio, performance dates and record distribution. You did it their way or not at all.

Rocky sensed this and arranged a partnership for me at the famed Basin Street East. We were running the largest jazz room in the world. Rocky was my biggest personal fan and friend, responsible for one of the happiest and most gratifying years of my life. We had the greatest artists such as Joe Williams, Peggy Lee, and the incomparable Ella Fitzgerald. Aside from being one of the world's greatest boxers, Rocky later surprised the world with his oil paintings. His work personified his champion qualities.

I wasn't lacking in offers because my name was known in every area of the beauty business: salons, styling, product manufacturers, platform work, and new open salon designs in the trade magazines. The deal came that I couldn't resist with Carl Stanley and Charlie Chirchirillo, known as Charlie Church. They owned budget salons, almost as many locations as I did. They asked me to join the team as international operational director. I decided to do a salon franchise and contacted my friend, Edie Adams.

"Edie, we're forming a nationwide chain of beauty salons. These will be affordable salons availing the housewife and worker to professional hair care. Franchises will be sold for territories, and they'll also own the service supply house for the salons."

It took quite a few meetings and a great deal of talking, but Edie eventually signed on.

Things didn't always go smoothly. "Edie is not doing enough PR work," Carl said. "I saw her last night on Johnny Carson, and she didn't mention the salons."

Naturally, Carl expected me to work this out.

"Edie, you know part of the terms in your contract is to mention the salons whenever you're on TV or in public forum," I said. "This is not a favor we're asking. You're being well compensated for this."

It took a few times, but eventually Edie remembered to mention the salons: Edie Adams Cut & Curl.

Whenever I was in the audience at one of her performances, she would introduce me. "Johnny, the man who made me millions without smoking a cigar."

I loved Edie. She was gracious and great to work with. Such a precious, honorable lady, she worked nonstop to pay off the debts of her husband, Ernie Kovacs, after he died.

The Cut & Curl company didn't know my true energy. I traveled to twenty cities every month.

Tony called me. "John, could you do me a favor and go to Texas? I have a new endeavor, a franchise opening called Tony Bennett Spaghetti House."

"Tony, why did you lend your name to this?"

"I want musicians to be able to come in and have a plate of spaghetti or something to eat without any charge."

The pro forma was a huge success until I found out the backers were not what I'd term the ethical type. It was with great trepidation that I recommended that Tony resign his name from the franchise. They were taking advantage of him.

When I left Cut & Curl, I got an offer to join a Midwest public company whose board was made up of bankers. I created twenty-eight more salons for them in the Dallas, Fort Worth, and Houston area.

I also opened a thousand-seat supper club in Houston and named it Mama Benedetto's after Mom. Tony gave me three beautiful drawings of Mom, himself, and me for the menus, and he performed on opening night. It was a full house for two shows — two thousand people.

Much later in life, 1994, I again crossed Lee Rizzuto. He is chairman of National Italian American Foundation. They wanted to name Tony man of the year, but his office said Tony didn't do ethnic events. So Lee asked me if I could persuade my brother to accept the honor.

I never involved myself in Tony's business decisions, but felt this was an exception considering myself a professional Italian, believing strongly in promoting Italian culture and charities, I spoke to Tony, who agreed to accept it.

CHAPTER TWENTY-SEVEN

The limousine drives Patricia and I to the gravesite.

I lay my head back and look at my wife as I slide back eleven months.

*****

Patricia and I were boarding a plane in Houston to Las Vegas. Upon landing, we were ushered to the new MGM Grand hotel and casino. It was massive, unlike Caesars Palace where I usually stayed. It was January, so the weather was perfect.

We had decided to forgo those gaudy chapels. The wedding was a nice little get-together in the judge's chambers with two friends, Joe and Clair Altman, as witnesses, During the ceremony, we discovered the judge was a part-time comic. I think he performed most of his show during our ceremony.

At the airport heading back home, Patricia hit the nickel jackpot. "Do you think we can take this weight on the plane?" she asked.

We enjoyed our time alone together, now we were heading back to Patricia's three young children: Judy, eleven, Colleen, nine, and Sean, six-oh, and our little dog, Pepsi. I was ready. I loved them all.

*****

Pent-up emotions rise to the surface at the gravesite. Good-byes to loved ones are deeper, more meaningful: lingering hugs, kisses, embracing physically and spiritually.

My eldest child, daughter Ann, a successful teacher, makes sure everyone in her life is all right. She was a love child born in the midst of our largest world war.

My daughter, Lynn, is forever the peacemaker, perhaps because she was born at the beginning of peacetime. She is blessed with four-year-old Melanie and new baby Michael, a special gift and a blessing.

My daughter, Patti, renamed herself Ciel. A genius on every level, she works internationally to better people's lives. I love her more than she'll ever know, because her anger gets in the way. She still shuns me for leaving her mother so many years ago.

My son, John, is the rebel. He's very successful, although not in the direction I foresaw. John always marched to his own drummer. I'm very proud of what he has achieved. Although he lives far away, he's remained close and protective of his sisters and mother.

Patti is not the only one filled with anger because I left their mother so long ago. I don't blame them. I was not a great husband.

I feel I shared time and love with my children, though. I recall our times together fishing, playing, caring, loving. I'm sad if they can't recall these happy times. I miss them all, I love them all.

I see my relatives whose past lives intertwined mine, the good and the bad. I've relived it all these past four days.

I begin to realize the great power I possess. It all started when I could hear beautiful music chords at will as a child. I could command whether I wanted to hear choral, orchestra, or both. Now I can relive any moment I choose. The hell of it is, though, I was doing this in sequence.

I finally relax. *Have I really relived my entire life in only four days?*

The priest's prayers pull me back to the gravesite. I observe the priest who always addressed Mom's spiritual needs. With her strong beliefs and saintly life, surely she could have taken the role of spiritual leader.

Saying good-bye to Mom today triggers memories of me leaving her so unexpectedly when I went to war, not knowing if I'd ever see her again. This time, I knew.

Ann drives us to the airport. We're exhausted when we board the plane, and Patricia falls asleep. We'd be back shortly to the children and our home in San Francisco. I think Tony named it for me, the Paris of America.

EPILOGUE

My husband, Giovanni Benedetto, now known as John Bennett began writing this book in November of 1977, at the death of his mother, Anna Benedetto.

Surely this writing began as a method of healing, dealing with his loss. It progressed as a tribute to his mother for her achievements, holding together a family during the turbulent Depression years, suffering the loss of her husband. It became a tribute to a certain group of people who remained strong, persevered, and accomplished an impossible task. They survived the Depression with determination, grace, and ethics intact, producing determined, confident, talented children to lead a new generation to a better world.

Perhaps my reasoning in tackling such an immense task was the same as John's reasoning thirty-five years ago. My way of facing life going forward, a method of healing, dealing with the loss. Hopefully, our efforts, progress as a tribute to John for his achievements as well as those of our family.

(Left: Giovanni, now John, WWII. Middle: John with his sister Mary. Right: John)

BENEDETTO

Follow us at:
        https://www.facebook.com/TheShadowOfHisSmile/
Email at: pbnem@bellsouth.net
Mail: P.O. Box 4111   Jupiter, Florida 33469-9998

A cd of Giovanni on the Al Jolson Shell Chateau Hour Radio Show featuring Joe Cook can be purchased at: I thank Jerry for finding the broadcast and creating cds. Jerry Haendiges Productions 13808 Sunset Drive Whittier, CA 90602
Phone: 562-696-4387
Fax: 866-593-1689
Website: www.OTRSite.com - Largest source of Old Time Radio Logs,
Email: Jerry@otrsite.com
Finally, as John's friend Paul Harvey would say, I was left to write "the rest of the story."

Made in the USA
Columbia, SC
10 November 2017

the longtime but recently terminated agency for Anheuser-Busch, was serving Coors beer to guests at his home. Seeing that I had two thoughts: first I was surprised and felt sorry for the fellow and, second, the item did not seem to ring true since while D'Arcy had lost the brewery's business and would soon close its local office, there was no way on earth that this fellow would do such a thing out of spite or otherwise. He was too smart for that, and he continued to hold out hope against hope of rewinning some brewery business.

Later that day, I got a call from the ad exec. "I thought we were friends," he said with an edge to his voice.

"I thought so too; why would you think otherwise?" I replied.

He went on to ask if I'd seen the item in Berger's column, insisted that it was a complete fabrication, swore he would never serve anything but an A-B product, and then the clincher: he had contacted Berger about it, and the columnist told him that the source was none other than yours truly.

I tried to assure my friend that Berger was not telling the truth and reminded him that I'd never been to his home and thus would have no basis, much less a reason, to concoct such a lie. Then I called Berger. Once I had him on the phone I called him several unprintable things and threatened him physically. He confessed that he'd made the story up based on some shaky information from a colleague who had visited the ad executive's home in connection with a feature story she was writing about one of his neighbors. At that point I blew; there were two *Post-Dispatch* reporters who lied, and I told Berger that if he did not contact my friend and come clean I would file a formal complaint with his editors, not to mention what I might do if I ran into him around town.

Berger complied with that demand, yet to this day I have no way of knowing if my friend was ever completely convinced that I had nothing to do with the dastardly columnist's evil deed.

Seventy-Three

"This is more up your alley than mine," my colleague Al Akerson insisted. He fielded a call from an executive with Saint Louis-based Enterprise Rent-A-Car, the family-owned company that had parlayed a lucrative niche in the rental car market into a formidable position within that industry. "Believe it or not they're about to overtake the big boys—Hertz, Avis, Budget, and the others—and they want the world to know it, so I'm handing it off to you," he said.

In an introductory meeting that followed, we learned that not only was Enterprise gaining on the household names in the car rental business, it was about to become number one based on fleet size and its number of US offices. Car salesman Jack Taylor started the company in the 1950s in the basement of a Saint Louis Cadillac dealership. He saw an opportunity to rent cars to people needing replacement vehicles while their own cars were being repaired, usually after collisions. He cultivated relationships with the leading casualty insurers, many of which were obliged to provide replacements for policyholders while their cars were in the shop. Enterprise offered deep-cut rates and would even deliver the rentals to their inconvenienced customers. Early on, Enterprise all but ignored the traditional vacation and business rental market and had almost no presence at major airports, opting to avoid the costly user fees associated with such operations.

During more than forty years in business at that point, Enterprise quietly amassed hundreds of offices coast to coast and a fleet of nearly two hundred thousand cars. While the company remained privately held, sources like *Forbes* magazine pegged the company's annual sales then at more than $2 billion and Jack Taylor's net worth to be several hundred million dollars. Charming, classy, and understated, Jack turned the operation over to his son, Andrew, who, while thoughtful and low-key like his father, made no secret of his aim to go head-to-head with the big boys. And he was determined to do so with aggressive yet carefully crafted advertising and public relations campaigns.

"The first hurdle we have to clear is that no one in the news media will believe or take your word for the fact that Enterprise is about to become number one," I cautioned Andy, who proved to be a very quick study.

"So what do we do?" he asked.

"We need to find an independent source to authenticate the company's industry position—someone capable of confirming the achievement who'd then be willing to comment credibly on the factors that enabled Enterprise to take the lead—ideally someone with an industry trade publication," I said.

Taylor explained that unlike other industries, the rental car industry is very small and that the one or two publications covering it were not exactly the most solid sources. "There are only six or eight players of any consequence, and several of them are owned by the automobile manufacturers or are subsidiaries of larger conglomerates, so there's not a lot of trade news reported," he added. Compounding the issue, hardly any Wall Street analysts follow the business. "That leaves Enterprise as the only operator that stands on its own, and of course we're privately held," he noted.

We had a staffer do some research. She came up with a San Diego-based publication that reported annually on the industry and its rankings. "However, the numbers they use are not independently audited, so their information is undocumented," Taylor said when asked about the trade journal.

"Well, they're all we have, so we need to establish a relationship with the editor and do what we can to make certain he gets it right," I said.

A relationship was cultivated, and when the next set of rankings was published, the editor got it right, and Enterprise and Fleishman-Hillard were ready to pounce. The agency contacted a number of the leading news organizations and encouraged them to do stories linked to the question, "What's America's number one rental car company?" They all bit. *USA Today* had it on the front page. *Time, Newsweek,* and *Business Week* all weighed in, as did the Associated Press and CNN's nightly business report.

While Hertz and Avis cringed, Andy Taylor was on cloud nine and no longer an unknown CEO. His advertising agency was ready too—with an offbeat, memorable television campaign featuring a car zooming along in a plain brown wrapper with the theme, "Pick Enterprise. We deliver," playing up the company's novel pledge to deliver cars to the customer's doorstep.

After its initial burst of notoriety, Enterprise kept growing rapidly, adding cars to its fleet and branch offices throughout the United States and then Canada and the United Kingdom. With growth came an almost inexhaustible need for young, motivated, college-educated men and women to staff the operations and care for an ever-increasing customer base. Soon, Enterprise's annual sales revenue surpassed $5 billion, and Jack Taylor reportedly was a billionaire and then some, according to *Forbes*'s annual listing of the world's wealthiest people.

"What do we do for an encore?" Andy Taylor asked.

"What's your number one need?" I asked.

"People."

"Then it's the people issue that we'll focus on."

We went back to work, this time helping secure Enterprise a prominent place in the 100 Best Companies to Work For series, followed by stories in *Fortune* magazine and elsewhere, emphasizing the need and commensurate opportunities for newly minted college graduates—the exceptional rewards that awaited the young men and women who make it through the company's rigorous boot camp training regimen.

The relationship with Enterprise continues to this day and has grown to become one of the F-H/Saint Louis office's signature clients

• • •

Public relations, unlike most other businesses, generally does not have a gender issue, certainly not in a big picture sense or in other ways that matter. Statistically there are more women in the PR field than men, and women occupy many of the top jobs, especially in the agency world. There is no glass ceiling in PR it's fair to say.

That, however, did not prevent a woman in marketing communications with Enterprise from point-blank accusing me of having difficulty working with women. The simple and specific truth was that I had a problem working with *her*. Admittedly I did not suffer foolish clients (or coworkers) well, and she sensed it as on more than one occasion I challenged her positions or bristled at her edicts on various issues. From what I'd observed, she was usually testy with everyone—men and women alike. I attributed her contentious behavior to a lack of confidence in her own competence and, perhaps, a bit of agency-client paranoia.

But her accusation disturbed me, so after giving the matter some serious thought I showed up at a meeting one day with a list containing the names and phone numbers of thirty-two women with whom I'd worked, both within the agency and on the client side—including many I'd hired and mentored. With a certain amount of glee I handed the list to my accuser and invited her to contact any or all of those referenced. "Ask them what I'm like to work with and, specifically, if there were any gender issues," I insisted. She vowed to do so, but very soon thereafter she was let go by her employer. Word was she was "just too difficult" to work with.

Seventy-Four

J ohn Graham appeared suddenly in my office doorway one day.
"I just had a call from Barry Beracha, your old friend and number-one fan from the A-B Fort Collins campaign and other adventures," he revealed. "He wondered if you were still with the firm and, if so, would you be able to help out with some big things he has in the works."

"Wow! I'd love to," I said, not knowing what Barry had in mind. After his stint as the engineering and facilities construction chief at Anheuser-Busch, Beracha was tapped to head the company's foundering bakery division, one of several acquisitions the company made in the 1980s and '90s that had not fully panned out. A-B had recently announced its intention to spin the business unit off, after which it would be an independent company once again. All I knew for sure at that point was that Barry Beracha was a good guy, a capable executive, and a straight shooter, and I was flattered to have been requested by him.

After a brief but warm reception in Beracha's office a few days later, the bakery bossman outlined the task at hand. "As you may know, Anheuser-Busch has decided to spin us off in a stock deal," he said. "What you may *not* know is that we plan to change our name, and we have a good idea what that will be. At the same time, we're revamping our corporate identity with a new logo and other elements—some of which will have implications for our product line—and, most importantly, we'll be taking the newly independent company public. There is a great deal of energy and enthusiasm in the employee ranks, I'm delighted to say. However, one of our first priorities must be communications help in connection with the fourteen or fifteen bakeries we'll be closing so as to get a better handle on our costs. Wall Street doesn't think much of our industry, mainly because we tend to have outdated, labor-intense facilities, and we'll be doing something about that before we're cut loose from Anheuser-Busch. It's the only way we can be competitive, and the only way the stock will have a prayer when trading begins. Once we get past the plant closings, we can get on with the fun stuff."

Beracha further disclosed he'd retained Anspach, Grossman, Portugal, a leading corporate identity and design outfit, to develop a new name for the organization, with sparkling new graphics to match. He gave me a preview. AGP recommended Earth Grains, a name already in use for some of the company's breads. It was a solid choice, and the accompanying graphics were impressive. The company's stock would be traded on the New York exchange as soon as the spin-off was complete. "Can you help us jump-start this baby?" he asked.

I huddled with Andy Woods, my trusted, capable sidekick from the Honda, Space, and Olympic Festival days. We roughed out a plan to take the wraps off Earth Grains, positioning it as a serious new contender in the baked goods category. We subcontracted with a group that produced glitzy trade shows and other presentations for the brewery and a host of other companies, and together we fashioned a spectacular liftoff for the new kid on the baked goods block.

The initial centerpiece was a rally at the Saint Louis Convention Center for several thousand headquarters and local bakery employees, customers, Anheuser-Busch shareholders, and stock analysts. The show was beamed live by satellite to branch bakeries and to a New York reception for media and other Wall Street representatives. To anchor the proceedings, we brought in popular television personality Regis Philbin. "Not only is he demographically perfect—our target consumers love him and watch *Regis and Kathie Lee*, his daily talk show—but downstream I could see him appearing in commercials for Earth Grains products," I maintained. At a key moment during the hoopla a battered bread delivery truck bearing the company's old logo came chugging and wheezing out onto the stage. "You may not know it, but I'm a bit of an amateur magician and illusionist," Philbin told the audience, and with that he gave a cue and the old clunker vanished in a cloud of smoke to be replaced by a gleaming new vehicle proudly displaying the chic new Earth Grains logo—to the delight and amazement of the audience.

The stunt worked so well with the celebrity emcee pulling the strings that video highlights were fed by satellite to television stations, celebrity gossip shows, and networks coast to coast, many of which used the footage—a rare occurrence given the unabashed commercialism and typical ho-hum white bread (pun intended) nature of the bakery industry.

A few days later Earth Grains' stock opened strong on the New York exchange; a delighted Barry Beracha was featured on FNN (now CNBC) and CNN, and he sat for interviews with several key business publications.

Earth Grains was off to a rousing start. And for the next couple of years Regis Philbin starred in TV commercials for Earth Grains refrigerated bagels.

(Five years later, Sara Lee Corporation would acquire Earth Grains. Beracha and a number of other key executives retired. They became quite prosperous in the process, deservedly so.)

Seventy-Five

Jim Bridges was a highly decorated Vietnam War hero and a confirmed idealist who ran a flourishing investment advisory boutique on the Saint Louis riverfront, but he was in big trouble. I'd first met him when he served as executive assistant to Anheuser-Busch chief financial officer Jerry Ritter as I was writing and producing several of the company's annual reports. Later on, by pure coincidence, our wives became friends and our kids attended grade school together.

By and by, Bridges was awarded the management of a $50 million piece of the Saint Louis Police and Firefighters' pension fund. The problem was that Jim was not an insider, and no sooner did he get the business than he was instructed to run any and all trades he made through a specific brokerage house. A righteous chap who took his fiduciary responsibilities seriously, Bridges balked at that idea, telling the fund's trustees he could do better for them if he was free to shop his trades for the lowest commissions. When the trustees made it clear they wanted no part of such an arrangement, Jim smelled a rat and tattled to the office of the US attorney for Eastern Missouri.

Funniest thing: once it was no longer a secret that the feds were investigating the matter, Bridges got word the pension fund no longer required his services. The termination letter falsely accused him of "churning," making unnecessary trades to generate extra income for himself. What was really happening was that the designated brokerage was rewarding some of the trustees with a percentage of their commission fees; in other words kickbacks.

Things got ugly. And serious. The key trustees were indicted. Their first line of defense was to publicly attack the name and reputation of Jim Bridges and to bring suit against him with much fanfare. He lost many of his other clients, had to close his business, endured threats of harm to himself and his family, had to hire an expensive defense attorney, and waited for the other shoe to drop.

Jim took me into his confidence and, whenever asked, I attempted to provide him with communications advice as the saga played out. When the criminal case went to trial he was, of course, the government's star witness, and anyone paying attention to the proceedings would have come away knowing that not only was Bridges not a culprit, he was the whistle-blowing hero of the case. The problem was that almost no one outside the courtroom was paying attention.

The accused trustees were found guilty and given prison sentences. And Jim Bridges for all his heroism and personal risk was allowed by the feds to twist in the wind—his reputation sullied and his business destroyed.

Finally, one day many months later, Bridges got a letter from FBI Director William Sessions thanking him for his role in bringing the kickback perpetrators to justice. I convinced him to let me take the letter to Kevin Horrigan, a local newspaper columnist, who wrote a beautiful piece summarizing the saga and giving Jim his due. Then I recommended that he make copies of the column and Sessions's letter and send them to former and prospective clients, as he had decided to rehang his shingle and return to the investment business. He did and was successful once again until, sadly, he was diagnosed with a terminal illness (Lou Gehrig's Disease) and forced to shut the venture down. Jim died quickly and tragically, an embittered soul who was twice a hero and one of the finest men I've ever had the good fortune to call a friend.

Book Three

Seventy-Six

Fleishman-Hillard was on the block.

John Graham sensed that if he and the other owner-partners of the firm were to realize true value for their holdings they would either need to capitalize their interests through an employee stock option (ESOP) program or an outright sale to a third party. The agency was growing dramatically and winning new business and accolades left and right. At the same time us growth-minded second generation partners were aging, so time was fast approaching to do something, Graham knew. Initially he considered the ESOP approach because it involved participation by a wide array of agency employees who would have a stake in the firm, but he backed off that approach, as it would have saddled us with an extraordinary debt load—one that would be difficult to service and in the event of default the company would end up with a new owner anyway, most likely a lending institution or some bottom-feeding investment outfit. Then there was the dilution factor; at that point ownership was confined to just fourteen partners or so, but there were hundreds of employees.

So a merger and acquisition firm was retained to shop the agency to communications conglomerates capable of swinging a deal for cash or stock. The universe was small, with only three or four high-probability suitors—holding companies with interests in advertising, public relations, and other less-mature but promising specialties such as e-commerce, Internet marketing, fund-raising, lobbying, and the like. Then there were other less likely candidates—acquisition-minded media empires, plus several F-H clients that might want to consider owning their own agency.

Graham did not hold out much hope for the media or client company options. Clearly he was thinking about cashing in for his own benefit as well as his partners. Just past age sixty, he was not ready to retire and was rightly concerned with what life might be like for the next five, seven, ten years or more working for a corporation with no feel for the PR business after decades of answering to no one and running his own show. Then there was the other consideration: how would Fleishman-Hillard function in dealings with other media interests if it were owned by one of their competitors or, alternatively, how would the agency fare attempting to represent other Fortune 1000 concerns if it were owned by a member of the same club?

Initially we weren't sure what the agency was worth in the open market. Sure, there was some idea based on what other agencies had sold for and on pro formas based on certain assumptions. The agency was essentially debt-free, had fifty offices worldwide, nearly two thousand employees, revenues of $135 million, and profit margins perennially of 20 percent or better—enviable and enticing for sure. We understood too that the true value of the agency must include all-important but less concrete blue sky metrics like reputation, goodwill, a blue-chip client list, and a talented workforce; for a service business those far outweighed traditional tangible industrial assets such as plants, equipment, or distribution systems.

Graham was anxious to find out and asked our representative to concentrate first on the major agency conglomerates—WPP Group, Interpublic, and Omnicom.

Seventy-Seven

B efore long, on a fragrant April Saturday morning, Graham summoned the Fleishman-Hillard senior partner group to a private meeting room at Saint Louis's Ritz-Carlton hotel. Collectively, those present managed the entire agency—every office, every practice group, every specialty area—and together they easily represented at least 95 percent of the firm's ownership.

Graham had big news. There was another person in the room, a stranger, and a screen and projector were at the ready, obviously for presentation purposes.

Graham opened: "Some time ago we retained Robert Cowin, who's with New Orleans-based Cari Capital Company, to test the waters on our behalf with a number of businesses that might have an interest in acquiring our firm. I believe all of you know why we're doing this—why we would consider foregoing the independence that has been so precious to us and so key to our culture. And you all know my feelings. We've been together now in some cases for more than twenty years. The firm we've built is the gold standard of PR agencies. We've won every award there is to win, our peers have picked us as the best full-service agency ten years in a row, and our employees say F-H is a great place to work. When it comes to financial management and long-range planning no other agency can hold a candle to us. There are two overriding issues now facing us: number one, how do we continue to grow this organization if we remain independent with the limited resources that are available to us? And number two: as we as individuals reach middle age and beyond, how do those of us who've worked so hard and so long capital-ize on the value of what we've created? As you know a few years back we took a look at an employee stock option program and backed away from that approach because there was too much downside. Clearly the acqui-sition route is the way to go provided we find the right partner and the right offer. Well, I can tell you that I think we've done just that, and I've asked Bob Cowin to pick it up from there."

Cowin: "Thanks, John. It's good to be with you this morning. Ladies and gentlemen, with the full blessing of John Graham and your CFO Royce Rollins, for the past several months I have been in contact with those agency conglomerates that logically and most likely would have an interest in Fleishman-Hillard. To no surprise, all of them expressed interest to one degree or another. We were at liberty to share your fi-nancials and other vital information with them and, after some prelimi-naries, John and Royce ultimately met with each of them. The upshot: It's our belief that one of the potential suitors is head and shoulders above the others. Omnicom Group is that organization. No doubt some of you are familiar with Omnicom. Last year as a group they had rev-enues of more than $1 billion. Their stock trades on the New York ex-change. They are a pure holding company, if you will. In the last few years they have made some astute acquisitions in both the advertising and PR fields—DDB Needham and TBWA Chiat-Day in the former cat-egory, Ketchum and Porter Novelli in the latter. They are something of a Wall Street darling. They have a track record of acquiring businesses and then leaving them alone, maintaining their cultures to compete against other agencies, including other Omnicom agencies, so long as their fi-nancial performance remains strong. They have made a tentative offer for Fleishman-Hillard. They would acquire the agency in exchange for Omnicom common stock worth in excess of one hundred million dol-lars. F-H of course would have to undergo an intense due diligence pe-riod. If everything checks out, and we're confident it will, the deal would close sometime in the fall. Then each of you would receive Omnicom shares for your stock in F-H according to a formula based on the number of shares you now hold. Of course you would not be able to trade those shares during the standard, SEC-mandated six-month restrictive period. The chart on the screen right now will give you an idea of what your stock would be worth in the exchange. John…"

Graham: "Thanks, Bob. There you have it, boys and girls. We've met with Omnicom, IPG, and WPP group, and I can tell you without hesitation that those other guys don't hold a candle to Omnicom. What's more, they want to see us grow, and with the resources that would be available, we'd be able to do just that. That's important to those of us who plan to stick around for a while. They are our kind of people. They're down to earth, and they know what they're doing. What's more, they really want us. We'd still be known as Fleishman-Hillard, based here in Saint Louis, and it's no exaggeration to say that we'd be the jewel in their PR crown."

After a remarkably brief question-answer period it was abundantly clear that everyone in the room strongly favored the sale. As the number two F-H shareholder, then in my early fifties, I could barely disguise my excitement.

(In the years since the merger, Fleishman-Hillard has indeed proven itself to be the crown jewel of Omnicom's PR holdings with a platinum-plated client roster; a seemingly endless stream of awards that are the envy of the industry; and a stable of brilliant practitioners as well as solid financial controls and both a short- and long-term planning focus about which other agencies can only dream. As such, I suspect that each of us who benefited from the buyout now look back with both gratitude and the certitude that Omnicom got itself a prize catch and, alas, quite a bargain.)

Seventy-Eight

L ater that day, back home, I tried to explain the pending Omnicom deal to a distracted Kathy. "I've believed for a long time that this day would come," I told her, adding I planned to retire soon after the buyout.

"With the boys grown and gone, this will enable us to do many of the things we haven't been able to do before."

"Like what?" she asked, unable or unwilling to disguise her skepticism.

"Kathy, look, we're going to walk away from this deal set for life. That's why I elected to borrow from the bank twenty years ago, to buy all that stock in the firm, so that when this day happened we'd have honest-to-goodness financial independence."

"Yeah, so that you can play golf, write crap, and do your big shot thing. I've never been part of that scene before. Why should I expect anything to change now?"

"I want to take a victory lap—to get in the car and visit people we haven't seen in years and to savor all this. Then I want to travel, play golf, read, and, yes, maybe do some writing, visit the kids, and generally enjoy life. Who knows, I might even teach or do some consulting. What's wrong with that?"

"Nothing, but where do I fit into that picture?"

Kathy had come to have her own interests, and more often than not they did not include me. Several years earlier she'd returned to school with my whole-hearted encouragement to become certified in psychological counseling. As a former elementary schoolteacher and mother with almost ten years of sobriety under her belt, she wanted to work with kids through the school districts as well as individual clients as a staff member of a private counseling service. She was fast becoming recognized as an accomplished alcohol and substance abuse therapist. She also had a passion for needlepoint and worked as a volunteer instructor in the craft at Sign of the Arrow, a fashionable suburban not-for-profit shop established by alumnae of the Pi Beta Phi sorority that raised funds for local charities while turning out literally dozens of belts and other trendy items. I was proud of her and thought she knew that.

Perplexed, I said, "Look, you have your thing and I have mine, so you do yours and I'll do likewise, and when our interests converge, they'll converge. Whether they do or not, you are not defined by who you're married to, which is a compliment. At the same time you haven't seemed to mind the perks that go with being my spouse, and you sure as hell don't mind the lifestyle we've been able to have and the things it's allowed you to do—with my full support, I might add."

"You're always telling me what I think and what I feel or should feel and what to do or not do; you don't have a clue," she countered.

Privately, I was growing weary of what seemed more and more like all-out verbal and psychological warfare with Kathy. I was frustrated as well with her nonstop passive-aggressive behavior that included spending or giving away large sums of money and other possessions behind my back. Besides, I was disappointed by her reluctance to revel in the sale of the agency and all that it would mean. What I thought would be an occasion for joy and celebration had instead become a garden-variety domestic spat.

Seventy-Nine

The sale to Omnicom closed in October. In accordance with the buy-out agreement, I swapped my shares of Fleishman-Hillard stock for a predetermined number of Omnicom shares, valued then at just under forty dollars each.

"Hallelujah, your ship has come in!" exclaimed a friend.

I wanted to begin working fewer hours with an eye toward retirement. An internal agency announcement indicated I'd give up my partner's title, cut my workload to twenty or twenty-five hours a week, and retire completely within a couple of years.

In December, at the firm's annual holiday party, I was recognized for twenty-five years of service and presented with a trip to the old Nicklaus-Flick Golf School in Boca Raton, Florida. Responding, I said, "The only thing I need more than help with my golf game is a gallon of Rogaine," a nod to a fast-receding hairline, and then proceeded with all sincerity to sing the praises of the firm, the privilege of helping to build a PR juggernaut and to work with so many exceptionally talented people. I mentioned that my retirement plans included travel, reading, golf, and writing—"for therapeutic purposes, rather than the good or enlightenment of mankind."

With the festivities in full swing, I accepted best wishes from many fellow employees. The procession of well-wishers included Connie Baumgartner (nee Simokaitis), the fetching creature I'd been smitten with years before. With the growth of the firm, I hadn't seen her in a long time, as she worked four floors away in the agency's business office. "You look fantastic," I said, reveling in her undiminished beauty. "Whatever it is you're doing, keep doing it." She gave me a good luck kiss on the cheek, thanked me, and we spoke for a bit. "Let's have lunch someday soon—for old time's sake," I suggested.

Six weeks later, we did. We lunched on The Hill, Saint Louis's Italian neighborhood famous for its restaurants, tidy bungalows, and old country-inspired red, white, and green striped fire hydrants. She brought me up to date on her family and career. She was married—had been for twenty-three years to the same fellow she'd wed about a year after joining the firm. In the meantime, she'd returned to college, completed her business degree, and had three children. She was the primary family breadwinner by a wide margin and had climbed the ladder in the F-H accounting group, attaining the rank of senior vice president.

I found her magically alluring. She was smart, funny, sweet, and gorgeous with smoldering blue eyes. As we returned to the office I confessed I wasn't sure if my intentions toward her were honorable. That didn't seem to faze her.

We had lunch again a few weeks later. For me, the old chemistry was still there and the spell continued. "I'm falling in love with you," I confessed. She said her life was too complicated to consider the implications of anything so extreme. "What you need is a kiss," I said. When we got back to the office in the privacy of an elevator lobby I gave her a long, slow, sweet kiss. It caused my knees to buckle and my breath to quicken. "You don't play fair," I told her. She feigned innocence.

We began seeing each other with increased frequency, and before long I popped the question, sort of. "Marry me," I more or less insisted. "If not I guess it'll be déjà vu all over again. We'll mess around and go our separate ways. You owe it to yourself to consider whether you're truly happy with your current situation, and so do I."

A short time later, with our divorces in the works, we spent a long weekend in Florida, staying at the big pink landmark Don Cesar resort hotel on Saint Petersburg Beach. Our engagement became official, and we whiled away the days around the pool, on the beach, and sight-seeing.

One evening after dinner we went for a walk on the beach. The moon was full. "This reminds me of that poem of yours," she said. "You know, the one you're always quoting with the ending that goes 'hand in hand on the edge of the sand they danced by the light of the moon.'"

Then we kissed, and we danced. Right there—on the edge of the sand.

Eighty

C onnie and I were married on December 18 in a small civil ceremony at the Saint Louis Ritz-Carlton. Her children attended. Mine did not; after the divorce my sons and I were estranged, and it was killing me. We moved into a handsome, renovated classic seventy-year-old brick and stone home in Saint Louis Hills, one of the city's nicer neighborhoods. In February, we honeymooned on Maui. In July we honeymooned again, this time with her kids—three days at Disney World, followed by a Caribbean cruise on one of the Magic Kingdom's luxury ships.

In October, we did a ten-day sweep of California with stops at the Del Coronado off San Diego, the Monterrey Peninsula, and San Francisco. At Pebble Beach we reveled as a bagpiper serenaded the sundown at Spanish Bay, prowled the shops of Carmel, and dined at Clint Eastwood's Mission Valley Ranch. Later on Nob Hill we had drinks and danced at the fabled Top of the Mark Hopkins Hotel. The city was shrouded in fog. "Let's see if I can get rid of the fog," I said, looking out the window toward the TransAmerica pyramid, which was completely obscured by the atmospherics.

"No way you can lift a fog, especially not San Francisco fog," she taunted.

"We'll see," I said, and with that I made a lifting gesture with both hands.

Within minutes the fog was gone and the brilliant San Francisco cityscape was there to behold, a trillion lumens strong.

"Life is pretty good," I said. "All we need to do to make this marriage really official is for you to meet my dad, and all I need is to get my boys back." That's when I surprised her with the details of an impending trip to Europe.

A few weeks later we flew to London. After several days stalking the ghosts of Whitehall, visiting Churchill's Cabinet War Rooms, dining and shopping in Mayfair, Notting Hill, and Knightsbridge, and attending a performance of "My Fair Lady" in the West End, we went by train via the Chunnel to Calais in the north of France. In a rented diesel-powered Peugeot, we headed west toward the heart of Normandy.

We bought flowers in the postcard-perfect fishing village of Port en Bessin and drove six miles west on Route 514, the coastal road, directly to Colleville sur la Mer and the American Cemetery at Omaha Beach.

"There is no more sacred place on earth than this," I said, making a beeline for the gravesites. I found my father's final resting place from memory, knelt, kissed his headstone, and said, "Dad, I'd like to present my bride. Connie, say hello to my dad, my hero, and your new father-in-law." We spent a couple of hours arm in arm, walking the solemnly still hallowed grounds, were moved to tears at High Noon when the carillon played the army, navy, and marine hymns, and then drove down into the bocage, hedgerow country, near the spot where Joe Sr. was mortally wounded. This time I knew for certain that we were in the right place. I climbed a wire fence and walked slowly around a farmer's pasture and said a little prayer as half a dozen head of dairy cattle grazed away unfazed.

The next day we were in Paris, the City of Lights, easily the most romantic city on earth. After a day of sightseeing, including, for vertiginous me, a tortuous trip to the top of the Eiffel Tower, shopping, and museum-hopping we strolled hand in hand along the Left Bank, directly across from the Louvre, and were swallowed up in the enchantment of time and place. We waved to folks passing by on one or two of the idyllic Bateaux-Mouches passenger barges and embraced. Thus inspired I threw an arm over her shoulder; and as we started back to the hotel I began to recite, "The Owl and the Pussycat went to sea…and hand in hand on the edge of the Seine, er, the sand…"

• • •

I'd had numerous dealings over the years with the late, legendary sportscaster Jack Buck, and just after our return from Europe I ran into his son-in-law, Jeff Brooks, in the hallway at my office. Jeff had degrees in both journalism and law and was working in our financial communications group at the time. I mentioned the trip and the visit to my dad's grave at the American Cemetery, and he asked if I knew about a book of Jack's poetry and writings that had just been published to benefit the Cystic Fibrosis Foundation. He said there was a poem in the book inspired by a visit to the cemetery that Jack had made several years earlier with Mike Roarty and their wives.

I got a copy of the book, found the Normandy poem, and sent Jack a note saluting his work along together with a snapshot of me at my dad's gravesite. Himself a World War II veteran (Ninth Infantry) and Purple Heart recipient, Jack called later to say he wished he'd known my dad was buried there and thanked me for the photo and the kind words.

Jack was a wonderful man and a phenomenal talent.

Epilogue

Working part time, I spent two and a half more years with Fleishman-Hillard before retiring altogether, at which point they had another nice reception, thanked me for my contributions to the firm, and told me I'd be missed. A couple of competitors asked me to throw in with them, but I politely declined. "I bleed Fleishman-Hillard surgically correct brushed nickel," I told them. "Besides, my bride still works there, and I would not want to put her in an awkward position." The truth was I was looking forward to doing whatever I felt like, and after having been with and helped build the (then) number-one agency in the world, I was pretty sure anything else would be a disappointment.

"Do you miss it?" a former colleague asked at lunch one day several years after I'd retired and he had followed suit.

"To me there's a difference between a collection of memories and experiences—even positive ones—and longing for something. Those were great, but I wouldn't go back for all the tea in the People's Republic where, by the way, there's bound to be at least one Fleishman-Hillard office by now. I left because I could; it was the right decision at the right time. The PR business has a high mortality rate when you play at the level we played at for as long as we did. I don't have to tell you that; I suspect you feel the same."

"No question about that," he agreed, changing the subject.: "So what do you think about the Graham succession derby? Do you think he'll ever step down?"

John Graham had headed Fleishman-Hillard for more than thirty years, deservedly becoming a legend in the process. Both the firm and the industry were abuzz with speculation about his plans. He was nearing seventy and had indicated, but not stated outright, that his successor most likely would be one of two people—either the F-H Washington general manager, a twenty-year F-H veteran who came up on the lobbying side of the business, or Dave Senay, another twenty-year man and my one-time protégé who'd worked for me on the Bert Parks/Liggett

& Myers project, the Acura introduction, and the Valvoline accounts. More recently he'd served with distinction on the AT&T account, as general manager of the Saint Louis headquarters office, and as one of the firm's six regional presidents. "No way it'll be the Washington guy," I ventured. "He's immature, transparently obsequious, not trusted by his own people and, horror of horrors, he's a lobbyist. Senay, on the other hand, I see as the real deal—savvy, a good manager, more mature, and he earned his stripes on the PR side of the business. I can vouch for him firsthand. He'll do a great job—if he can just keep his ego in check."

Meantime, I found marriage, stepfatherhood, and retirement rewarding and was grateful for a second chance to get it right. After some fits and starts, I was able to forge solid relationships with Connie's kids—Jane, Peter, and Becky—who eventually came to introduce me to others as their stepdad with relative ease. I took great pride in that, but it left me yearning all the more for my own sons. I returned to counseling for the first time in years and spoke openly of the estrangements and the associated pain in therapy sessions and at AA meetings. "Be patient, pray, take advantage of opportunities to let your boys know your love for them is undiminished and unconditional, and keep your expectations in check; eventually they will come around," a recovering friend advised.

Tragically, Kathy was diagnosed with late-stage throat cancer. Radical surgery and a regimen of radiation and chemotherapy proved too little, too late. We were back on relatively good terms when she turned for the worst. I spent the better part of a week on and off at her hospital bedside as she clung to life. Notwithstanding our troubles, the loss of my first true sweetheart and the mother of my sons, memories of times shared and the fine young men we created together, was devastating. Our sons of course were wracked with grief, but battled back, emerged from the abyss, and ever so slowly let me back into their lives, almost as if their mom had granted them permission to do so from the grave.

Twelve days after Kathy's death our first grandchild was born. Matt was practicing law in Los Angeles, and his wife, Suzanne, gave birth to a little girl, Megan. Four months later Brendan and his wife, Maureen, had a son; they named him Brady (her maiden name). Armed with his MBA from Washington University's Olin School of Business, Brendan's career with Anheuser-Busch was gaining momentum. Before long, there were two more grandkids. Matt and Suzanne, who in the meantime had moved to the Denver area, had a son, also named Brendan, and "Big" Brendan and Maureen a daughter, Kathleen. Since then there've been two more—Matt's Michael and Brendan's Claire.

Patrick, my youngest, remained single. He enlisted and saw major action as an infantryman with the vaunted First Battalion, Fifth Marine Regiment, initially in Desert Shield, the 2003 invasion that toppled Saddam Hussein, and two subsequent Iraq deployments, seeing action in Fallujah and Ramadi. He earned a battlefield promotion, two navy/marine corps combat achievement medals, and three Purple Hearts.

At an AA meeting one evening after time had passed and wounds had begun to heal, I spoke of the joy of being reunited not only with my father, so to speak, but with my sons and their families, and thanked the group for the encouragement and wisdom that saw me through the major changes—the estrangements, retirement, divorce, remarriage, and the death of my first wife. "Everything good that's happened to me since 1990 has been thanks to sobriety and this program," I asserted, "and everything not so good (i.e., a 2011 prostate cancer bout and more recent stage IV-A throat cancer) has been manageable—again thanks to Alcoholics Anonymous."

● ● ●

The Power of True? The F-H I joined on February 1, 1972, with twenty-four employees and billings of less than $1 million is today the most celebrated international agency and ranks as one of the largest PR firms in the world with eighty offices, twenty-six hundred employees, and billings of more than a half billion dollars.

In May 2013, Fleishman-Hillard undertook a bold rebranding initiative, which included the adoption of what I regard as a silly, almost indecipherable new hyphen-free logo; a hackneyed and nebulous new slogan, "The Power of True"; and entry into or expansions of a number of specialty areas—advertising, research, analytics, social media, and even video game development.

My take: The move may make sense as F-H wrestles with a market saturation issue in its traditional business areas as well as the huge, technology-driven revolution in new media. But it's not without risk. In the 1980s when ad agencies began gobbling up PR firms or starting their own PR departments, they justified the idea by touting the virtues of something they called integrated services, the concept being that clients could have all their communications needs met under one organizational umbrella. But it met with significant client resistance, indifference, or confusion as well as account roster conflicts and was more or less quietly mothballed.

Granted, this is another era, but that should be a history lesson as F-H hits the reset button and embarks in new directions. Assimilating people from advertising and other new disciplines into the agency's culture, carefully cultivated as it's been for some seventy years, is another challenge to be faced. And the converse could be true for its PR incumbents worldwide if and as the agency's center of gravity begins to move away from its core competencies. This, of course, is to say nothing of that most important of all considerations—client acceptance.

• • •

"No, I don't miss working," I told my former F-H colleague. "On the other hand, I wouldn't trade the experience for the world. It seems like only yesterday that I was standing atop the coke ovens blissfully breathing in the toxic fumes at Granite City Steel—fat, dumb, and chomping at the bit to make it big."

Before long the guessing game of who would take John Graham's place climaxed with word that Dave Senay would indeed be the firm's new president and chief executive officer. Graham would continue to serve as chairman, at least for the time being. I told my ex-colleague and confidant that upon hearing the news, I'd sent Graham a note congratulating him on the choice of Senay, and that it read in part, "The other guy didn't have a chance; he didn't have me as a mentor."

"You didn't really say that to Graham, did you?" he asked.

"No, but I thought about it. As you know so very well, us old PR men never die...we just keep on spinning."

In November 2015, after nine years in office, in a rather curious move, Dave Senay stepped down as Fleishman-Hillard CEO. He was replaced by former F-H/ Europe head, Irishman John Saunders. I had been concerned that if things didn't work out with Senay, his replacement might come from another Omnicom-owned agency—a stranger to the culture; that would be unfortunate, perhaps even disastrous. In my view John Saunders is the perfect choice to succeed Senay. He is a smart, capable executive, a good people person, and he's thoroughly imbued with the F-H culture, to say nothing of his abundant Irish energy, wit, and charm. And after about a year in his new position, by all accounts, he has agency morale up and the business humming on all cylinders.

Special Thanks

Looking back, I was incredibly fortunate throughout my career to have landed, with no special prior connections, in the midst of some supremely gifted and patient bosses, mentors, and life coaches. In 1966 and 1967 at the Auto Club, it was Ron Jacober who helped get me started before going on to a remarkable career of his own in sports broadcasting with a major assist from his number two, Don Constantine. For the next three and a half years at UMSL, Robert E. (Bob) Smith shared his abundant and colorful life experiences, guidance, and contacts with me. Then at Fleishman-Hillard, Harry Wilson, Bob Hillard, and especially John Graham all poured forth with priceless jewels of wisdom, savvy, and career-growth opportunities. Their generosity, their genius, their insights, and their intellects were pure fate, helped along by a loving God and the teachings and talents inherited from a mother who was taken from us all too soon. I will never forget or be anything but grateful for them—the gifts they shared, the freedom they granted, and the trust they bestowed to me, first to learn and then to do my thing.

About the Author

Joseph Townsend (Joe) Finnigan spent thirty-five years in the public relations business, most of it in Saint Louis as an award-winning executive vice president and senior partner with Fleishman-Hillard, Inc., helping to build it into one of the world's largest, most successful, and admired agencies. A native of Springfield, Illinois, he is a 1966 graduate of the Marquette University College of Journalism. Retired since July 2000, he spends time playing golf, traveling, and writing—mostly social commentary and doggerel. He and his wife, Connie, live in the Saint Louis suburb of Ladue.

Made in the USA
Middletown, DE
27 May 2017